Screening

MW00387871

Screening Text

Critical Perspectives on Film Adaptation

Edited by SHANNON WELLS-LASSAGNE
and ARIANE HUDELET

McFarland & Company, Inc., Publishers
Jefferson, North Carolina, and London

Acknowledgments. Our thanks go out to all the people and institutions that made possible this volume and the conferences that inspired it, particularly the Université de Bretagne Sud and its research group HCTI, the Université de Paris III — Sorbonne Nouvelle and its research group ARIAS, and the Université de Paris–Diderot and its research group LARCA.

ISBN 978-0-7864-7230-7
softcover : acid free paper ∞

LIBRARY OF CONGRESS CATALOGUING DATA ARE AVAILABLE

BRITISH LIBRARY CATALOGUING DATA ARE AVAILABLE

On the cover: movie film reel, old books (iStockphoto/Thinkstock)

Manufactured in the United States of America

McFarland & Company, Inc., Publishers
Box 611, Jefferson, North Carolina 28640
www.mcfarlandpub.com

Table of Contents

Introduction

Shannon Wells-Lassagne and Ariane Hudelet

> Il ne s'agit plus ici de traduire, si fidèlement, si intelligemment que ce soit, moins encore de s'inspirer librement, avec un amoureux respect, en vue d'un film qui double l'œuvre, mais de construire sur le roman, par le cinéma, une œuvre à l'état second. Non point un film "comparable" au roman, ou "digne" de lui, mais un être esthétique nouveau qui est comme le roman multiplié par le cinéma.
> —André Bazin, *Qu'est-ce que le cinéma?*[1]

Whether it be the inevitable new adaptation of a British classic, the edgy interpretation of a recent bestseller, or simply the newest comic book film, the success of film adaptations is unarguable. Indeed, Robert Stam's comments in his collection *Film and Literature* ring even more true today than when the book was originally published in 2005: "Not only do literary adaptations form a very high percentage of the films made [...] but also almost all films can be seen in some ways as 'adaptations' [...] virtually all films, not only adaptations, remakes, and sequels, are mediated through intertextuality and writing."[2] One might argue that the scores of adaptations and reinterpretations of previous works is in fact a glut, reminiscent of what certain theorists have suggested is the postmodern inability to create, but only recreate, or deconstruct; indeed Bazin's comment given in the epigraph is a response to New Wave French critics who feared the tendency to bow to the supposed primacy of the written text would keep directors from becoming the *auteurs* that cinema needed to establish its own status as the seventh art. However, as the essays in this book will make clear, rather than limiting film, the inspiration of a written text often inspires innovation, creating new meaning for both source text and screen adaptation.

1

Film adaptation is of course simply the latest avatar of the desire to rein-habit a beloved story, a tendency that dates back at least to Homer, and which perhaps came to a head in the Victorian period, whose "bootleg" renditions of the latest novel in forms that included clothing, jewelry, pamphlets, plays, etc. show that the remakes that regularly grace our screens are far from a purely contemporary phenomenon. The study of adaptations, however, is still somewhat recent, due largely to the inclusion of film adaptations of classic British literature into university literature classes, and the source text has loomed large in adaptation studies ever since, too often taking precedence over the later film in what has come to be known as the "fidelity debate"—the success of said film being chiefly dependent on its faithfulness to the orig-inal text. Likewise, in attempts to theorize the nature of adaptation, critics must inevitably examine the fundamental natures of the two media in order to hypothesize on the essential aspects of the transfer from one to the other. As a consequence, all too often studies of adaptation, from George Bluestone's *Novels into Film*[3] onwards, focus on the ultimately insuperable barrier that separate the two media, whether they choose to differentiate between the three tenses of the novel as compared to film's single present tense,[4] between what is "temporal" and "visual," or "perceptual" and "conceptual,"[5] all in an attempt to theorize on the process necessary for transferring a written text to the screen. Though as editors Deborah Cartmell and Imelda Whelehan mention wryly in their introduction to their collection, "The publication of *The Cambridge Companion to Literature on Screen* confirms the fact that Literature on Screen has finally arrived,"[6] much remains to be done to establish adaptation as a field of film study in its own right, distinct from the literary studies that long dominated the field. It was largely thanks to critics like Cartmell and Whele-han,[7] Brian McFarlane,[8] James Naremore,[9] and Robert Stam,[10] among others, that adaptation theory has come into its own, and this theorization of the dis-cipline has come into fruition with recent books by Kamilla Elliott,[11] Linda Hutcheon,[12] and Thomas Leitch.[13]

The example of Thomas Leitch's *Film Adaptation and Its Discontents* seems particularly pertinent to this collection: indeed, rather than attempting an abstract analysis of adaptation, Leitch chooses to organize his study with case studies that each exemplify a given problem in adaptation, be it fidelity, the adaptation of sacred texts to secular celluloid, or the film preceding the source text in terms of primacy. Theory, then, is the attempt to generalize, to strip away the excess to arrive at the essence of a phenomenon: but with a process as nebulous and heterogeneous as film adaptation, theory must arise from practice, from concrete details that rise above the particular to convey something more global about the discipline. As such, we hope that these different essays, each focusing on different works and different aspects of the transfer from the blank page to the silver screen, will allow the reader to come away with a better understanding of the complexities and intricacies of film adaptation.

The book begins with two introductory texts by prominent scholars in adaptation studies: Deborah Cartmell, co-author of the recent *Cambridge Companion to Literature on Screen* and *Screen Adaptation: Impure Cinema*, among many others, and Kamilla Elliott, author of *Rethinking the Novel/Film Debate*. These two essays function in tandem, examining apparently diametrically opposed phenomena: Cartmell's harkens back to the early twentieth century's first sound adaptations, while Elliott's examines postmodern adaptations from the beginning of the twenty-first; Cartmell deals with the English language's most venerated of literary source texts, Shakespeare's plays, while Elliott focuses on adaptations of problematic or hybrid forms (literary nonfiction and autobiographical comic-books). However, the seemingly disparate analyses in fact serve to lay bare two of the core tensions in adaptation studies: the fraught relationship between what Cartmell refers to as the "verbal and non-verbal," and the problematic nature of the status of the author. Thus early sound adaptations of Shakespeare plays are characterized by their simultaneous pride in maintaining the text, and fear of "words getting in the way of entertainment"; rather than allowing a new means of ingress into the plays, the spoken text actually unbalances the filmic content, and ultimately hinders the viewer's enjoyment. This of course contradicts the belief held by critics as estimable as Virginia Woolf and Henry James that the visual generally usurps the primacy of the verbal[14]; on the contrary, sound in the new "talking pictures" is manifestly not as unproblematically universal as its advocates pretend. By juxtaposing Shakespearean words with Shakespearean images, films seemingly dilute the impact of both, resulting in critical and commercial failure. Of course, the very emphasis on the source text is linked to the prestigious nature of the playwright, whose famed words (and their difficulty) both attract and repel prospective filmmakers and audiences. Cartmell's savvy use of marketing material from the period, like pressbooks, demonstrates the schism between the aims of the studio and the product they are supposedly promoting, (often unsuccessfully) straddling the divide between art and popular culture.

As befits a study of postmodern adaptations, Elliott's essay examines *Adaptation* and *American Splendor* in the light of poststructuralist theory, specifically the postulate of the "death of the author" that Roland Barthes popularized in 1967, as it pertains to adaptation in general and autobiographical adaptations in particular. Though some have attributed the recurrent denigration of adaptations to the Romantic notion of the author,[15] thus implicitly suggesting that the "death of the author" would free adaptations from this stranglehold, Elliott makes it clear that things are not so simple: "Literary film adapters occupy an ambivalent position under Barthes's formulation: as readers of literary texts, they are born ushering in the deaths of literary authors; as authors of films based on those texts, even as they affirm Barthesean intertextuality, they too are pronounced dead by Barthes as authors." Here the debate no longer focuses on the text's accessibility to the audience, but on the very survival of the source text and its author, both of whom must seemingly "die" to make way for the filmic interpretation, in the wake of theoretical and industry abnegation of authorial presence (either as screenwriter or author). As Elliott aptly demonstrates, by recognizing the lack of a stable identity for the author and at the same time foregrounding his or her persistent presence in the adaptations, these films manage to defer traditional questions about the fidelity of the film to the source text, instead focusing on the relationship between the film and reality, indeed between fact and fiction: how true is the film to the author's experience? Which media best express this experience?

In a sense these two essays are indicative of adaptation studies as a whole, encompassing wildly diverse works and time periods, but grappling with fundamental and enduring questions like the relationship between text and image, or between author, text, and adaptation. Likewise, though the specter of fidelity remains, it is largely peripheral to more fruitful avenues of analysis. As such, these contributions provide a useful gateway to the case studies that follow.

As recent works like those of Cartmell and Whelehan, Julie Sanders,[16] or Linda Hutcheon make clear, the term "adaptation" is nothing if not ambiguous. Just as genre films have been crucial in establishing the importance of *auteur* theory in film studies, so adaptation studies must take into account the importance of genre when analyzing the problems inherent in the transposition of text(s) to screen. It seems appropriate therefore that Kevin Dwyer open our analysis of genre in adaptation studies; by turning his attention to the adaptation of non-fiction, he is in fact examining an extreme example of the problem of authorship that has traditionally plagued film in general, and adaptation in particular. After all, as he himself notes, "The very process of adaptation creates fiction from non-fiction [... though] mainstream film urges us to believe in fictions, and even to take them for true stories." Likewise, Dwyer also highlights the tightrope being constantly walked by filmmakers between the desire to make films authentic, and wanting to make them compelling: authorship and fidelity, two of the most troubling areas of adaptation study, are thus immediately brought to light. Fidelity remains the *bête noire* of adaptation studies, and the authors of this collection choose to treat the subject by examining other critical parameters in the transposition to the screen, notably in the possibilities and the limitations of genre. In so doing, of course, they are able to broach the topic of the relationship between source text and film adaptation in new and promising ways.

Delphine Letort and Gilles Menegaldo navigate the nebulous field of *film noir*, whose generic expectations are sometimes so strong as to curtail identification with the original text. Letort's essay deals with the extent to which Robert Siodmak's *The Killers* manages to convey, not Ernest Hemingway's story as such, but rather the author's writing style, especially given the choice of *film noir* tropes. Letort posits that the genre actually allows Siodmak to delve more deeply into some of Hemingway's central preoccupations, all while varying the form and content of the source narrative. Menegaldo's close analysis of the incipit and conclusion of Hammett's novel *The Maltese Falcon* and three of its screen adaptations exemplifies the unlimited possibilities available even in the apparently rigid codes of *film noir*, though his conclusion suggests that increased adherence to the *noir* tropes coincides with both a more convincing adaptation and a more coherent tone, resulting, it is suggested, in a more successful film.

The final essay in this examination of genre focuses on the most widely adapted of authors, who has in a sense created a genre for himself: Shakespeare on film was after all the first truly "respectable" area of adaptation studies, and the ways filmmakers must navigate the demands of genre and source text in creating the screen versions examined here is thus particularly complex. Sarah Hatchuel's essay on the epic nature of Kenneth Branagh's *Hamlet* deftly assimilates the ambiguity of the term; she shows how Branagh both conforms to and subverts generic expectations in his film adaptation by fusing the theatrical vision of "the epic" with the filmic definition of the term. This creates a sort of generic "odd couple," since, as Hatchuel affirms, "much as epic theatre is designed to appeal to the audience's reason, epic movies are meant to create emotions." This blurring of boundaries may be seen as a testimony to the manner in which Branagh manages to blend theatre and film in his adaptation, limiting himself to neither, but availing himself of the resources of both.

Again and again our authors suggest that context is all, that even direct transposition from one medium to another might have an entirely different meaning given the possibilities and constraints of film. Likewise, this twenty and twenty-first century context renders some aspects untranslatable without sacrificing audience sympathies, whether they be those of the general public (as in the class issues of Austen) or of the Hays Office (as is obvious in the different characterizations of Sam Spade before and after the reinforcement of the Production Code). This context is brought to the fore in the second section of the book focusing on the sociocultural nature of adaptation.

Perhaps inevitably in a volume on Anglo-Saxon film, race is first among the political issues addressed by film adaptations. While Joyce Goggin examines the way race was erased in the classic Hollywood adaptation of *Wuthering Heights*, Donald Ulin demonstrates how casting has foregrounded that same issue, making *The Shawshank Redemption* into a reading of one of America's foremost texts on race, Mark Twain's *The Adventures of Huckleberry Finn*.

Hélène Charlery brings to light the ever-changing complexities of race issues by examining the nuances of changing mores in two adaptations of *Shaft*, charting the movement towards the mainstream, though the freedom from overt racial tension allowed by the precepts of political correctness hides an underlying sexual tension in the insuperable barrier of more personal interracial relations. Charlery's description of the problematic politics of race and sexuality are an apt transition to Shannon Wells-Lassagne's analysis of Deborah Warner's adaptation of Elizabeth Bowen's *The Last September*, where a changing political landscape and a hope of reconciliation between Irish Catholics and Protestants results in a dramatically altered plot, and a love story that aspires to reconcile "two houses, both alike in dignity."

This postcolonial rereading of *Romeo and Juliet* leads us to another more overt example of "Empire writing back"; Florence Cabaret's look at the recent Bollywood version of Austen's classic *Pride and Prejudice*, Gurinder Chadha's *Bride and Prejudice*, highlights the political ramifications of this transposition to modern-day India. It is a classic example of postcolonial adaptation — both a willing subversion of a canonical British text by a minority director, and a fond tribute to that same culture, and its successful fusion with Bollywood tropes.

Adaptation criticism often focuses on the plaguing question of fidelity (from Bluestone onward), as well as ideology (particularly in the works of Higson, Monk, and Sargeant), but the aesthetics of the transfer of the text to the screen is a more recent object of study. These artistic implications of adaptation, and their relationship to these other areas of criticism, are in the spotlight in our next section. In so doing, the authors concentrate on the innovations used by some filmmakers in adapting film's strengths to express textual nuances: each author focuses on aspects initially seen as untranslatable from one medium to another, be it the idea of surface in Nicole Cloarec's analysis of Cathal Black's *Korea*, the unseen in Karim Chabani's look at *Howards End* and *The Remains of the Day*, or Lessing's traditional distinction of the visual medium as a spatial one, and the textual as a temporal medium, an issue brought to light in Laurent Mellet's work on Merchant Ivory adaptations of E.M. Forster. Each of these essays offers stimulating discussions of the possibilities and limitations of the different art forms, and suggests that even though film and text have their inevitable specificities, the creativity of artists in both text and film are constantly seeking to blur the boundaries separating the two arts, and on occasion manage to overcome these limitations.

The forces both personal and financial that inspire adaptation of course are also at the root of the phenomenon of *re*adaptation, the subject of our third section; however, rather than streamlining or simplifying the process, in the sense of "practice making perfect," there is a sense that readaptation actually complicates an already complex and convoluted process. We are after all multiplying the referents, the influences, the expectations, and the allusions. The texts chosen by our next four authors testify to the power and the protean nature of the source texts, each an inexhaustible fount of inspiration for generations of artists and filmmakers.

Sébastien Lefait and Charles Holdefer argue convincingly that the prominence of the work of Shakespeare and the myth of *Don Quixote* in Western culture goes without saying, and though *Heart of Darkness* and *Scarface* may be more modern additions to this canon, the iconic status of "the horror" that Gene M. Moore examines or the gangster that Dominique Sipière presents seem obvious, whether it be in the acclaim received by the recent reworking of the mob mentality on *The Sopranos* or the mocking homage made to Coppola's film in *Tropic of Thunder*. In the end, readaptation is dependent on and created by myth, and the epic stature of tales like Conrad's and Cervantes's are obvious, while the legends of Al Capone and Shakespeare have made the wild living of the one and the creative genius of the other unquestionably "larger than life," something each generation attempts to capture for itself.

Finally, the informal talk given by producer Roger Shannon at the French conference in 2007 that was the inspiration for this book allows us to resituate the preceding essays as an addendum to the filmmaking process. By sharing both his own experiences as a producer and the comments of writers whose work has been adapted, we're brought back full circle to the creation of film through the basis of writing. These valuable perspectives allow us to peek beyond the ivory tower to the artists whose work we admire, reminding us that it is after all due to a variety of personal, professional, financial and societal influences that different adaptations see the light of day, and suggests future horizons for adaptations to come. It is perhaps appropriate that French scholars, whose critics did so much to establish cinema as the seventh art, would take up the task of examining its typically less-esteemed sister adaptation.

Without presuming to hope that this collection will have the same impact as texts like that of André Bazin, quoted in the epigraph, the variety and creativity displayed and analyzed here by our authors reveal that rather than limiting the cinema, as certain French New Wave critics feared, adaptation can give new inspiration to explore the possibilities of the intersection of text and film, and as such, it would seem, adaptation studies has many happy days yet to come.

NOTES

1. "The point here is not to translate, however faithfully, however intelligently, and it is even less to take lovingly respectful inspiration from the text, so as to create a film that will mirror the source, but rather to construct from the novel, through the cinema, a second-level work—in no way a film comparable to the novel, or worthy of it, but a new aesthetic being that is like the novel multiplied by the cinema" (editor's translation). André Bazin, "Le *Journal d'un curé de campagne* et la stylistique de Robert Bresson," *Qu'est-ce que le cinéma?* (1975), Paris: Éditions du Cerf, 2002, 124–126.

2. Robert Stam, ed., *Literature and Film: A Guide to the Theory and Practice of Film Adaptation*, Malden, MA: Blackwell, 2005, 45.

3. George Bluestone, *Novels into Film* (1957), Berkeley: University of California Press, 1968. Bluestone's was the first book-length study of the phenomenon.

4. This is the argument used by Bluestone to justify the ultimate futility of film adaptation in its attempt to capture the spirit of the original text.

5. Brian McFarlane, *Novel to Film: An Introduction to the Theory of Adaptation*, Oxford: Oxford University Press, 1996, 27. McFarlane goes on to say that since both media are involved with narrative, this allows for a "meeting of minds" between the two.

6. *Cambridge Companion to Literature on Screen*, Cambridge: Cambridge University Press, 2007, 1.

7. *Adaptations: From Text to Screen, Screen to Text*, London: Routledge, 1999.

8. *Novel to Film: An Introduction to the Theory of Adaptation*, Oxford: Oxford University Press, 1996.

9. *Film Adaptation*, New Brunswick: Rutgers University Press, 2000.

10. *Literature Through Film: Realism, Magic, and the Art of Adaptation*, Oxford: Blackwell, 2005.

11. *Rethinking the Novel/Film Debate*, Cambridge: Cambridge University Press, 2003.

12. *A Theory of Adaptation*, New York: Routledge, 2006.

13. *Film Adaptation and Its Discontents: From* Gone with the Wind *to* The Passion of the Christ, Baltimore: Johns Hopkins University Press, 2007.

14. Kamilla Elliott discusses their views in chapters 2 and 3 of *Rethinking the Novel/Film Debate*.

15. See for example Linda Hutcheon, *A Theory of Adaptation*, 3–4.

16. Julie Sanders, *Adaptation and Appropriation*, London: Routledge, 2006.

Adaptation, Sound and Shakespeare in the 1930s

Deborah Cartmell

In the retro silent film *The Artist* (2011), a voice-test of a leading actress, reading from Shakespeare, is dismissed by the hysterical laughter of the stubbornly silent leading man. The coming of sound to Shakespeare movies is accurately represented here; it was met with a mixture of anxiety, amusement and contempt, possibly the reason Louis B. Mayer, head of Metro-Goldwyn-Mayer Studios, reportedly proclaimed that Shakespeare films were "box office poison."[1] The stakes were loaded against early talking Shakespeare films: unlike their silent predecessors, talking Shakespeare films ostracized a global audience through the employment of complicated English, insulted "purists" who insisted that Shakespeare be spoken in full and with an English accent and outraged cineastes who regarded Shakespeare's language and theatrical expression as damaging to the potential of cinema. Sound was bad news for the Shakespeare film and by association film adaptation. No matter how they are pronounced, changed or ignored, words — or more precisely, long, archaic, obscure, or thought-provoking words — are a guarantee of box office failure. Film adaptations of Shakespeare in the new age of sound posed the ultimate challenge for film adaptation — with the Shakespearean words both defining and, to borrow Louis B. Mayer's term, poisoning the movies, condemning adaptations as either too wordy or not wordy enough.

The acquisition of sound, or more precisely, words, transformed the way that Shakespeare adaptations were regarded in the early silent period and beyond. As I have argued, Sam Taylor's *Taming of the Shrew* (the first mainstream Shakespeare talkie of 1929) enacts a flirtatious tussle between sound and silent film, especially through its employment of the omnipresent silent-inducing whips that simultaneously make an impressive noise for those seeking

9

the thrills of sound cinema while asking the Shakespearean speakers to be silent.[2] In opposition to the film's valorization of silence over words, the publicists of the film enthusiastically greeted the "all talking sensation" as the first ever adaptation of Shakespeare, implying that what went before wasn't Shakespeare at all, and that to be an adaptation, the words of the author must be spoken. In spite of earlier silent adaptations of the play, the film's pressbook repeatedly makes the claim: "in this screen story of the Bard's immortal comedy, brought to the screen for *the first* time in the history of motion pictures" (my italics) or "the glorious comedy which has come finally to motion pictures after four centuries of success on the legitimate stage.[3]" The Shakespeare films that followed in the thirties made similar claims about their position as the first adaptations of the plays (and the necessity of speaking the author's words to qualify as an adaptation) while reflecting anxieties about the introduction of Shakespeare's words into mass media entertainment.

At the beginning of the sound era, Shakespeare — given his cultural status, his perceived Englishness and the complexity of his language — must have represented the biggest challenge for film adaptors. In fact the extraordinarily daring *Taming of the Shrew* did much to warn off any further attempts to film Shakespeare during the following years. As Scott Eyman has observed, the film was the beginning of the end for its stars Mary Pickford and Douglas Fairbanks[4]; it provided a cautionary tale for all stars of the silent screen not to aim too high — not to attempt Shakespeare before they had proven that they could talk at all. Indeed shortly after its release the film was undeservedly reduced to a laughing stock; according to Scott MacQueen, in the early thirties Hollywood fell to sniggering about the first Shakespearean "train wreck" of talking cinema.[5] This attitude to the film is still prevalent in the relative neglect the film receives in Shakespeare and film criticism, regardless of its status at the first mainstream "talkie" adaptation of Shakespeare, not to mention the audacious claim in the publicity materials that this is the first ever Shakespeare film adaptation.

While there was a spate of sound adaptations following *The Taming of the Shrew* (for instance *All Quiet on the Western Front* [1930], *A Farewell to Arms* [1932], *Little Women* [1933], and the biopics *The Private Life of Henry VIII* [1933] and *The Barretts of Wimpole Street* [1934]) it was not until 1935 that another major Shakespeare adaptation appeared: Max Reinhardt and William Dieterle's *A Midsummer Night's Dream*, produced by Warner Bros., featuring the contract actors of the company, including James Cagney (Bottom), Olivia de Havilland (Hermia), Dick Powell (Lysander), Joe E. Brown (Flute) and Mickey Rooney (Puck). But prior to the extravaganza of *Dream* there were some shorter and less adventurous attempts at talking Shakespeare.

Nineteen twenty-nine saw each studio presenting a variety act film, each showcasing their big stars and their newly found talking abilities. Two of these attempted Shakespeare. Norma Shearer appears as Juliet in MGM's *Hollywood Revue* (1929) followed by John Barrymore as Richard III in Warner Bros.' *Show of Shows* (1929). Both performances are amidst an array of vaudeville, acrobatic, music and comedy acts. Both performances situate Shakespeare in relation to popular entertainment, a sign of things to come. *The Show of Shows* presents a talking John Barrymore as Richard III on top of a hill of bodies (one disturbingly moves at the end of the sequence); his dramatic, highly theatrical recitation is preceded (and undermined) by an introduction in which we're informed that Richard will dispose of his enemies "with the graceful impartiality of Al Capone.[6]"

Hollywood's efforts to make Shakespeare accessible in the sound era are explicitly mocked in the first of these variety extravaganzas, MGM's *Hollywood Revue*, which features two versions of the balcony scene with Shearer as Juliet and John Gilbert (star of the silent screen and whose career was ruined by the talkies) as Romeo.[7] After a "straight" rendition of the scene, the pair are congratulated by director Lionel Barrymore who simultaneously receives "a wire from New York" which reads "don't change a thing, but the main title and the dialogue"; in a film now re-titled "The Necker," the two dutifully repeat the scene in 1929 slang ("Now listen, boyfriend, you have a nice line in chatter but how do I know you care for me in a big way?"/"Julie baby, I'm ga-ga about you"). Dismissed as a "shrivelling failure" by Scott Eyman,[8] the skit jokingly forecasts that Shakespeare may confront even more insurmountable obstacles than those of the film actors playing him in making the transition from silence to sound.

A Midsummer Night's Dream can be seen to take heed of this warning and on one level is defiantly anti-theatrical in its choice of cast (none of whom have significant theatrical pedigrees), deliberately employing a decidedly cinematic style of acting. A similar "wire" to that sent in the 1929 *Hollywood Revue* was delivered to Irving Asher, head of Warner Bros.' London studio, asking that the play be rendered "more colloquial" for the 1935 film.[9] Accompanied by Mendelssohn's *Midsummer Night's Dream*, the trailer begins "America applauded! Europe cheered! Asia thrilled! The whole world hailed this screen masterpiece! And paid $2.20 to see it. Now at last it comes to you at popular prices." The trailer stresses the film's democratic credentials, appealing to a global audience, oblivious to its use of Shakespeare's notoriously difficult language, and emphasizes its price, so as to capitalize on film's potential to provide culture for next to nothing. (Indeed a major departure from the play is the democratization of the *dramatis personae*, with Bottom — played by

James Cagney — reinvented as a character to be applauded rather than laughed at for his social presumptuousness.) As it has been argued, the choice of the play, on one level, may be a response to the imposition of censorship on the cinema (with Warner Bros. productions very much in the fray in their alleged glorification of violence through their popular gangster films); normally thought of as one of Shakespeare's "safer" plays, this adaptation brings themes of sexual violence and repression disturbingly to the forefront of the production, commencing with the explicit allusions to Hippolyta's violent abduction by Theseus and ending with a menacing Puck (played by a teenage Mickey Rooney) sneakily following Theseus and Hippolyta into their bedroom at the film's conclusion; these themes of enslavement or imprisonment and perverse surveillance could strike a chord at a time in which Jewish filmmakers, including Reinhardt and Diertle, were banned from working in Germany.

One aspect of this film forgotten today is the fact that it was made within the first decade of sound cinema and that like its predecessor, *The Taming of the Shrew*, it juxtaposes verbal with non-verbal sequences in a playful confrontation between the two styles. The 1935 film begins with a possible allusion to the 1929 film in the figure of the silenced Hippolyta. Like Katherine at the end of *The Shrew*, Hippolyta is in the last stages of her taming (having been "wooed by the sword") and she is introduced into the film as what only can be described as a quivering wreck, wearing a tight-fitting chain-mail helmet and a snake entwined around her neck which restrains her right arm in a loose form of a straitjacket. The snake is a possible reference to the whips in *The Taming of the Shrew* and a visual correlative to Oberon's description of Titania's bower where a "snake throws her enamell'd skin,/ Weed wide enough to wrap a fairy in" and Hermia's account of her nightmare (revealed to an absent Lysander in which a "serpent ate my heart away,/ And you sat smiling at his cruel prey").[10] While the original screenplay included a prelude or back-story of the conquest of the Amazons by Theseus, the initial impression of Hippolyta here compactly retains the story of a woman who has reluctantly surrendered, now visually crestfallen and conquered.[11] The back story is also omnipresent throughout the film in Theseus's fantastic palace with its phallic undulating pillars, which Jack J. Jorgens describes as contributing to the film's dark, post–Freudian reading of the play.[12] Allegedly Verree Teasdale, the actress who plays Hippolyta, was heard to exclaim a "hundred times during the lengthy production," "my kingdom for the privilege of sitting down for five short minutes,"[13] as her first costume contained rings which cut into her flesh if she created too much movement. The life-like snake featured in the first costume reappears as an artificial one in Hippolyta's next appearance, where she wears a dramatic sculpted black and silver dress with an ornamental snake outlining the bodice. While stunningly majestic, she remains a prisoner of the costume. She ends the film in a third dress — a lighter and sparkling gown with pronounced fairy-like ruff. However, Theseus's all too proximate dark caped figure seems to swallow her up at the pair's departure, possibly recalling the now famous "Nocturne" sequence in which Oberon's billowing black cape envelopes and brings darkness to the fairy world.

The film's daring, explicitly disturbing opening — like the subject matter of *The Taming of the Shrew*—concerned with the silencing of a woman, is extended throughout this adaptation, in arguably one of the most "outspoken" of all Shakespeare movies. Without doubt, the most memorable sequence in this film is the "Nocturne" choreographed by Bronislava Nijinska which thematically mirrors the message of the opening sequence through the invasion of the male fairies and subsequent subduing of Titania. In the play, Oberon — who is depicted in a black jumpsuit full of sparkles, evocative of a "Prince of Darkness"— opens Titania's eyes to the reality that she is in love with an ass (both Bottom and Oberon himself) and at the same time demanding "Silence awhile" (IV.1.79). In the film, he engulfs her with his snake-like black mantle, bringing, with his dark costumed entourage, a masculine darkness to the world of the female fairies. The stunning sequence is easily the most memorable in the film, bringing silence to a world of sound, an ominous message for Titania and her troupe; it nonetheless provides a bold and defiant display of how images can speak more eloquently than words, even Shakespeare's words.

The film's use of sound, or employment of words, was met with a mixed response. Graham Greene praised the cinematic fairy sequence while condemning the spoken poetry as serving merely to delay the action.[14] In other words, Greene liked the action but hated the words. Harley Granville-Barker in "Alas, Poor Will" (*The Listener,* 1937) ranted that the filmed words "not merely mutilated, but were occasionally even re-written from Elizabethan English into plainer American. What is one to say of such an outrage?"[15] Alfred Hitchcock, while defending the film in opposition to Harley Granville-Barker's "purist" attack, observed, too, that the words get in the way and the "general public will not be talked at."[16] No one could be more horrified by Shakespeare's words spoken on screen than art historian Erwin Panofsky, who singled out the Reinhardt-Dieterle film of *A Midsummer Night's Dream* (1935) as "the most unfortunate film ever produced"[17] in its falling victim to the pitfalls of the "talkies" in its over-reliance on theatrical rather than filmic traditions — that is, its dependence on words. Allardyce Nicoll found in the film hope for Shakespeare on screen and in sound the potential to achieve a new type of "quality" film,[18] but, generally, Shakespeare films were seen as either too theatrical by those proclaiming film as art (Panofksy) or as too unfaithful (or filmic) by those in the field of literature and theatre (Granville-Barker).

But the publicity materials proclaim otherwise — the film is regarded as both popular entertainment as well as educationally uplifting. The pressbook insists on the film's pedagogical value, echoing Nicoll's yearning for "quality" audiences, setting up a club to endorse the film for a certain "class of people," and features a section entitled "Spreading the News Round Schools" with plenty of ideas as to how to inspire youthful attendance at a Shakespeare film without "'forcing' it down their throats."[19] The educational value of the film, marketed to parents, is extended through the production of study guides and teachers' manuals "for school tie-ups on this picture"[20] and the pressbook even includes a photograph of "Professor" Reinhardt with the cast, sitting around a table, studying the play. It seems that the pressbook is trying to persuade its readership that this film "is the real thing" due to the fact that it's speaking Shakespeare's language. Claims of its uniqueness — that this is a first — are not understated in the pressbook. Exhibitors are told "THREE HOURS OF ENTERTAINMENT THAT WAS THREE CENTURIES IN THE MAKING," "THE SHOW THAT THE INVENTOR OF MOTION PICTURES DREAMED SOME DAY WOULD BE MADE" and "WARNER BROS., WHO BROKE THE SILENCE OF THE FILMS WITH TALKING PICTURES, NOW BRINGS THE MIGHTY VOICE OF SHAKESPEARE TO THE SCREEN."[21] The implied association between Warner Bros. ("WHO BROKE THE SILENCE OF THE FILMS") and Shakespeare's "MIGHTY VOICE" suggests that this is Shakespeare's language with a modern twist, that is, accessible to all. Exhibitors are encouraged to lure the public to the movie with statements such as:

> That Shakespeare wrote for all the people rather than any one class is being proven twice a day at _____ Theatre where the Bard's greatest comedy, "A Midsummer Night's Dream" is playing. Students of grade schools sit beside professors of literature and taxi drivers touch elbows with dignified solons, in common enjoyment.[22]

Suggestions for reviews include the likes of "'It's the swellest show I ever attended,' reported _____ who drives Yellow Taxi No. _____."[23]

The chief selling point of this film seems to be the accessibility of Shakespeare, with words spoken with a new accent — that is, in the language of Hollywood. The trailer celebrates the film's global appeal and cheap prices, the film's stars' introductions to the film proclaim it to be a significant moment in Hollywood; for both Jean Muir (Helena) and Frank McHugh (Quince), the film is "as new to the talking screen as sound was to the silent." The extraordinarily eccentric and irreverent promotional 20-minute film *Shake,*

Mr. Shakespeare, directed by Roy Mack, goes one stage further, presenting a screenwriter at his desk having been tasked with reading all of Shakespeare following the imagined stupendous overnight success of *A Midsummer Night's Dream*. Faced with the newspaper adverts, "coming," *Macbeth, Julius Caesar, Othello, Hamlet,* the writer falls asleep and visions appear. Typically "loud-mouthed" American Shakespearean characters pop out of their books, dancing to "We're Going Hollywood," "modernising" their characters so that Romeo sings a ditty, "Romeo and Hollywood, what sublimity/ Does anyone know if Miss Garbo/ Has a bal-con-y?" and Hamlet performs a jazzy dance sequence backed by a group of Hamlet-ettes and Antony entertains with a song and dance number which begins "Friends, Romans, and Countrymen, lend me your feet/ To the tune we love, the rhythm of Forty-Second Street." Finally Shakespeare himself appears, complaining, "Is it for this that I spilled so much magic ink?" and Hamlet concludes, "Today the screenplay is the thing."[24]

Reinhardt's declared suspicion of American talkies and his prioritizing of the music, as suggested by his desire to keep Erich Wolfgang Korngold — who arranged the music for the film — on the set, intimate that Shakespeare's language was of secondary importance.[25] Indeed the actors were asked to speak to the music, almost as if they were singing their words to Korngold's score. The universal language of music and the emphasis on visuals serve to upstage the words and in this respect the film harks back to the silent period of film-making in its attempt to appeal to a global audience. The flippancy of the promotional films, especially *Shake, Mr. Shakepeare* insisting on the translation of Shakespeare into "American," reveals an anxiety about the words and the realization that they would (and did) stand in the way of the film's box office appeal.

Undaunted by the mixed success of *A Midsummer Night's Dream,* the following year saw the release of two other adaptations of Shakespeare: George Cukor's *Romeo and Juliet,* starring Leslie Howard and Norma Shearer, and the British film, *As You Like It,* directed by Paul Czinner, with Laurence Olivier in the role of Orlando. Within the short period of sound cinema, much had changed. While in 1929 promoters of *The Taming of the Shrew* repeatedly boasted verbal authenticity, by 1935 it was clear that words were getting in the way of entertainment. Like Warner's *Midsummer Night's Dream,* MGM's *Romeo and Juliet* betrays anxieties about promoting the words in its publicity materials, focusing on the universal appeal of the well-known story. Nonetheless, like *A Midsummer Night's Dream* before it, promoters were not shy to boast originality with the pressbook opening with the assertion that the film will be a "first": "Boy Meet Girl —1436 / ROMEO AND JULIET— 1936" followed by the claim that "now, after five hundred years [*Romeo and*

Juliet], has for the first time been transformed in all its beauty and breathless excitement to a medium perfected for its reception — the motion picture screen,"[26] thus claiming the film to be the first adaptation of the play in spite of the numerous versions of *Romeo and Juliet* that went before.[27] The promotional short film "Master Will Shakespeare" tells the story of Shakespeare's journey to London in search of recognition, made explicitly analogous to those who currently seek their fame and fortune in Hollywood: the voiceover compares Shakespeare's ambitions with Hollywood hopefuls: "You've heard that call little stage-struck Sally, haven't you? And you too footlight fascinated John, who has a play tucked away as Master Will Shakespeare had."[28] While making the obligatory comparisons between Shakespeare's stage and Hollywood film (in particular, the smoking and portly Burbage is unmistakably evocative of a Hollywood mogul), the film is less "American" than its predecessor, *A Midsummer Night's Dream*. The mainly British cast (among the most notable exceptions to this is Andy Devine, whose broad American accent was an abomination to British reviewers[29]) was something of a risk. The film's producer, Irving Thalberg (Shearer's husband and model for F. Scott Fitzgerald's Monroe Stahr, the *Last Tycoon*), takes most of the credit for the film which, like *A Midsummer Night's Dream*, is marketed in the trailer through its value for money; first performances were a staggering $2.20 but we are now reassured that the film is available "at popular prices." The price distinction between premiere prices and normal seats is shorthand for the marketing of the film as cultural bargain, erasing the division between high and low culture, elite and mass entertainment. The cover of the pressbook, as Russell Jackson observes, forecasts the film's (misguided) sense of its marketability: "The World's Greatest Love Story Becomes Your Guaranteed Box-Office Attraction."[30] With pictures of the leading pair Norma Shearer and Leslie Howard, the trailer humorously reduces the plot to a typical Hollywood Romance with "This Girl, This Boy" (ironically they were aged 33 and 43, respectively).

Their performances are marred — perhaps due to their advanced ages — by an underlying sense of embarrassment throughout and thus the film lacks emotional conviction. The restraint of the central pair may be a response to the Motion Picture Production Code, a reserve reflected in the interior shots, which are cold, clinical, and church-like. Juliet's bedroom with pulpit-shaped balcony, her Madonna-like poses and the elaborate Botticelli-inspired but unrevealing costumes contribute to an overall lack of passion. This highly "respectful treatment" of Shakespeare is evident in the pre-eminence given to the literary consultant, Professor William Strunk, Jr., of Cornell University, in the film's opening credits. For the most part, the language is heavily punctuated with action as if to give viewers a break from the words. Even more pronounced than in *A Midsummer Night's Dream* are the contrasting film styles — wordless, visually stimulating sequences (the dances in Capulet's feast) with scenes that are heavily theatrical and seem overly wordy (for example John Barrymore's [Mercutio's] Queen Mab speech is spoken with indecent haste, as if to get it over with as quickly as possible). The quietest of all scenes, Juliet's funeral, is stunningly shot with numerous mourners zigzagging down a dramatic hillside lined with cypress trees.

Harley Granville-Barker regarded the pretension to academic scholarship an offense to Shakespeare. Not deigning to name Professor Strunk, Jr., he refers to "a gentleman placarded upon the screen as a Literary Advisor."[31] In writing of this so-called academic, he vents his hostility to the translation of Shakespeare's words to screen: "Was it he who advised them to leave out more than half the text, or occasionally to hand a speech belonging to one character over to another, or to chop the verse into pieces, and time and time again quite wantonly to cut the rhyme out of the rhymed couplets?"[32] Although poles apart, it is as clear to Granville-Barker as it is to Louis B. Mayer that Shakespeare's words do not mix with film:

> Of the cinema's second-best foot — so to call it — the mechanical reproduction of speech, there is little that need yet be said. The delicate colouring and fine gradations demanded by the speaking of poetry are still beyond its technique (in that filmed "Romeo and Juliet" a surprising proportion of the inhabitants of Verona seemed indeed to be afflicted with cleft palates). But bring it to perfection, it will still hardly oust the picture side of the cinema from pride of place.[33]

These views, that of the Hollywood mogul and the literary critic, on Shakespeare films as being too wordy and not wordy enough are possibly why Hollywood drew a halt to what Granville-Barker calls "the mechanical reproduction of [Shakespeare's] speech." In the mid-thirties there were plans for other Shakespeare films, a Warner Bros.' *Twelfth Night* (directed by Max Reinhardt) and *As You Like It* (from the MGM studios with Shearer suggested as Rosalind and John Barrymore as Jaques), but tellingly there were no further Hollywood Shakespeare adaptations for a decade. As a measure of *Romeo and Juliet's* failure, Leslie Howard's theatre production of *Hamlet* the following year was deemed a flop, eclipsed by the rival John Gielgud performance. Howard failed to cash in on his starring role as Romeo and we can only assume that those who saw him as Romeo didn't want a repeat Shakespearean performance.

Produced in the same year as *Romeo and Juliet*, *As You Like It* rarely gets more than a few words in Shakespeare and film criticism but it deserves to be considered alongside the above films produced between 1929–36 as a Shakespeare product of the new sound era. As with the previous films, there is a noticeable distinction between the movie itself and how it is marketed; the reverential and serious tone of the production is clearly at odds with the emphasis in the promotional materials on the film's popularity. *As You Like It,* the first Shakespeare talkie filmed in England (Inter Allied/20th Century–Fox), was hailed as a star vehicle for the now virtually forgotten actress Elisabeth Bergner, with co-star Laurence Olivier. Like Norma Shearer, Bergner's role in the film may have been compromised by the involvement of her husband (the film's director) and she fails to live up to the hype of the pressbook, which applauds her performance on every page. Although, like its predecessors, the film promoters tried to capitalize on the pedagogical uses of the movie, they were also anxious to attract a global market — the pressbook notes the foreign accent of the star as an asset for universal appeal[34] while the posters and advertisements "protest too much" about the film's easy intelligibility. One "review," for instance, reverts to the film's combination of authenticity and accessibility: "With an astonishing lack of reverential awe with which everyone ordinarily views Shakespeare, the producers of 'As You Like It' have brought the play to the screen as Shakespeare intended it should have been produced in one of the screen's great achievements."[35] In contrast to the pedagogical activities suggested to exhibitors, the promotional advice featured in the pressbook insistently proclaims, "Highbrow? Art-y? Forget it! Shakespeare is fun."[36] Cartoon images include two girls in twin beds assessing the film ("BUT DID YOU EVER SEE A MAN LIKE THAT ORLANDO BEFORE? HO-HUM! PLEASANT DREAMS!"), a young boy eagerly accompanying his mother to the film and men at work, with an overly muscular tattooed and toothless builder affirming that *As You Like It* is a film totally suited to his tastes ("YEAH I THINK IT'S FULL OF EXCRUTIATINGLY COMIC OVERTONES!").[37]

The lengths that the pressbook goes to in order to stress the accessibility of this production reflect a concern that the film would indeed be perceived as too highbrow and too British.

The idea that Bergner's foreign accent would appeal to a global audience could not be more misguided — it's hard to imagine a more unlikable Rosalind. She bellows out her lines incomprehensibly and in the guise of Ganymede irritatingly waves a duster-shaped twig at everyone she encounters. Her performance is excessively theatrical, as if she's speaking to a huge audience with gestures to match. The immaculately dressed forest party seem not to lack in any comfort and thus it is no surprise that so many arrive for the lavish wedding party at the end. Olivier, perhaps unwittingly, upstages Bergner (even though he felt the film a failure[38]) but he also seems to keep at arm's length from her throughout, never allowing us to believe in a love story. Kenneth

Rothwell disagrees, seeing in Olivier's performance "a sullen pupil called on to read aloud in class."[39] In truth, he does appear to distance himself from the role, even the poster image for the film shows him looking beyond Rosalind, a strange image to select for a romantic movie.

In spite of a treatment suggested by J.M. Barrie and a score by William Walton, the film is disappointing compared to its American counterparts. Bergner's performance, rather than liberating the film from the difficulties of Shakespeare's language, magnifies its incomprehensibility. She may look the part, but she sounds dreadful. Among the survivors of this film are David Lean (the then-young film editor) who went on successfully to direct adaptations of *Great Expectations* (1946), *Oliver Twist* (1948), *Doctor Zhivago* (1965) and *A Passage to India* (1984), and Laurence Olivier, who was to later become identified with cinematic Shakespeare, but who at this stage of his career felt that Shakespeare and film did not mix, reminiscent perhaps of those in the late twenties and early thirties who were similarly cynical about the longevity of sound.[40] For almost a decade afterwards, this view that Shakespeare was un-filmable prevailed.

These 1930 talkie adaptations of Shakespeare's plays were marketed for both their retention of Shakespeare's words (making them the "first" adaptations of the plays) and their global appeal, special selling points which were, in hindsight, a contradiction in terms. Words were indeed both requisites and poison for the translation of Shakespeare to screen, and these contradictory requirements would haunt the entire field of adaptation studies for most of the 20th century. While continuing to claim film's pedagogical potential, filmmakers needed to look at "lesser" writers for source material. In this early era of sound film, Shakespeare was at his best when silent.

NOTES

1. Quoted in Robert F. Willson, Jr., *Shakespeare in Hollywood 1929–1956*, Madison, NJ: Fairleigh Dickinson University Press, 2000, 7.

2. See Deborah Cartmell, "Sound Adaptations: Sam Taylor's *Taming of the Shrew*" in *The Blackwell Companion to Literature, Film and Adaptation*, Deborah Cartmell, ed., Oxford: Blackwell, 2012.

3. *The Taming of the Shrew* pressbook, 1929, 9,10.

4. Scott Eyman, *The Speed of Sound*, Baltimore: Johns Hopkins University Press, 1997, 276.

5. Scott MacQueen, audio commentary on *Taming of the Shrew* (1929), DVD, Turner Entertainment Co. and Warner Bros. Entertainment Inc., U.S.A., 2007.

6. *The Show of Shows*, John G. Adolfi, dir., Frank Fay, J. Keirn Brennan, scr., Warner Bros. Pictures, 1929.

7. This sequence is available on YouTube, http://www.youtube.com/watch?v=vbMDp 80kU7E (accessed 19/02/12).

8. Eyman, *The Speed of Sound*, 315.

9. Scott MacQueen, audio commentary on *Taming of the Shrew*.

10. II.2. 255–256 and II.2.148–149, respectively.

11. For an account of this, see Russell Jackson, *Shakespeare Films in the Making: Vision, Production and Reception*, Cambridge: Cambridge University Press, 2007, 28.

12. Jack J. Jorgens, *Shakespeare on Film*, Bloomington: Indiana University Press, 1977, 51.

13. "Shakespearean Art Makes 'Martyrs' of Film Stars," *A Midsummer Night's Dream* pressbook, 1935, 26.

14. *The Spectator,* 18 October 1935, in *The Graham Greene Film Reader: Mornings in the Dark,* David Parkinson, ed., Harmondsworth: Penguin, 1993, 38.

15. *The Listener* XVII, 425, 3 March 1937, 387–389, 425, 387.

16. "Much Ado About Nothing," reprinted in *Shakespeare on Film, Television and Radio: The Researcher's Guide,* Olwen Terris, Eve-Marie Oesterlen, Luke McKernan, eds., London: British Universities Film & Video Council, 2009, 145–148.

17. Erwin Panofsky, "Style and Medium in the Moving Pictures," in *Film Theory and Film Criticism: Introductory Essays,* Gerald Mast, Marshall Cohen, Leo Braudy, eds., Oxford: Oxford University Press, 1974, 233–248, 238.

18. Allardyce Nicoll, *Film and Theatre*, London: George G. Harrap, 1936, 28–29.

19. "Spreading the News Round Schools," *A Midsummer Night's Dream* pressbook, 1936, 6.

20. "'Teachers' Manuals' from Hays Office," pressbook — see *A Midsummer Night's Dream*, E. Edward Edleson, ed., New York, 1936, 6.

21. "Catchlines," Pressbook, 21.

22. "All Ages and All Classes Join in Praise of 'Dream,'" *A Midsummer Night's Dream* pressbook, 29.

23. *Ibid.*

24. Available on the DVD special features on *A Midsummer Night's Dream.*

25. Scott MacQueen, audio commentary on *Taming of the Shrew.*

26. "Boy Meets Girl —1436, ROMEO AND JULIET—1936," *Romeo and Juliet* pressbook, 1936, np. The authors of this go on to claim that a film of *Romeo and Juliet* was previously impossible, as there was not a producer who could rise to the challenge before Irving Thalberg came along.

27. The IMDB lists 11 with matching titles alone.

28. "Master Will Shakespeare," Jacques Tourneur, dir., Richard Goldstone, scr., *Romeo and Juliet* (1936), Turner Entertainment Co., 2007.

29. Jackson, *Shakespeare Films in the Making*, 159.

30. *Ibid.*, 154.

31. *Ibid.*, 388.

32. *Ibid.*

33. *Ibid.*, 425.

34. "Bergner's 'Rosalind' Her Best-Loved Role," *As You Like It* pressbook, 1936, 14.

35. "*As You Like It* Grandest Fun Ever Brought to Screen," *As You Like It* pressbook, 15.

36. "So you *think* you don't like Shakespeare?," *As You Like It* pressbook, 11.

37. *Ibid.*, 11–12.

38. Samuel Crowl, *Shakespeare and Film*, New York: Norton, 2008, 8.

39. Kenneth Rothwell, *A History of Shakespeare on Screen: A Century of Film and Television*, Cambridge: Cambridge University Press, 1999, 50.

40. See Crowl, *Shakespeare and Film*, 8, and John Cottrell, *Laurence Olivier*, Upper Saddle River, NJ: Prentice-Hall, 1975, 101–103.

BIBLIOGRAPHY

Boose, Linda, and Richard Burt, eds. *Shakespeare the Movie.* London: Routledge, 1997.

Buchman, Lorne Michael. *Still in Movement: Shakespeare on Screen.* Oxford: Oxford University Press, 1991.

Cartmell, Deborah. "Sound Adaptations: Sam Taylor's Taming of the Shrew." *The Blackwell Companion to Literature, Film and Adaptation,* Deborah Cartmell, ed. Oxford: Blackwell, 2012.

Clayton, B. "Shakespeare and the Talkies." *English Review,* XLIV (1929) 739–52.

Collick, John. *Shakespeare, Cinema and Society.* Manchester: Manchester University Press, 1989.

Davies, Anthony. *Filming Shakespeare's Plays: The Adaptations of Laurence Olivier, Orson Welles, Peter Brook, and Akira Kurosawa.* Cambridge: Cambridge University Press, 1990.

Davies, Anthony, and Stanley Wells, eds. *Shakespeare Survey 39.* Cambridge: Cambridge University Press, 1987.

Donaldson, Peter. *Shakespearean Films / Shakespearean Directors.* London: Unwin Hyman, 1990.

Eyman, Scott. *The Speed of Sound: Hollywood and the Talkie Revolution, 1926–1930.* Baltimore: Johns Hopkins University Press, 1997.

Jackson, Russell. *Shakespeare Films in the Making: Vision, Production and Reception.* Cambridge: Cambridge University Press, 2007.

Jorgens, Jack J. *Shakespeare on Film.* Bloomington: Indiana University Press, 1977.

The Listener XVII, 425, 3 March 1937, 387–389, 425, 387.

A Midsummer Night's Dream pressbook, 1935.

Parkinson, David, ed. *The Graham Greene Film Reader: Mornings in the Dark.* Harmondsworth: Penguin, 1993.

The Show of Shows. John G. Adolfi, dir., Frank Fay, J. Keirn Brennan, scr., Warner Bros. Pictures, 1929.

The Taming of the Shrew (1929). DVD, Turner Entertainment Co and Warner Bros. Entertainment Inc., U.S.A., 2007.

The Taming of the Shrew pressbook, 1929.

Terris, Olwen, Eve-Marie Oesterlen, and Luke McKernan, eds. *Shakespeare on Film, Television and Radio: The Researcher's Guide.* London: British Universities Film & Video Council, 2009.

Willson, Robert F., Jr. *Shakespeare in Hollywood 1929–1956.* Madison, NJ: Fairleigh Dickinson University Press, 2000.

Postmodern Screened Writers
Kamilla Elliott

The paper that I presented at the Lorient conference has evolved into two essays. "Screened Writers"[1] expands the first part of that paper, addressing representations of canonical British authors in films that adapt their works; this essay expands the second part, turning from dead British authors to address living[2] American writers screened in films that adapt their works.[3] Charlie Kaufman wrote the screenplay for *Adaptation* (2002),[4] also writing himself into the film as a character played by Nicolas Cage. Although Harvey Pekar did not write the screenplay for *American Splendor* (2003),[5] the film adapts his autobiographical comic books and he appears in the film in various forms.

Both essays investigate how undead screened writers run up against traditional and poststructuralist notions of dead authors. In "The Death of the Author," Roland Barthes declares that

> writing is the destruction of every voice, of every point of origin [...] the voice loses its origin, the author enters into his own death, [when] writing begins [... There is] no other origin than language itself, language which ceaselessly calls into question all origins [...] it is language which speaks, not the author [... A] text is not a line of words releasing a single "theological" meaning (the "message" of the Author-God) but a multi-dimensional space in which a variety of writings, none of them original, blend and clash [...] a text is made of multiple writings, drawn from many cultures and entering into mutual relations of dialogue, parody, contestation, but there is one place where this multiplicity is focused and that place is the reader, not [...] the author [...] the birth of the reader must be at the cost of the death of the Author.[6]

Literary film adapters occupy an ambivalent position under Barthes's formulation: as readers of literary texts, they are born ushering in the deaths of literary authors; as authors of films based on those texts, even as they affirm

Barthesean intertextuality, they too are pronounced dead by Barthes as authors.

One would expect dead British literary authors to resist Barthes's post-structuralist authorial death, depending as they do on older theories of author-ship and death for their immortality and canonization. Conversely, one would expect films espousing postmodern and poststructuralist ideologies and aes-thetics to support Barthes's concepts. Both *Adaptation* and *American Splendor* foreground postmodern concepts of authorship and identity: neither allows its screened writer an autonomous, individual, core, stable identity. Kaufman divides himself into author and character, and gives the latter a fictitious screenwriting twin brother, Donald, also played by Nicolas Cage.[7] Pekar takes many more forms than Kaufman in his film, appearing in *propria persona* in newly filmed and archival footage (nominated REAL HARVEY and HUMAN HARVEY in the screenplay) and represented in his own words, whether the words of his autobiographical comics, responses to filmed interviews, or on the DVD commentary. He also appears represented by others, reading voiceover scripted by screenwriter-directors Robert Pulcini and Shari Springer Berman; played by actors Paul Giamatti, Daniel Tay, and Donal Logue (nom-inated HARVEY, KID, and STAGE ACTOR HARVEY in the screenplay); drawn by some of the more than 70 illustrators of his comics (nominated CARTOON HARVEY in the screenplay); he is further represented as a name in the phone book and as a rag doll made and sold by his wife (nominated HARVEY RAG DOLL in the screenplay).[8]

Both films are further postmodern in that they are self-reflexively con-cerned with their own making. *Adaptation* is about its own writing, drama-tizing Kaufman's attempts to adapt Susan Orlean's *The Orchid Thief* (2000)[9] to itself; *American Splendor* is a docu-drama tracing Pekar's life and life writing and featuring *faux* documentary scenes of its own making.

And yet these postmodern films challenge as much as they affirm post-structuralist theories of authorship. Both films multiply representations of writers to shore their fragments against the postmodern ruins of Barthes's "death of the author" and against cultural devaluations of screenwriters and comic book writers.

Postmodern screened writers function further to shift discourses of literary film adaptations from its usual suspects. Depicting screened writers writing auto-biographical texts on which films are based shifts the focus from adaptation as product to adaptation as process; it sidelines questions of how true the films are to the books they adapt, displacing them with questions of how true the films are to the life of their writing and to the life of their writers; it fore-grounds questions of which medium is closer to life or reality, books or films.

The Death of the Screenwriter

"You. You're in the eyeline. Can you please get off the stage?"—Thomas Smith[10]

Long before Barthes, screenwriters have had to struggle more than other writers with being pronounced dead. While Barthes represents the death of authors as part of a cycle of death and birth, theories of screenwriting could be described as murderous. More than a decade before Barthes, New Wave film theorists (most notably François Truffaut) were declaring the death of the screenwriter as author of films and the birth of the director-*auteur*.[11] The writing of screenwriters has also been murdered by film theory. Throughout film history, theorists and aestheticians have made the destruction of written language (whether the words of literary texts or of screenplays generally) a cardinal principle of filmmaking. After surveying numerous scholars who propound this process, I concluded: "The process of filmmaking is one of de-verbalizing, de-literarizing, and de-wording verbal language to make film 'language.' This is not translation but evisceration into images. Indeed, one could argue that the destruction and dominance of the word constitutes a principal aesthetic of film theory."[12] Such aesthetics persist, shifting the debate over representational authority from Barthes's triad of author, text, and reader to a battle between words and images and writers and filmmakers.

In *Rethinking the Novel/Film Debate*, I traced the marginalization of screenwriters in the film industry before and after New Wave theory.[13] The film *Adaptation* begins by dramatizing this marginalization. The opening scene unfolds as *faux* behind-the-scenes documentary footage on the set of Charlie Kaufman's previous film, *Being John Malkovich* (1999), a dramatization based on his real life experience.[14] Lead actor John Malkovich, assistant director Thomas Smith, and cinematographer Lance Acord each evince creative and directive authority, telling actors and extras what to do. When Kaufman appears to watch the filming, no one knows who he is and he is promptly ordered off the set: "You. You're in the eyeline. Can you please get off the stage?"[15] The task of the screenwriter is to remain unrecognized and to make sure that he and his writing are *not* visible in the finished film. The writer and his writing, then, are not to be screened. The death of his writing as well as himself as author of the film here marks a greater death than Barthes proscribes.

Kaufman's next film, *Adaptation*, puts the screenwriter and his writing squarely in the eyeline, making him the film's protagonist and its central plot his struggle to adapt Susan Orlean's literary nonfiction, *The Orchid Thief* to a screenplay, featuring almost everyone else (Orlean, John Laroche the orchid thief, the film's producer, screenwriting teacher Robert McKee, Kaufman's agent, and his own twin brother) as his antagonists. The film presents itself as an act of live literary film adaptation, unfolding as a non-linear, self-reflexive, postmodern pastiche of Charlie's many attempts to adapt the book. We witness Charlie typing and audio-recording drafts of the screenplay; we hear them as voiceover; we read them as typeface; we see filmed scenes shot from the screenplay as shooting script. At times, we see scenes being written *after* they have been screened; at others, we see them being written *as* they are being screened. *Adaptation*, then, resists the death of the screenwriter in both Barthesean and film theory senses: it shows the writer writing; it refuses to produce a final script that will allow his death; it refuses to follow conventions that make the destruction of screenwriting the grounds of filmmaking. Refusing to let the process of writing end before the film begins, ending the film with Charlie intending to write the ending, and having the author speak in voiceover (which also violates mainstream film and screenwriting conventions of the time) all resist the destruction of the screenplay as the basis of film and the death of the screenwriter either in verbal language or film images.

Kaufman has explained his interest in screening writers engaged in acts of live writing as a response to the *death* that he perceives in films:

> There's something about movies that's very safe because they usually play out in a certain way, and also because they're done. They're dead. It's not like theater where anything can happen [...] It's just this dead thing that you're watching and I don't like that about it.
> Take real people and take the person who really wrote it, and make them characters, and have the experience of watching them write it be the experience that the moviegoer has.[16]

Adaptation figures mainstream Hollywood conventions as another sort of death, set against "life." In his meeting with producer Valerie Thomas (Tilda Swinton), which Kaufman has said was based on a real-life meeting, Charlie resists conforming his screenplay to Hollywood conventions:

> I just don't want to ruin it by making it a Hollywood thing. [...] Like an orchid heist movie [...] changing the orchids into poppies and turning it into a movie about drug running [...] I don't want to cram in sex or guns or car chases [...] Or characters learning profound life lessons. Or growing, or coming to like each other, or overcoming obstacles to succeed in the end.[17]

Charlie wants "to let the movie exist, rather than be artificially plot driven." He justifies his resistance to Hollywood conventions by his aspiration to be faithful to the book: "the book isn't like that," he protests; he wants to "remain true" to the book. But he goes further to equate the book, a work of literary nonfiction, with life, extending his aspiration to fidelity from the book to life: "the book isn't like that, and life isn't like that. It just isn't."[18] The singular "it" here conflates book with life and assigns Hollywood to negation and unreality. Later in the film, Charlie makes the same protest against screenwriting guru Robert McKee's principles. When McKee (Brian Cox) counters that real life is full of sensational stories that feed Hollywood conventions,[19] Charlie begins to reconsider his equation of Orlean's book with real life and Hollywood with fictionality.

The Hollywood screenwriting conventions that Charlie resists are championed by McKee and gormlessly and enthusiastically adopted by Charlie's simple-minded twin brother, Donald, an aspiring screenwriter. Donald takes the diametrically opposed view that the book is not true to life, while Hollywood is. Not only does he script his screenplay according to McKee's principles, he also scripts his own life (as far as possible) according to Hollywood film. When Charlie, paralyzed by writer's block (which paradoxically keeps the author alive) turns to Donald for help, Donald not only adds the very elements Charlie refused to introduce into the screenplay (changing the orchids into drug-producing plants, cramming in sex and guns and car chases, showing characters learning profound life lessons and growing and coming to like each other and overcoming obstacles to succeed in the end); he also conforms his own life and death to them. Indeed, Donald's death at the end is a Barthesean as well as Hollywood death, since he has finished his version of the screenplay.

Literary Nonfiction, Film and Life

"[O]nce you meet somebody that you're writing about it becomes very hard to [...] separate."— Charlie Kaufman[20]

Donald will not allow that Hollywood conventions are fictional fabrications. Rather, he maintains that his fictional screenplay is truer to life than Orlean's nonfiction book. He insists that Charlie has failed to adapt *The Orchid Thief* not because he is inept or because the book is "uncinematic," but because the author is a liar and her book is a lie. His evidence that Susan is "lying" is based on the fact that "she said everything right" and "people who answer questions too right are liars."[21] The appearance of absolute verbal truth, Donald insists, must screen a lie.

Donald represents his additions to Charlie's screenplay as investigative journalism truer than Orlean's journalism: as filmic exposures of the lying author and her secret life. The truth of the author's life is, amazingly, identical to and indistinguishable from the formulaic sensationalized plots of mainstream Hollywood film. The author, then, is screened as personified Hollywood film, while her own representation of herself in her nonfiction book is largely screened off, and what is represented is figured as fiction and lies.

Donald displaces his infidelity to her book onto her marital, professional, and criminal infidelities. "'The movie,' Orlean has said, 'goes from faithful to crazily unfaithful' which, ironically, is exactly the trajectory of her on-screen self."[22] In Charlie's script, Susan is an elite author, successful, insightful, and professional. In Donald's script, she violates her professional ethics, her marriage vows, and Title 21, Section 841 of the United States Controlled Substances Act. She has sex with a subject, takes illegal drugs, posts pornographic pictures of herself on the Internet, and tries to kill Donald and Charlie to prevent them from exposing her in/through their screenplay/film.

Donald's adaptation does not simply adapt the author to Hollywood clichés; it further undertakes principles of literary film adaptation propagated by mass market screenwriting books, most notably McKee's *Story*.[23] Donald's script crassly literalizes poetic verbal metaphors and undertakes the crudest of word-to-image translations. Donald believes that literary metaphors express neither abstractions nor subjectivities, but rather secrets and lies.[24] Rather than expressing a higher truth, literary metaphors hide literal truth, and Donald avers that the way to expose that truth is to literalize the metaphors. Orlean's poignant and amorphous yearning to feel passion akin to the passion that her subjects feel for orchids translates in Donald's script to passionate sex with a subject and physical passion for a drug extracted from orchids, called "Passion" in an earlier version of the script.[25] When, towards the end of the shooting script, Charlie gazes on a wailing, exposed Susan (Meryl Streep), she is described as an incarnation: "this person, this concept turned flesh before his eyes."[26] Donald has done more than incarnate her, however: he has carnalized her.

Donald similarly adapts the author to film via a crude, formulaic approach to adaptation as word-to-image translation. Charlie's earlier attempts to adapt *The Orchid Thief* show the book as a legible document, illuminated with yellow highlights, flagged with yellow post-its, and edged with marginalia, refusing to dissolve into film or be adapted to screenplay format. Once Donald has rejected the book as a lie, he discards it and subjects the author to cinematic surveillance to expose "the truth," spying on her through lighted rectangular windows that look like film screens, pulling her into cinematic close-ups via binoculars. Donald, then, screens off the book and screens the writer using film techniques. Donald displaces her image from the book onto Laroche's Internet porn site. As Orlean profited from writing about her subject, the orchid thief Laroche (Chris Cooper), Laroche now profits from screening her image on his web site.

Yet for all its irreverence to the author and departures from her book, in apparent contrast to Charlie's earlier attempts to adapt it, Donald's screenplay does not differ much from Charlie's. Donald's adaptation is as much a literalization and carnalization of Charlie's script as it is of *The Orchid Thief.* The seeds of Donald's pornographic author are in Charlie's script when he masturbates to the author's photograph on the book jacket. Charlie's masturbatory fantasy has already carnalized the author as muse and conventions that figure literary film adaptation as adapting the spirit of a text. The photo materializes in his fantasy to Susan (Streep) herself and the author copulates with the screenwriter, achieving a simultaneous orgasm, representative of harmonious adaptation.

The seeds of Donald's violent showdown with the author are also in Charlie's script. Charlie's admiration of Susan's writing as "great, sprawling New Yorker stuff" has already evolved into exasperation with "that sprawling New Yorker shit" in a later discussion with agent Marty Bowen (Ron Livingston).[27] Donald's script carnalizes Charlie's verbally expressed frustration with Orlean's words as physical combat. The author, whom Charlie has been too terrified to meet, turns out, in Donald's literalization of his fear, to be extremely dangerous in the flesh. When Charlie finally joins Donald in spying on Susan, violating her scopic space, the author retaliates by pulling him violently into her physical space. Although Susan fails in her attempt to kill the twin screenwriters, Donald dies in a car crash fleeing the murderous author and Laroche, the incarnation of the book's title, the orchid thief, is killed by an alligator. Following the death of the subject and the fictional screenwriter, only the literary author and original screenwriter remain. With guns sunk in the swamp, their final showdown is, appropriately, a battle of words. Susan turns from attempted murder to hurling insults; Charlie turns from physical flight to verbal defense and attempted verbal murder, repeatedly telling the author to "Shut up!"[28] Charlie's diction of self-loathing—"loser," "fat," and "bald"—leveled at himself throughout the film, now flies at him from the mouth of the author who had, in his masturbatory fantasy tenderly contradicted his verbal self-abuse. The slurs "fat" and "bald" are physicalizations of Charlie's writerly excess and lack, his authorial grandiosity and failure. Confusing the two identities further, many of the insults Charlie hurls at Susan are abuses he has also inflicted on himself: "lonely," "old," "desperate," and "pathetic."[29] But there is revenge as well as projection in the verbal combat: Susan calls Charlie "a fat piece of shit" just as he called her writing "sprawling *New Yorker* shit."[30]

The rhetorical projections of this scene attach to plot-based projections. The author's attempt to kill the screenwriter lest he reveal her professional and personal failures is itself a projection: it is the screenwriter who wants to murder the author for exposing *his* professional and personal failures (and an earlier version of the screenplay did kill off the author).[31] The final version of the film, however, rejects the death of both author and screenwriter and instead settles for the death of the book, epitomized by the death of "the orchid thief," John Laroche, and the death of the conventional Hollywood screenwriter, Donald, himself a fiction that Hollywood believed in for some time, as I detail below. The personified allegory of adaptation, then, emerges not so much as the death of her as the author made flesh, crassly, carnally, and according to Hollywood conventions of illicit sex, drugs, and violence. Donald's adaptation represents her attempted (and failed) life rather than her death. The film leaves the literary author bemoaning her life and yearning impossibly to return to her origins: "Oh, my God. It's over. Everything's over. I did everything wrong. I want my life back. I want it back before it all got fucked up. I want to be a baby again. I want to be new. I want to be new."[32] The representation resists the author as literary origin from which the film has strayed, substituting an author who has strayed from and betrayed her life as represented by her book: from her own literary identity and origins.

Her attempted and failed life is tied integrally to her attempted and failed murder of the screenwriters. Although Donald is accidentally killed fleeing from the author, the happy ending of the film is that both Hollywood conventions and the prestigious literary author have failed to kill off the marginalized screenwriter. Yet his is no unilateral triumph. Equations of writing with life and representations of both literature and film as life writing that keep authors alive are shot through with writer's block that threaten his birth as author of this project, let alone his death. Throughout the film, Charlie equates his failure to write with his failure to live life. After McKee challenges Charlie's idea of what real life is and Charlie begins to reconsider his aesthetics, he also begins to reconsider the way he lives his life so introspectively and self-reflexively, like a piece of postmodern literary nonfiction afraid to become a screenplay: afraid to act, speak, or commit to anything outside of his own head (or anything within his own head). He tells McKee, "What you said was bigger than my screenwriting choices. It was about my choices as a human being."[33] Charlie's resolve to live more like a McKee script forms the tongue-in-cheek moral of the screenplay, in which real life aspires to be more like Hollywood film.

The final ending of the film is not Donald's: it is Charlie's. Just as the film leaves Susan impossibly longing to return to her literary self as origin, so too it leaves Charlie impossibly writing the ending of the film without actually ending it, resolving to act without actually acting, resolving to change without actually changing. The film thus ends much where it began, with Charlie resolving in voiceover to change and improve himself, as an attempted and impossible return to origins that lies between attempted murder and attempted birth, epitomized by the author's yearning to be born again and the screenwriter's *ourobouros* (a snake swallowing its own tail) — his self-consuming communion of tails/tales and heads, of ends and beginnings.

The ending of *Adaptation*, however, does not exactly return to its beginning. It goes further to make a conclusion about the relationship between the life of the writer and the life of the writing. The ending shows the eternal life of writing: the writer alive in the writing, his lived life being written into the writing. It shows the writer resolving to end the film, writing the end of the film as voiceover, acting out the film he is writing. As the writer adapts his life to the writing, the writing adapts to his life, each feeding the other to resist the death of the author. *Adaptation*, in the final analysis, does not sacrifice the author for the life of the text, as Barthes does, or set the biographical life of the writer at odds with the author function, as Foucault does, but rather figures adaptation as *ourobouros*: as attempted murder that feeds attempted life. The film further sets *ourobouros* against Barthes's successional life cycle, in which "the birth of the reader must be at the cost of the death of the Author,"[34] where the author dies giving birth to the reader. By representing the author as reader of his writing throughout the film, reading what he writes as he writes it, he keeps himself alive.

Kaufman's screenplay also shifts the grounds upon which book to film adaptations are usually addressed: "Even though you're watching the movie as a story that plays as a story, there's the constant nagging thing that's 'Is this real, is this not real?'"[35] Most reviews, articles, and interviews on *Adaptation* set aside the usual comparisons of book and film in favor of comparisons between real and reel life, probing the film's intersecting levels and layers of invented and real-life people, constructed and actual events, and fictional and autobiographical writing.[36] Kaufman, then, has shifted the question from "How is the film faithful or unfaithful to the book?" to "How is this film faithful or unfaithful to real life?"

Kaufman's screenplay, however, does not simply concede to conventional postmodern conclusions that everything is a fiction. Indeed, when journalists all too ready to use the film to champion postmodern omnifictionality express conventional skepticism that there is anything "real" in the film, Kaufman contradicts them:

> [T]he sweating, pacing, fretting Kaufman we see on screen, barely articulate in an interview with an executive, could well be an exaggeration, even a caricature, of the real one. Or, indeed, a complete fabrication. Put simply, the more we

think we know about Hollywood's most intriguing screenwriter, the more opaque and mysterious he becomes. Kaufman, perhaps unsurprisingly, disagrees: "I think the personality traits you see on screen are an aspect of myself and that writing seems to make me focus on that side of myself more. There are exaggerations and fabrications but the personality traits are actual. I've been in that meeting and been trapped in a total feeling of self consciousness and awkwardness."[37]

The disclaimer at the end of the film also acknowledges the co-existence of the "actual" and the "fictitious" rather than yielding to a postmodern omnifictionality:

> This story is based upon actual events. However, some of the characters, incidents portrayed and some of the names herein are fictitious, and with respect to such characters and incidents, any similarity to the name, character, or history of any person, living or dead, or any actual event, is entirely coincidental and unintentional.

In the film, "actual" people play themselves, such as John Malkovich, Catherine Keener, and John Cusack. Other "actual" people are played by actors, such as Charlie Kaufman, Susan Orlean, Valerie Thomas, John Laroche, and Robert McKee. Still others, are fictitious characters with no biographical counterparts, most notably Donald Kaufman. Extradiegetically, Donald is credited as though he were an actual person, as co-screenwriter of the film along with Charlie Kaufman. For some time, interviewers besieged a tight-lipped Kaufman with questions about Donald's existence or non-existence. He was nominated along with the actual Charlie for both Golden Globe and Academy Awards for screenwriting (although the "brothers" were informed that if they won they would have to share an Oscar statuette).[38]

Between the script and the finished film, in the production process, lie further interplays between fictionality and actuality. The actual Charlie Kaufman served as a stand-in for the actor who plays him, both reversing the concept that the actor stands in for the real-life character and counterpointing his own fictional representation of Kaufman being told to get out of the eyeline and off the stage.[39] Nicolas Cage's brother, Marc Coppola, served as a stand-in for him, both realizing and reversing the fiction created by one actor playing two brothers, since two brothers stand in for one actor. The actual Susan Orlean was cast as a supermarket shopper in a scene that was cut from the final version of the film. The author of the book, then, was first screened as not-author and then screened off from the finished film, a real-life correlative to her fictionalization and conquest by the fictional screenwriters.[40]

Adaptation, then, sets fiction and actuality in specific, orchestrated relations to restore the screenwriter and screenplay to film aesthetics and to challenge conventions of which medium, literature or film, is closer to life, and to redirect the questions conventionally asked of literature to film adaptations.

Life Writing and the Death of the Author

"Anything that doesn't kill me could be the basis of one of my stories."
— Harvey Pekar[41]

A year later, the film *American Splendor* sets life-writing against the death of the author even more didactically than *Adaptation* does. Like Charlie, Pekar is threatened by and must overcome bodily death in the film. The happy ending of the film depicts him celebrating his defeat of death from cancer and his ongoing life as author. While other recent films of screened writers, including *Adaptation*, figure sexual libido and romantic partners as inspirations for writing,[42] *American Splendor* makes fear of death Pekar's initial motivation for writing. While Pekar himself has indicated that his inspiration was intertextual (he was inspired to write after reading Crumb's comics),[43] the film minimizes this impetus in favor of an older tradition of authorship and death: that fear of death compels authors to seek immortality through writing. In a fictional scene not based on his comics, Pekar (Paul Giamatti), a file clerk in a hospital, comes across the death record of a fellow file clerk. Seized with awareness of his own future death by analogy, he begins to write his life. This scene, in which consciousness of death gives birth to life writing, can be read as a defense against Barthes's "death of the author," as writing produces authorial life as language and text, which Barthes allows to live. Both film and comics additionally reverse and subvert Barthes's argument that "writing is the death of every voice,"[44] since Pekar writes in response to losing his voice: "I lost my voice for three months. [...] So I started writin' stuff down — stories an' things, my points a' view, ideas."[45]

Subsequently, when Crumb offers to illustrate Pekar's comic, Pekar regains his voice.[46] If writing is the death of every voice, illustration, it seems, restores it. Images more substantially resist the death of the author in language, through portraiture's conventions of immanence, in which a subject inheres and is present in his portrait.[47] As I have argued elsewhere, representations of authors as/by images destabilize Foucault's location of the author function in the proper name:

> For Foucault, the author function is located in the proper name, which subjects it to discourses, beliefs, and practices that surround and attach to that proper name, governing the production, circulation, classification, and consumption of

texts. Yet to locate the author function in his or her name is *itself* a discourse of authorship that expresses beliefs about authorship that are too narrowly linguistic, literary, and discursive and do not sufficiently account for some cultural practices. For millennia, the author function has manifested in *images* of authorial bodies as well as proper names — in portraits, statues, photographs, film, television, and digital media.[48]

Moreover, Foucault differentiates "the individual named" from "the author's name": "[...] the author's name, unlike other proper names, does not pass from the interior of a discourse to the real and exterior individual who produced it; instead, the name seems always to be present, marking off the edges of the text, revealing, or at least characterizing, its mode of being."[49] Autobiographical writing complicates Foucault's segregation, since its "mode of being" is integrally bound up in representing "the real and exterior individual who produced it." "The Harvey Pekar Name Story," written by Pekar, illustrated by Crumb, and animated in the film, illustrates this complexity. Pondering another Harvey Pekar in the phone book, Pekar concludes that, because the other man's entry has no middle initial, "his was a purer listing." The phone book undermines Pekar's name with a rival "purer" version of the authorial name that belongs to another who is not author.[50] That the name does not refer to the author Pekar only accentuates its dilution of the authorial name. In the film, as the actor playing Pekar dramatizes this comic, the actual Pekar crosses the scene behind him and vanishes in a filmic dissolve.

That Pekar is represented by others — whether by phone book compilers or illustrators or actors or screenwriters or a doll — both augments and diminishes him as author. As he becomes subject to representations authored by others, he loses authorial authority; yet as he becomes part of their texts, he is allowed to live, even as they die producing him. That they represent him *as* an author only intensifies the paradox.

The film's screenwriters have this author affirm their representations of him. Early in the film, Pekar reads their scripted voiceover: "Different artists draw me all kinds of ways but hey I'm also a real guy. And now there's this guy playing me in a movie. Here's our man; here's me; here's the guy playing me anyway, though he don't look nothin' like me, but whatever"[51] While "The Harvey Pekar Name Story" ends with the unanswered question, "Who is Harvey Pekar?"[52] the screenplay makes him give an answer, affirming all of the film's representations of him as authentic: "I keep tellin' ya, all of 'ems me."[53]

However, the apostrophes in this speech and throughout the screenplay undermine his authority, othering his language as dialect. The inverted commas suggest that his own words are lacking (literally missing letters); they also gesture to other uses of inverted commas that mark speech as quotation. By contrast, the screenwriters represent their own descriptive narration in standard English. In his comics, Pekar uses standard English to represent his speech.

The screenplay further undermines his writing and authorial authority with poststructuralist concepts of authorship. The film opens with Pekar announcing in scripted voiceover: "This is the story about comic books, an' a guy who made a whole life outta them."[54] While both the comic books and their author are declared to be the film's subjects here, the comic books take temporal priority. The life made "outta" comic books upends the theories of expressive authorship that Pekar himself espouses, in which life provides the raw material for autobiographical writing; it substitutes constructionism, asserting that comic books are the materials from which Pekar has made his life as well as his living. The screenplay figures the comics as "his life": "PANELS from Harvey's comics begin to float over his head, his life literally passing before his eyes in comic book form,"[55] further representing his life as the construction of comics: "The following montage chronicles Harvey's illness by cutting between comic art depicting key events and shots of HARVEY, JOYCE and FRED creating the book."[56] It invents a sequence in which Pekar, following his encounter with the dead clerk's medical file, is not so much inspired to write by his life as by his comic book persona:

> Instead of still comic panels with balloons, the Cartoon Harvey now rants directly into the camera. [...] The Human Harvey seems oblivious to his cartoon replica. [...] The Cartoon Harvey turns to address the Human Harvey, who actually looks him in the eyes. It now seems Human Harvey can actually hear his cartoon alter ego.
>
> CARTOON HARVEY: Wake up! Your whole life's gettin' eaten away by this kinda crap! What kind of existence is this? Is this all a workin' stiff like you can expect? Ya gonna suffer in silence fer the rest a' yer life?! Or ya gonna make a mark. Huh? Huh?
>
> IN AN INSTANT, THE CARTOON HARVEY DISAPPEARS AND THE LIVE ACTION SCENE TAKES OVER THE WHOLE FRAME. [...]
>
> CUT TO:
>
> INT. HARVEY'S KITCHEN — NIGHT
>
> Bursting with ideas, Harvey (wearing his undershirt and boxers) starts storyboarding his first comic with stick figures.[57]

Later, when Harvey faces cancer, Pulcini and Berman script a scene in which his wife, Joyce (played by Hope Davis), figures autobiographical writing in poststructuralist terms as a mechanism that *distances* and *defers* life rather than manifests or makes it: "You'll make a comic book out of the whole thing. You'll document every little detail. And that way you'll remove yourself from the experience until it's over."[58]

But the film is not entirely poststructuralist in its links between authorship and death. Just as the film is a pastiche of conventional and *avant garde* film conventions, so too it is a pastiche of older and newer theories of authorship. The pastiche, however, amplifies rather than reduces the power of death over the author. Diagnosed with cancer, Pekar ponders: "Am I some guy who writes about himself in a comic book? Or am I just — am I just a character in that book? When I die, will 'dat character keep goin'? Or will he just fade away?"[59] Pekar's questions express a hybrid blend of postmodern and Romantic concepts of authorship and death. From a Romantic view, physical death threatens the life of the character, dependent as it is on the life of the author for its continuation as an expression of authorial life, rather than bestowing immortality upon him after death. From a poststructuralist view, blurring the line between author and character through autobiography paradoxically forefends against Barthesean authorial death, since the author-as-character is part of the text, which Barthes allows to live. Yet Barthesean theory also insists that the character kills the author, since the author dies at the moment of writing himself as character. The film's Romantic-poststructuralist theoretical pastiche, then, proves more lethal than either separately, since it threatens the death of both author and author-as-character.

Reel and Real Life

"Who is Harvey Pekar?"—Harvey Pekar[60]

Like *Adaptation*, *American Splendor* shifts the usual questions asked of book to film adaptation from the filmic fidelity to literature to the fidelity of both film and literature to life and to relations between fact and fiction within both forms. Autobiographical writing and documentary film always raise questions of relations between representation and life and between fact and fiction, especially when autobiographical writing takes the form of a comic book and documentary film incorporates dramatic scenes and cartoon animation. Both hybrid media and adaptation add an element of competition over which mode of representation is closer to life. Questions arise: Do some media, forms and genres appear more real than others? Does documentary film appear closer to life than autobiographical comic books? Does archival footage appear more realistic than dramatic film scenes? Does voiceover narration create a more authentic sense of interiority than a surrealistic dream sequence?

The answers to such questions depend in large part upon theoretical ideologies and cultural conventions and expectations. As with its theories of authorship, *American Splendor* does not come down decisively on the side of any one view, but creates a pastiche of several. It includes many media and forms: shots of Pekar's comics, dramatic scenes, documentary filming, animation, archival footage, and more, all of which are in competition with each other as representatives of reality. At times the screenplay and film imply that one mode of representation is more real than another:

INT. REHEARSAL STUDIO — PRESENT — DAY
  HIGH DEFINITION VIDEO DOCUMENTARY FOOTAGE
  A few items indicating film production are in the frame.
  At a table in the foreground, BOB THE DIRECTOR discusses the character of Joyce with the ACTRESS playing her. The actress just nods as the director goes on.
  We can see THE REAL JOYCE sitting with THE REAL HARVEY in the distance. [...] THE REAL JOYCE and REAL HARVEY listen curiously — sometimes pleased, sometimes displeased — as their personalities are dissected and boiled down to a few phrases.
  CLOSER SHOT OF REAL JOYCE AND HARVEY
  The REAL JOYCE puts in her two cents about the actress playing her. She rants about what it's like to be portrayed in a movie, and having a character arc imposed on her life.[61]

Yet this illusion of a reality beyond than the dramatic scenes is itself scripted and filmed as a dramatic scene.

If the real here makes the dramatic scenes less real by comparison, elsewhere, infusing dramatic scenes with the real makes them more realistic. To create continuity between archival and dramatic scenes, Giamatti wears Pekar's clothing. Other infusions were inessential. Judah Friedlander, who plays Pekar's friend, Toby Radloff, wears a "genuine nerd" button given to him by Radloff, even though the production team had made a replica of it. Radloffs's remarks on the DVD commentary figure it as a token bonding the two Radloffs; indeed, Radloff, discussing the button, nominates Friedlander his "twin brother."[62] Madylin Sweeten, who plays Joyce's and Pekar's adopted daughter, Danielle, wears one of Danielle's hair ties, again tokenistically tying the real to the fictional.[63]

Elsewhere, however, the film subverts realist conventions. The present-day documentary scenes, conventionally deemed more real than dramatic scenes, voiceover narration, or animation, were filmed to accentuate their artificiality. Berman remarks: "We took all the props from a real space and put them in a fake space"; Pulcini attests: "We wanted the documentary moments in the film to be the most artificial looking and to kind of resemble a comic book panel"; Berman adds: "And they were shot in high definition; everything else was shot on 35 mm, so that it was very punchy as opposed to the browner look of the rest of the film."[64]

Contests among representational forms over their relative realism are further undermined by hybridizing them. The film animates Pekar's comics, making them more like film; conversely, from its opening credits on, filmed sequences are shot to appear look like comic books, as these screenplay extracts illustrate:

> We are now in a large, empty room similar to a blank comic book panel.[65]
> With the window framing these guys, the scene FREEZES, looking just like a comic book panel.[66]

Some dramatic scenes were shot in silhouette to resemble Sue Cavey's illustrations for the comics and cartoon "drawings were done to be a cross between Harvey and Paul."[67]

In addition to hybridizing media, the film frequently shifts between and juxtaposes forms. For example:

> INTERCUT HARVEY WALKING WITH COMIC BOOK PANELS OF THE CARTOON HARVEY IN ACTION.[68]
> The LEFT SIDE OF THE FRAME remains Harvey at the supermarket deliberating over the check-out lines. However, the RIGHT SIDE OF THE FRAME now contains a CRUMB STYLE COMIC PANEL DEPICTING THE EXACT SAME SCENARIO. A BUBBLE appears over CARTOON HARVEY'S head revealing his thoughts.... SUDDENLY, THE RIGHT SIDE OF THE SCREEN BECOMES FULLY ANIMATED.[69]

Do hybrid representations seem more realistic than single-medium representations? On the one hand, they manifest greater representational plenitude; on the other, they can seem to protest too much, heightening artifice through unfamiliar forms of multimediality.

Similar questions can be and have been asked of adaptations. In Platonic discussions of representation and realism, a prior representation is deemed closer to life than subsequent representations, which are the shadows of a shadow of reality. Thus adaptations are less real than the works they adapt; actors-as-characters are less real than the literary characters they play; dramatized reenactments of written events are less real than the prose. But from a nineteenth-century point of view, adapting symbolic to pictorial and audible and embodied modes of representation "realizes" representations, rendering them more real.[70] Actors bring characters to life; iconic images and sounds make symbolic words real representational flesh. Representational plenitude increases the sense of realism. Modernism, however, takes the view that multifarious representations become artificial and conventional. Streamlining representation, retreating from incarnate excess to ascetic, aesthetic, existentialist minimalism, advocating monomedial purity against both hybridity and intermedial adaptation, modernism locates reality in subjectivity and interiority. Postmodernism restores hybridity and multiplicity, but not as reality or authenticity. It does so to debunk both earlier and modernist claims to the real in any location or form, fragmenting representations to undermine the real and dislocating them from any referents apart from other representations, rendering master narratives and objective truth impossible. Whether adaptations and hybrid representations augment or diminish realism, or whether they present one mode of representation as more real than others, or all of them as equally real or unreal will reside in the eyes and mind of the audience. While Romantic expressivist, Victorian realist, and modernist audiences may locate the real in or under or between these representations, the birth of the postmodern and poststructuralist audience must be at the expense of the real, which dies along with the author. Yet beyond these alternatives, it is possible to envision a post-postmodern audience for whom everything is a hybrid of the fictional and the real, rather than more flatly and reductively not real.

The last word of this essay concerns the last word. There is a further tradition in which whoever had the last word, whoever comments about what has gone before, is the most real, the most true. Thus, although postmodernism denies reality and truth, its denials are taken to reflect a superior truth and greater reality to what came before. If we cannot imagine a universal audience with one view, we can turn to consider who in *American Splendor* has the last word. The DVD ends with a shot of the comic book that adapts *it*: Pekar's and Brabner's *Our Movie Year*, published after the release of the film in 2004. Yet that is not the last word on the DVD; the DVD audio commentary is. It provides further insights into the relations between fiction and reality constructed by and obscured by both comics and film. Not only does Berman admit, "We made that scene up, it's not an *American Splendor* story," Pekar also admits to making up stories that he presented as autobiographical in his comics. Pulcini and Berman sound genuinely surprised to hear this. Radloff's mobile phone goes off several times during the recording of the commentary, adding a delicious note of nerdy unintentionality amid all the savvy, self-reflexive commentary.

The DVD commentary unveils aspects of navigating between fiction and reality remote from poststructuralism's confident, celebratory, always already proclamations and postmodernism's dispassionate, casual, skeptical, parodic siding with the fictional over the real. Authors of the comics and film speak practically about the making and unmaking of lines between fiction and reality on the set: "We'd say [...] real Harvey or stage Harvey or film Harvey [...] we have to keep them all straight."[71] Far from the clinical diagnostics of academics, Joyce and other commentators speak with emotion about their encounters with fictional scenes of themselves, expressing pain when the real and the fictional coincide and betrayal and disappointment when they do not. Watching actors play dramatized scenes of Pekar's cancer treatment, Joyce Brabner comments: "This hurts because it's so real." As the sentimental, conventional, and considerably fictionalized ending of the film unfolds, depicting Hope Davis as Joyce and Madylin Sweeten as Danielle dancing together, the actual Danielle says wistfully, "I wish this could have happened in real life." Intersections between fiction and reality also produce pleasure: when the actual Joyce, Harvey, and Danielle embrace in the scene depicting Harvey's retirement party, Joyce remarks: "That hug at the end is one of my favorite moments in the movie because it's real."

Postmodern screened writers, then, support and undermine postmodern and poststructuralist theories of authorship and representation, alternately resisting them and espousing them; serving as proof texts for them and revealing their blind spots, omissions, and limitations; and debunking and resurrecting the older theories that postmodernism and poststructuralism thought had died along with the author.

Notes

1. Kamilla Elliott, "Screened Writers," in *The Blackwell Companion to Literature, Film and Adaptations*, Deborah Cartmell, ed., Oxford: Blackwell, 2012.

2. Pekar died in 2010.

3. The sections of this chapter addressing *Adaptation* were presented at the conference "From the Blank Page to the Silver Screen: Film Adaptation in the English-Speaking World," Université de Bretagne Sud, Lorient, France, 8 June 2006. The sections addressing *American Splendor* were written in 2012.

4. *Adaptation*, Spike Jonze, dir., Charlie Kaufman and Donald Kaufman, scr., Columbia Pictures, 2002. Donald Kaufman is a fictional persona.

5. *American Splendor*, Robert Pulcini and Shari Springer Berman, dirs. and scrs., Good Machine, 2003.

6. Roland Barthes, "The Death of the Author" (1967), *Image — Music — Text*, Stephen Heath, trans., New York: Hill & Wang, 1977, 142, 143, 146, 148.

7. To avoid confusion among the three screenwriters, this essay refers to the extradiegetic author of the screenplay as "Kaufman" and to the diegetic screenwriters as "Charlie" and "Donald."

8. Robert Pulcini and Shari Springer Berman, *American Splendor: The Shooting Script*, The Daily Script, www.dailyscript.com/scripts/American_Splendor.pdf.

9. Susan Orlean, *The Orchid Thief: A True Story of Beauty and Obsession*, New York: Ballantine, 2000.

10. Charlie Kaufman and Robert McKee, *Adaptation: The Shooting Script*, New York: New Market Press, 2002, 3.

11. François Truffaut, "A certain tendency of the French cinema" (1954), in *Movies and Methods*, Bill Nichols, ed., Berkeley: University of California Press, 1976, 224–35.

12. Kamilla Elliott, *Rethinking the Novel/Film Debate*, Cambridge: Cambridge University Press, 2003, 129.

13. *Ibid.*, 79–83.

14. Doreen Alexander Child, *Charlie Kaufman: Confessions of an Original Mind*, Santa Barbara, CA: Praeger, 2010, 61.

15. Kaufman and McKee, *Adaptation*, 3.

16. Rob Feld, "Q & A with Charlie Kaufman and Spike Jonze," in *Adaptation: The Shooting Script*, Charlie Kaufman and Donald Kaufman, eds., New York: New Market Press, 2002, 128–129.

17. Kaufman and McKee, *Adaptation*, 5–6.

18. *Ibid.*, 6.

19. *Ibid.*, 68–69.

20. *Ibid.*, 58.

21. *Ibid.*, 76–77.

22. "Who's the Proper Charlie?" *The Observer*, 9 February 2003, http://film.guardian.co.uk/interview/interviewpages/0,,891854,00.html.

23. Robert McKee, *Story: Style, Structure, Substance, and the Principles of Screenwriting*, New York: Methuen, 1999.

24. Kaufman and McKee, *Adaptation*, pp. 74–75.

25. Charlie Kaufman and Donald Kaufman, *Adaptation: Second Draft*, 24 September 1999, http://www.imsdb.com/scripts/Adaptation.html.

26. Kaufman and McKee, *Adaptation*, 97.

27. *Ibid.*, 50–51.

28. *Ibid.*, 96.

29. *Ibid.*

30. *Ibid.*, 50.

31. Kaufman and Kaufman, *Adaptation: Second Draft*.

32. Kaufman and McKee, *Adaptation*, 97.

33. *Ibid.*, 70.

34. Barthes, "The Death of the Author," 148.

35. Feld, "Q&A with Charlie Kaufman and Spike Jonze," 128.

36. In addition to reviews and interviews, see the entry for *Adaptation* on "Reel Faces" at ChasingtheFrog.com: Chasing after the truth behind movies based on real stories, http://www.chasingthefrog.com/reelfaces/adaptation.php.

37. Danny Leigh, "Let's make a meta-movie," *The Guardian*, 14 February 2003, http://www.guardian.co.uk/film/2003/feb/14/artsfeatures?INTCMP=ILCNETTXT3487.

38. See the Internet Movie Database, http://www.imdb.com/title/tt0268126/trivia.

39. "Interview with Spike Jonze and Charlie Kaufman," 25 October 2002, http://www.chasingthefrog.com/reelfaces/adaptation_intview4.php.

40. See photos of Orlean's deleted scene on the blog *Regarding Adaptation* at http://www.susanorlean.com/adaptation/behind/adapt_behind01.html.

41. Harvey Pekar, "Payback," in *Best of American Splendor*, illus. Dean Haspiel, New York: Ballantine, 2005, 3.

42. I am thinking of the films *Shakespeare in Love, Bright Star, Iris, Becoming Jane*, and *Mansfield Park* (1999).

43. Harvey Pekar, "Comics Are My Thing," in *American Splendor: Our Movie Year*, Gary Dumm, illus., New York: Ballantine, 84–85.

44. Robert Pulcini, and Shari Springer Berman, *American Splendor: The Shooting Script*, The Daily Script, www.dailyscript.com/scripts/American_Splendor.pdf, 142.

45. *Ibid.*, 20.

46. *Ibid.*, 28.

47. See, for example, Joanna Woodall, ed., *Portraiture: Facing the Subject*, Manchester: Manchester University Press, 1997.

48. Elliott, "Screened Writers."

49. Michel Foucault, "What Is an Author?" in *Modern Criticism and Theory: A Reader* (1969), David Lodge, Nigel Wood, eds., Edinburgh: Pearson Education, 1988, 280–293.

50. Harvey Pekar, "The Harvey Pekar Name Story," in *American Splendor and More American Splendor*, Robert Crumb, illus., New York: Ballantine, 2003, 1–4.
51. Pulcini and Berman, *American Splendor*, 13.
52. Pekar, "The Harvey Pekar Name Story," 4.
53. Pulcini and Berman, *American Splendor*, 97.
54. *Ibid.*, 5.
55. *Ibid.*, 93.
56. *Ibid.*, 89.
57. *Ibid.*, 24–25.
58. *Ibid.*, 86.
59. *Ibid.*, 92.
60. Pekar, "The Harvey Pekar Name Story," 4.
61. Pulcini and Berman, *American Splendor*, 57.
62. Toby Radloff, audio commentary on *American Splendor* (2003), DVD, Optimum Home Releasing, U.S.A., 2004.
63. Danielle Batone, audio commentary on *American Splendor*.
64. *American Splendor* DVD commentary.
65. Pulcini and Berman, *American Splendor*, 93.
66. *Ibid.*, 26.
67. Pulcini and Berman, audio commentary on *American Splendor*.
68. Pulcini and Berman, *American Splendor*, 4.
69. *Ibid.*, 24.
70. Martin Meisel, *Realizations: Narrative, Pictorial, and Theatrical Arts in 19th-Century England*, Princeton: Princeton University Press, 1983.
71. Joyce Brabner, audio commentary on *American Splendor*.

BIBLIOGRAPHY

Adaptation. Spike Jonze, dir., Charlie Kaufman and Donald Kaufman, scr. Columbia Pictures, 2002.
American Splendor. Robert Pulcini and Shari Springer Berman, dirs. and scrs. Good Machine, 2003.
Barthes, Roland. "The Death of the Author." *Image—Music—Text*. Trans. Stephen Health. New York: Hill & Wang, 1977, 142–148.
Becoming Jane. Julian Jarrold, dir., Kevin Hood, scr. HanWay Films/UK Film Council/Bórd Scannán na hÉireann, 2007.
Bright Star. Jane Campion, dir., scr. Pathé Renn Productions/BBC Films/Screen Australia, 2009.
Child, Doreen Alexander. *Charlie Kaufman: Confessions of an Original Mind*. Santa Barbara, CA: Praeger, 2010.
Elliott, Kamilla. "Screened Writers." *The Blackwell Companion to Literature, Film and Adaptations*, Deborah Cartmell, ed. Oxford: Blackwell, 2012.
Foucault, Michel. "What Is an Author?" *Language, Counter-memory, Practice*, trans. D.F. Bouchard and S. Simon, ed. D.F. Bouchard. Ithaca: Cornell University Press, 1977, 124–27.
"Interview with Spike Jonze and Charlie Kaufman." 25 October 2002, http://www.chasingthefrog.com/reelfaces/adaptation_intview4.php.
Iris. Richard Eyre, dir., John Bayley, Richard Eyre, scrs. BBC/Fox Iris Productions/Intermedia Films, 2001.
Kaufman, Charlie, and Donald Kaufman. *Adaptation: Second Draft*. 24 September 1999, http://www.imsdb.com/scripts/Adaptation.html.

Kaufman, Charlie, and Robert McKee. *Adaptation: The Shooting Script*. New York: New Market Press, 2002.

Leigh, Danny. "Let's Make a Meta-Movie." *The Guardian*, Friday, 14 February 2003, http://film.guardian.co.uk/interview/interviewpages/0,6737,891854,00.htm.

Mansfield Park. Patricia Rozema, dir., scr. Arts Council of England/BBC/HAL Films, 1999.

McKee, Robert. *Story: Substance, Structure, Style, and the Principles of Screenwriting*. New York: HarperCollins, 1997.

Meisel, Martin. *Realizations: Narrative, Pictorial, and Theatrical Arts in 19th-Century England*. Princeton: Princeton University Press, 1983.

Orlean, Susan. *The Orchid Thief: A True Story of Beauty and Obsession*. New York: Ballantine, 2000.

Pekar, Harvey. *American Splendor: Our Movie Year*, illus. Gary Dumm. New York: Ballantine.

_____. "The Harvey Pekar Name Story." *American Splendor and More American Splendor*, illus., Robert Crumb. New York: Ballantine, 2003, 1–4.

_____. "Payback." *Best of American Splendor*, illus. Dean Haspiel. New York: Ballantine, 2005.

Pulcini, Robert, and Shari Springer Berman. *American Splendor: The Shooting Script*. The Daily Script. www.dailyscript.com/scripts/American_Splendor.pdf.

Shakespeare in Love. John Madden, dir., Marc Norman, Tom Stoppard, scrs. Miramax Films, 1998.

Truffaut, François. "A Certain Tendency of the French Cinema" (1954). *Movies and Methods*. Bill Nichols, ed. Berkeley: University of California Press, 1976, 224–235.

"Who's the Proper Charlie?" *The Observer*, 9 February 2003, http://film.guardian.co.uk/interview/interviewpages/0,,891854,00.html.

Woodall, Joanna, ed. *Portraiture: Facing the Subject*. Manchester: Manchester University Press, 1997.

True Stories: Film and the Non-Fiction Narrative[1]

Kevin Dwyer

We live in a world ruled by fictions of every kind [...] For the writer in particular it is less and less necessary for him to invent the fictional content of his novel. The fiction is already there. The writer's task is to invent the reality.[2]

This essay focuses on questions of genre, authorship, and realism in mainstream Hollywood film adaptations of non-fiction writing. My goal is to bring us closer to the very boundaries of the fatal attraction between fiction and non-fiction, so we can better measure to what extent our non-fictions are potentially fictions, and at what point our fictions become history. Is not all non-fiction, through the process of adaptation, destined to become fiction? I will posit here that it is the very process of adaptation that creates fiction from non-fiction, eroding the latter into the form of a palatable story, fit for dissemination in many different forms. It is my contention that mainstream film urges us to believe in fictions, and even to take them for true stories.

I will be relying in my analysis on five non-fiction books and their filmed adaptations, which all currently bear the same title. *Midnight Express*[3] is the story of Billy Hayes, an American imprisoned in Turkey for possession of hashish, and his subsequent escape from the hell of Turkish jails. *In Cold Blood*[4] recounts the murder of four members of the Clutter family in Holcomb, Kansas, and the capture and execution of the two men who committed the crime. *Alive!*[5] is the story of the survivors of a 1972 plane crash in the Andes who had to resort to cannibalizing the bodies of the dead to survive. *The Right Stuff*[6] follows the lives of American Air Force test pilots who broke speed and altitude records in the 1950s, some of whom later became involved as astronauts in the first American space program. *Schindler's List*[7] is the story of Oskar Schindler, a Nazi businessman who managed to save the lives of the Polish Jews working in his factory.

The best-selling literature under study in this paper relies, in most cases, on accounts from numerous sources, for the most part, from participants in one or another of the events recounted. The author's work in these cases was journalistic, and involved crafting a compilation of the various accounts. Although the filmed versions take as their point of departure the written text (or at least the phenomenon of the best seller), we will see how many of them go back to (and use) the original participants and places of the events recounted not only for consultative purposes, but also as a way to emphasize the veracity of the filmed story and to be able to promote the film as a true story.

Based on a True Story: A Genre?

What does "based on a true story" mean? As non-fiction is a genre of writing in and of itself, adaptations of such works may also fall into a genre of their own. It usually means a compelling story of human beings struggling in extreme circumstances. The central figures are predominantly male. Although action and suspense are present to varying degrees, the films have a tendency to be more character-driven, as they are examinations of people in exceptional circumstances.

While we can define some generic characteristics of based-on-a-true-story films, this is more difficult with pure fiction adaptations, for they will always be associated with the genre generated by the type of story adapted — whether it be, for example, a thriller, detective, or western. This may also apply to the post-modern practice of parody, self-reflexivity and cross-genre productions. While we might not be very surprised to see the Dracula story made into a western or *The Scarlet Letter* as a martial arts movie, it might be more surprising if one day we were to see a musical made of *In Cold Blood*. This is due to the fact that there is an air of integrity around true stories that must not be violated and this inevitably shapes their filmic adaptations.

Although there is a respectful side to the based-on-a-true-story labeling that does not readily invite parody, satire or misrepresentation, based-on-a-true-story is nonetheless a slogan typically used by another genre, i.e., the exploitation movie, where lurid true tales (often based on newspaper articles or police arrest reports) about the looming menace of sex, drugs, crime, teenagers exploit the fears, anxieties and ignorance of viewers with the alleged purpose of educating the public, despite the fact that they primarily serve to provide titillation and vicarious thrills. Although the tales and films of true stories tend to be character-driven, it is the promise of action, of witnessing human suffering, "[...] the fury of conflagrations, the excesses of cruelty and suffering, and unspeakable lusts"[8] that equally compels people to read the books and, to a greater extent, to watch the films, these aspects being very effective in a visual medium and especially in the context of mainstream film production.

This is very clear in the example of *Midnight Express*, which is written in an as-told-by format. The film has completely appropriated the story at the expense of the source text. The screenplay was "taken over" by a writer with a much more forceful voice, screenwriter Oliver Stone. Stone, who won the Best Screenplay Oscar for *Midnight Express*, took questionable liberties with the story as recounted in the book, adapting it into a film that more crassly exploits the based-on-a-true-story label, notably by introducing elements of exploitation — xenophobia and homophobia in regard to the depictions of Turks, for example — that are nowhere to be found in the Hayes story. Stone, however, did fashion the story to be more in keeping with the masculine orientation of the genre.

The mainstream adaptations under study here exhibit both a tendency toward awe-struck reverence of the subject matter while, at the same time, exploiting the sensational aspects of the stories. Both tendencies entail a loss of complexity vis-à-vis the original — in terms of both narrative and characterization.

Authorship

Stories belong to story-tellers, but in these non-fiction tales, perhaps more than in works of fiction, which can be more easily ascribed to one particular mind or consciousness, locating the story-teller can be fraught with complexity. In the case of non-fiction narratives, we are indeed confronted with what are at the very least "thrice-told tales"[9]: firstly recounted by the various participants, the story is then arranged in a book by the author, and then filmed as a feature-length movie. As the tales go through the process of adaptation from one medium to another, the original experience gets diluted, adapted, revised and becomes something less of a true story and something closer to fiction. The reality of the stories experienced — and then told — has been filtered through many interpreters, very much like the Whispering Game. (This game, in which a sentence is whispered in turn in the ears of a group of people to see how it is distorted by the time it reaches the last person, would also serve as an apt analogy for adaptation.) The maddening *mise en abyme* of the adaptation process comes through very clearly if we consider the raw event experienced by the actual participant as it gets mediated by the succession of story-tellers, each with their own agendas, viewpoints, and narrative styles.

Both *In Cold Blood* and *The Right Stuff* were written by two highly stylized writers, Tom Wolfe and Truman Capote, who have produced both fiction and non-fiction, and who have well-established reputations for their sense of wit and irony, as well as being two flamboyant dandies of the South who attained a level in notoriety in the social circles of New York. It is only Wolfe and Capote who openly transgress the stories by injecting their strong authorial voices over the "facts" as related by their interviewees. Because of the evident style and panache with which their books were written, the filmed versions of *In Cold Blood* and *The Right Stuff* interact with the source texts to a greater extent than the other books which claim to rely solely on the facts. For example, the opening titles of *In Cold Blood* overtly announce the film as "Truman Capote's *In Cold Blood*." Filmed in black and white, under a sometimes overbearing Quincy Jones soundtrack, the film attempts to capture the frontal, blow-by-blow quality of Capote's account while, at the same time, working within the conventions of *film noir*. The filmed version of *The Right Stuff* recreates the author's tone by concentrating on the more comic episodes and characters involved in the tale, especially in the depictions of Vice President Lyndon Johnson and the NASA administrators, one of whom speaks with a German accent. However, in order to best capture the tone of the books, the filmmakers resorted to the "artificial" introduction of additional sounding-board characters, in both cases journalists, who serve a dual authorial function, both as ironic observers and as commentators, who facilitate plot explanation at different points in the stories.

Although these transgressions and authorial interventions move the stories in both their filmed and written versions closer to a sort of fiction, we can witness the same phenomenon when we look at texts and films which claim to be absolutely true to the true story. In the cases of *Alive!* and *Schindler's List*, there is an aura of reverence about the tales that has not allowed for irony or transgression, but which has, on the other hand, allowed the filmmakers to opt for sentimentality. The "miraculous" tales of *Alive!* and *Schindler's List* are imbued with spiritual qualities, with both films concluding on "inspiring" panoramic shots over redemptive, religious music.

Piers Paul Read claims in the introduction to *Alive!* "[...] the story was so strong that it was best told unadorned. It was not for the author to tell the reader what to think, but for the reader to decide for himself."[10] Likewise, Thomas Keneally, the author of *Schindler's List*, claims:

To use the texture and devices of a novel to tell a true story is a course that has been frequently followed in modern writing. It is the one I chose to follow here [...] I have attempted, however, to avoid all fiction, since fiction would debase the record, and to distinguish between reality and myths which are likely to attach themselves to a man of Oskar's stature. It has sometimes become necessary to make reasonable constructs of conversations of which Oskar and others have left only the briefest record. But most exchanges and conversations, and all events, are based on the detailed recollections of the [Schindler Jews], of Schindler himself, and of other witnesses to Oskar's acts of outrageous rescue.[11]

Speaking about the filmed version of *Schindler's List,* Steven Spielberg for his part has said: "This was one subject that did not need manipulation [...] I did not want to bring melodrama into it. I tried my best to stay to the side and just present the facts."[12]

Such claims to eradicate the voice of the author in favor of letting "the facts speak for themselves" are clearly made to bolster the authenticity of the books and films. However, we cannot take these claims at their face value, for they deny the subjectivity of author and filmmaker alike. Once an author is in the process of selecting words to describe a story, he/she could not be engaging in a more manipulative process. And once a director is making choices about casting, filming in black and white, and music, we can readily see how claims like Spielberg's, as well as Keneally's and Read's, are manipulative in and of themselves. It would be atypical of writers like Tom Wolfe and Truman Capote to make such claims, for they are obviously offering their very own stylized version of the "facts" as presented to them.

Stories belong to the storytellers and not to those left out of the story. Although the films were made with the complete endorsement of the written original, the original books were not always written with the complete collaboration of those involved in the story. In so doing, the films revisit and re-appropriate the stories without attempting to revise them in any way. In each of these true stories, we follow one or a group of the participants more closely than the others. Thus *Alive!* becomes the story of Nando Parado, who became the spokesman for the group of survivors and technical consultant for the film, and not the story, for example, of Bobby François, the one survivor who experienced extensive trauma due to the experience. Nando Parado is also the only survivor who fully approved of Read's text at the time of its writing while all of the others had objections.[13] Truman Capote clearly appropriated the *In Cold Blood* story as his own and remained by the side of the Clutter murderers until the moment of their execution. The story that he chose to tell is of the murderers and not the tale of the Clutters, whose homey, small-town all–American family life he subtly mocks. While *The Right Stuff* revels in the trials and tribulations of the first seven NASA astronauts, the real

Scott Crossfield, who appears as one of the un-chosen test pilots in *The Right Stuff*, always firmly denounced the book and the film as being totally unrealistic and exploitative.[14] (He appears as one who lost out on the chance to be one of the seven). Finally, we can wonder why the protective disclaimer, "This is a work of fiction," appears on the copyright page of *Schindler's List*, despite the author's clearly articulated claims of letting the facts speak for themselves.

Realism

Film is a great creator of artifice, if nothing else, and this perhaps explains the great lengths to which the films go to verify the authenticity of the tales that unfold on the screen. Just as the original books were written based on interviews, many participants in the original stories were used as consultants or extras for the films — e.g. Chuck Yeager for *The Right Stuff*, Nando Parado for the *Alive!* story, the townspeople of Holcomb, Kansas for *In Cold Blood*, and many of the Schindler survivors for *Schindler's List*.

In the books, photographs are widely used to illustrate the story and provide pictures of the participants and places in the events. These photographs go a long way in shaping the imagery and *mise en scène* of the films. Most of the photographs that can be found in the books are recreated in the films down to the very details of gesture and *mise en scène*, either as sets or as passing images. For the reconstruction of sets we can consider the examples of the Washington Post office in *All the President's Men*, the concentration camp of *Schindler's List*, as well as the mountain-top plane crash site of *Alive!*

The photographs of participants are also used in the choice of actors, who, through make-up, costume, lighting, and acting technique, resemble photographs of the original participants as much as possible while at the same time retaining the glamour reserved for mainstream film actors. Authentic locations and filming conditions are present not only to impress potential filmgoers but also to provoke realistic performances from the cast. The cast of *Alive!* were placed on a low-calorie diet throughout the shooting of the film. The murder scenes of *In Cold Blood* were filmed in the actual Clutter house where the crimes took place. The sets of *Schindler's List* were built on location in Germany, Poland and former Czechoslovakia. Much of the extra-filmic material — press releases, "Making of" features, film reviews — goes to great lengths to emphasize the effort made to imbue the films with the tint of authenticity. This is accomplished through interviews, comparative photographs, and confrontations between the actual participants and the actors on the sets of the films. The "Making of" feature of the Columbia TriStar *Midnight Express* DVD shows Billy Hayes walking through the Turkish prison set, expressing his amazement at how it so easily re-plunges him in the past. Likewise, in the "Making of" feature of the Paramount Home Entertainment DVD of *Alive!*, a number of the survivors are brought by helicopter to the set in the Canadian Rockies and are filmed in close-up, pensively contemplating the reconstructed plane carcass where they lived for 72 days.

History belongs to the storytellers. There is indeed the danger in these stories of (mis)taking fiction for reality, the film for the real event, and the actors for the real people. Liam Neeson is Oskar Schindler. Redford and Hoffman are Woodward and Bernstein. On the cover of the Time-Warner paperback edition of Hayes's *Midnight Express*, we find not a photograph of Billy Hayes but of actor Brad Davis.[15] In an upstream version of the same phenomenon, the recent Vintage edition of *In Cold Blood* carries a sticker advertising the *Capote* motion picture, with a picture of Philip Seymour Hoffman in the role of Truman Capote. Even adaptations of fiction are prisoners of realism. We can consider the recent production of *Oliver Twist* or any other period film based on a literary work, which will rely greatly on teams of historians, anthropologists and other non-literary experts for creating the atmosphere of the film, perhaps even more than they would on the original literary text.

Conclusion: Recipes for Adaptation

True stories are never quite true, and adaptations of true stories are even less so. I would like to add yet another, alternative, analogy for adaptation, one that allows for the myriad factors that present themselves in the adaptation process — the analogy of the recipe. This analogy works on two levels. Firstly, if all cooks in the world were to use the same recipe, there would be as many different dishes made from that recipe as there are cooks. Each cook modifies/interprets/adapts a recipe in ways that suit his or her needs and desires, with more or less garlic, more or less salt. A single recipe, whether it is simple and straightforward or drowned in discourse — can produce a range of interpretations that will depend on countless factors such as the disposition of the cook, location, season, available ingredients. The same multi-faceted dynamic applies to the adaptation process.

On a second level, if we consider the diversity of discourses embedded in different types of recipes — from cookery programs to women's magazines to cookbooks — it is possible to see several levels of authorial intervention that bring a recipe away from being a "true story" and closer to fiction. The most bare-bones recipe simply lists the required ingredients and the steps necessary to make a dish out of them. There is no artifice, no fiction about them. Neither is there any manipulation of the reader of such recipes, nor any indication of how the recipe should be interpreted. Would it be possible to approach such a recipe in the spirit with which Keneally, Read and Spielberg approached the true stories of *Alive!* and *Schindler's List* ("unadorned," "avoiding all fiction," "without manipulation")?

Other types of recipes are embedded in a discourse, they are "told" with a "voice." For example, a recipe by Marcella Hazan for pork stuffed with calf liver[16] already contains a deep discourse that directs the reader to think about the food and approach the recipe in a certain way. Here the author of the recipe has created a story around it, and we are clearly moving further away from a bare description of ingredients and closer to a story with its own narrative and *mise en scène*. A further example of recipes for dog, cat and rat from *The Decadent Cookbook*[17] confronts us with recipes that none of the readers of the cookbook are likely to be able to or even want to produce, and here we are once again in the realm of fiction.

This trend to fictionalization is even more apparent in the case of recipes accompanied by illustrations, which take us closer to a fictive imaginary world, guided not only by words but also by the images used to illustrate the recipe. The cook of these recipes inevitably holds up the prepared dish to these words and images and thus begins the fidelity debate: how many times have we heard or expressed ourselves, dismay at not producing a dish that looks like the picture? The photographs that accompany recipes are there to guide us perhaps, but they end up at the same time fooling us into believing that the image is or should be the real thing.

Are all of our true stories destined to become fictions? And is fiction, for that matter, destined to be shaped by history? Mainstream cinema provides the pretty pictures that allow our imaginaries to experience the true stories that others have lived through, without the mess, without the boredom, and thus urges us to believe the fictions it creates out of true experience, more than the true stories themselves.

NOTES

1. This article was written thanks to resources made available by the Belgian Royal Film Archives in Brussels.

2. J.G. Ballard, *Crash*, London: Vintage, 1995, 4–5.

3. Billy Hayes and William Hoffer, *Midnight Express* (1977), London: Time-Warner Books, 2005. *Midnight Express*, Alan Parker, dir., Oliver Stone, scr., Casablanca Filmworks, 1978.

4. Truman Capote, *In Cold Blood* (1965), New York: Vintage International, 1994. *In Cold Blood*, Richard Brooks, dir., scr., Columbia Pictures, 1967.

5. Piers Paul Read, *Alive!* (1974), New York: Harper Perennial, 2005. *Alive!*, Frank Marshall, dir., John Patrick Shanley, scr., Film Andes S.A., 1993.

6. Tom Wolfe, *The Right Stuff* (1979), New York: Bantam, 2001. *The Right Stuff*, Philip Kaufman, dir., scr., The See Ladds Company, 1983.

7. Thomas Keneally, *Schindler's List* (1982, orig. title *Schindler's Ark*), New York: Simon & Schuster, 1993. *Schindler's List*, Steven Spielberg, dir., Steven Zaillian, scr., Universal Pictures, 1993.

8. Sigfried Kracauer, *Theory of Film*, quoted in Gerald Mast, *Film, Cinema, Movie: A Theory of Experience*, Chicago: University of Chicago Press, 1983, 40.

9. Mbye Cham, "Oral Traditions, Literature and Cinema in Africa," in Robert Stam and Alessandra Raengo, eds., *Literature and Film*, Malden, MA: Blackwell, 2004, 298.

10. Read, *Alive!*, xiv.

11. Thomas Keneally, "Author's Note," *Schindler's List*, 10.

12. Quoted in James O. Jackson, "Schindler Shock," *Time Magazine*, March 14, 1994, 63.

13. "Only Nando Parado remained calm," "Introduction," Read, *Alive!*, xiii.

14. See Crossfield's obituary by Christopher Reed in *The Guardian Weekly*, May 5–11, 2006.

15. This is especially surprising given that dark, straight-haired Davis in no way resembles the blond curly-haired "original," Billy Hayes.

16. Marcella Hazan, *Marcella's Italian Kitchen*, New York: Alfred A. Knopf, 2001, 233.

17. See, for example, recipes for "Dog à la Beti" and "Cat in Tomato Sauce," in Medlar Lucan and Durian Gray, *The Decadent Cookbook*, Sawtry: Dedalus, 1995, 122–123.

BIBLIOGRAPHY

Alive! Frank Marshall, dir., John Patrick Shanley, scr. Film Andes S.A., 1993.
All the President's Men. Alan J. Pakula, dir., William Goldman, scr. Warner Bros., 1976.
Ballard, J.G. *Crash*. London: Vintage, 1995.
Bernstein, Carl, and Bob Woodward. *All the President's Men*. New York: Simon & Schuster, 1974.
Capote, Truman. *In Cold Blood* (1965). New York: Vintage International, 1994.
Cham, Mbye. "Oral Traditions, Literature, and Cinema in Africa." Robert Stam and Alessandra Raengo, eds., *A Companion to Literature and Film*. Malden, MA: Blackwell, 2004, 295–312.
Crash. David Cronenberg, dir., scr. Alliance Communications Corporation, 1996.
Hayes, Billy, and William Hoffer. *Midnight Express* (1977). London: Time-Warner Books, 2005.
Hazan, Marcella. *Marcella's Italian Kitchen*. New York: Alfred A. Knopf, 2001.
In Cold Blood. Richard Brooks, dir., scr. Columbia Pictures, 1967.
Jackson, James O. "Schindler Shock." *Time Magazine*, March 14, 1994, 61–63.
Keneally, Thomas. *Schindler's List* (1982). New York: Simon & Schuster, 1993.
Lanzmann, Claude. "Why Spielberg Has Distorted the Truth." *The Guardian Weekly*, March 4, 1994, 14.
Lucan, Medlar, and Durian Gray. *The Decadent Cookbook*. Sawtry: Dedalus, 1995.
Midnight Express. Alan Parker, dir., Oliver Stone, scr. Casablanca Filmworks, 1978.
Read, Piers Paul. *Alive!* (1974). New York: Harper Perennial, 2005.
The Right Stuff. Philip Kaufman, dir., scr. The See Ladds Company, 1983.
Schindler's List. Steven Spielberg, dir., Steven Zaillian, scr. Universal Pictures, 1993.

Siclier, Jacques. "L'Histoire au risque de la fiction." *Le Monde*, April 20–21, 1997.
Steimatsky, Noa. "Photographic *Verismo*, Cinematic Adaptation, and the Staging of a Neo-
    realist Landscape." Robert Stam and Alessandra Raengo, eds., *A Companion to Lit-
    erature and Film*. Malden, MA: Blackwell, 2004, 205–228.
Wolfe, Tom. *The Right Stuff* (1979). New York: Bantam, 2001.

The Writing of a *Film Noir*: Ernest Hemingway and *The Killers*

Delphine Letort

Ernest Hemingway's novels started to arouse the interest of Hollywood studios when *The Sun Also Rises* was published in 1926 and met with great public acclaim. Hemingway's reputation was confirmed and even enhanced by the publication of *A Farewell to Arms* in 1929 based on his experience as an ambulance driver during the First World War in Italy. "The dramatic possibilities of the book for screen treatment"[1] were revealed by a Broadway musical that enticed Paramount Pictures' producers into buying the screen rights both to Hemingway's novel and to Laurence Stallings's script which was used as a primary source for the film scenario.[2] From the very beginning, dealing with Hollywood made Hemingway deeply frustrated, as he was to be neither consulted for the film projects made from his writings, nor warned or financially compensated if there were to be any remakes.[3] Hemingway felt Hollywood producers and directors assumed a patronizing attitude towards his work: once a studio had acquired the rights to a novel, they were not held accountable to the writer for any change in the script. Most film adaptations distorted Hemingway's original intent, fuelling his bitterness and resentment against the studio system as Frank M. Laurence explains: "Hemingway's initial disappointment with movie adaptation had been in 1932, when Frank Borzage filmed *A Farewell to Arms* for Paramount. That was when Hemingway first learned that Hollywood only made the kind of pictures that people wanted to see, and the public had bad taste."[4]

Drawing on his personal experience, Hemingway wrote about the throes of the Great War shattering individuals' values and most intimate beliefs. In

the film, the war context becomes nothing more than a background dramatizing the love story between the hero (Frederick) and a nurse (Catherine),
who are cruelly torn apart by the conflict. Hemingway's dark view of life was
censored into "melodramatic mush,"[5] leading Gene D. Phillips to posit that
no film was ever able to capture the embedded layers of deeper meaning pervading Hemingway's books: "The stories made 'good copy.' But their true
inward significance, that subtle quality which was Hemingway's genuine, personalized imprimatur, never quite survived translation, unless momentarily,
from printed to dramatized version."[6]

Hemingway's relationship with Hollywood was grounded in a financial
agreement, which he depicted bitterly as a violent, aggressive negotiation that
deprived him of any sense of authorial pride: "You throw them your book,
they throw you the money, then you jump into your car and drive like hell
back the way you came."[7] However numerous the writers taking part in film
projects in the 1930s and 1940s might be, discontent was a widespread feeling
among them.[8] Whether they were hired as screenwriters, like Raymond Chandler, James M. Cain, William Faulkner, or Horace McCoy,[9] or sold their
motion-picture rights as authors, many of them complained about the degrad-
ing job they were expected to do. Their creative literary art was depreciated
even though they provided the film industry with original screenplays. Labeled
thrillers (*Double Indemnity*, Billy Wilder, 1944, adapted by Billy Wilder and
Raymond Chandler from James M. Cain), psychological melodramas (*The
Woman in the Window*, Fritz Lang, 1944, adapted by Nunnaly Johnson from
J.H. Wallis), hard-boiled detective films (*The Maltese Falcon*, directed and
adapted by John Huston from Dashiell Hammett in 1941) or gangster films
(*Asphalt Jungle*, John Huston, 1950, adapted by Ben Maddow and John Huston
from W.R. Burnett), the films made from their works gave birth to a new
genre dubbed *film noir*, the popular success of which also helped hard-boiled
writers to gain recognition. Hemingway's writing style displays many features
which characterize Dashiell Hammett's hard-boiled fiction — including terse
prose, sharp dialogues and vivid images furthering the plot.[10]

Yet surprising as it may be, only one short story by Hemingway was
adapted as a *film noir*: Robert Siodmak shot *The Killers* in 1946, working from
the screenplay by Anthony Veiller and John Huston[11] who expanded the story
into a full-length scenario. As a German expressionist-inspired film artist,
Robert Siodmak managed to translate the elliptic writing of Hemingway into
a picture that did not betray the tension contained in the original, enigmatic
story, which could account for the writer's attachment to the film — he would
relentlessly play it whenever his friends visited him in La Finca, his Cuban
home.[12] Because *film noir* was characterized by "visual dissonances" emerging

from *chiraoscuro* lighting, unbalanced frame compositions and curious camera angles,[13] it was able to stylize the hidden forces pervading Hemingway's writing. Aldous Huxley pointed out how difficult it was for a director to visualize it: "Hemingway's gift is that he writes in the white spaces between the lines."[14] Also branded the iceberg theory, the suggestive power of this writing technique was echoed in the expressionist lighting of film noir. No doubt Hemingway's sense of disillusionment appealed to those German and Austrian directors who had fled Nazi-dominated Europe[15] and who vented their existential malaise in "stories about the loss or the impossibility of individual freedom" with "images of death, of relentless fate"[16] that reflected Hemingway's concern for man's uncertain fate and psychological obsessions.

First published in 1927,[17] "The Killers" belongs to *The Nick Adams Stories,* a collection of short stories about Nick Adams, whose adventures are part and parcel of a process of initiation into adulthood. The meeting with the two hitmen mentioned in the title of "The Killers" is but one stage in the development of the main character, who is no more than an observer of the events related. In this particular episode, Nick Adams witnesses the arrival of two gangsters determined to kill Ole Anderson. No explicit motive is given for the murder of this ex-prizefighter who is resigned to dying, making the story an even darker tale.[18]

The Iceberg Theory and the Expressionist Artist

Robert Siodmak's German career allowed him to assimilate the dramatic effect of chiaroscuro contrast, using the expressive value of light and dark to fathom the psychology of his characters.[19] According to Gene D. Phillips, "the expressionist artist seeks the symbolic meaning that underlies the facts. To be more precise, Expressionism exaggerates surface reality in order to make a symbolic point."[20] Siodmak's American films bear the impact of this cinematographic concept, which shaped the photographic vision of *The Killers.* The director resorts to expressionist lighting and *mise en scène* to convey the mood of a story built on the principles of the iceberg theory, which Hemingway defined in these words on the last page of *Death in the Afternoon*[21]:

> If a writer of prose knows enough about what he is writing about he may omit things that he knows and the reader, if the writer is writing truly enough, will have a feeling of those things as strongly as though the writer had stated them. The dignity of movement of an iceberg is due to only one-eighth of it being

above water. A writer who omits things because he does not know them only makes hollow places in his writings.[22]

Hemingway's writing technique relies on the suggestive power of allusion, the visible tip of the iceberg metaphorically hinting at the hidden part. At a narrative level, this concept implies an elliptic style with narrative gaps emphasizing the crisis around which the story revolves. The film structurally reflects the iceberg theory with the opening sequence introducing us to the main characters and the following eleven flashbacks delving into the past of the Swede through the investigation of the insurance detective Jim Reardon. The writer drops a whole section of the story as he describes the facts without mentioning the reasons lying behind them. These missing elements yield the impression that the murder happens for no reason at all, which lays stress on the absurd killing Nick has to confront. The viewer instead of the young man is invited to take the initiatory voyage in the film as he reconstructs the events surrounding the man's demise under the guidance of the detective. Although the film may provide some information about the Swede's past, it darkens the whole story into a tale of cold violence as the ironic detachment of the writer is lost in a *mise en scène* that highlights the ruthlessness of the underworld.

A change of perspective accounts for this shift in the translation of words into images. The short story starts inside Henry's diner where two gunmen suddenly drop in and dominate proceedings by indulging in male banter. In keeping with the iceberg theory, Hemingway endeavors to express emotion obliquely, using details to build up an atmosphere instead of dwelling on the characters' state of mind.[23] The tension that permeates the short story climaxes into a feeling of entrapment as the text is fraught with repetitions laying stress on the pervasive presence of both hitmen. Their repetitive gestures and reiterated questions point out the gangsters' rigid code of conduct and produce a tension that paralyses the other characters into observers ("They sat down at the counter. [...] The two men at the counter read the menu. [...] They sat leaning forward, their elbows on the counter").[24] The same effect is achieved through a symbolic displacement in the film as the killers' aggressive instinct is revealed by the opening shot of their arrival in town. The viewer is drawn into the heart of the action as the camera adopts his viewpoint from the back seat of the car which hurtles into the night. The forward movement conveys a sense of impending doom as nothing can be made out but the killers' shadowy silhouettes against the moving landscape of the road leading to Brentwood, New Jersey. The film starts like a road movie with the gleam of the headlights emphasizing the high-speed race. Driving against the clock, the men become two anonymous figures as they wander across the sleeping town, standing silhouetted against the streetlight glow or with their faces distorted in the light falling from the windows of the diner. The light and dark pattern creates depth of field and helps identify the men as outsiders. Emerging from the darkness, the two men symbolize a threat coming from the outside, from the big city (Chicago). Both enter the diner through opposite doors: one looms in the background whereas the other gangster joins him at the counter from the foreground. The long shot used to signify Nick Adams' viewpoint at the other end of the counter conveys a sense of entrapment as all the characters are suddenly surrounded and made prisoners inside the diner. In the film the threat comes from outside with the gangsters embodying urban evil whereas in the short story the tension spreads from one character to another inside the diner.

The narrator of "The Killers" urges the reader to pay attention to details which connote the gangsters' idiosyncratic style. The description highlights their stereotypical behavior as they act alike, repeating each other verbally and physically. Both men are dressed alike, yet this resemblance makes them look grotesque instead of endowing them with charismatic qualities. The repetition introduces an ironic distance that undermines the gangsters' authority — their coats don't fit them ("He wore a derby hat and a black overcoat buttoned across the chest. [...] Both wore overcoats too tight for them"). Yet at the same time, they look all the more dangerous as they are stuck in their habits, wearing gloves like a second skin which they can't take off to eat ("He wore a silk muffler and gloves. [...] Both men ate with their gloves on"). The words further express a deep-rooted violence that makes them unable to communicate. Once again they repeat each other's phrases in a dialogue that negates the Other's presence aggressively and stubbornly ("So you think that's right? [...] So he thinks it's all right [...] He thinks it's all right. That's a good one"). Their counterparts are trapped by this confusing discourse as they ask the same question three times in a row without getting a straight answer ("What's the idea?"). Unlike the short story, the film increases the tension of the power struggle opposing the gangsters to George (the owner of the diner), Sam (the cook) and Nick (the customer). Few camera movements are used during the scene and the same shots are repeated with the camera using the same angles, thus adding to the already oppressive atmosphere. The ironic detachment sensed in Hemingway's writing is lost in the film: the gangsters' stiffness turns into cruel cynicism as they enjoy recounting what the Swede may expect if he comes in as usual for dinner. When a customer unexpectedly drops in and George tells him the cook has gone out, the camera adopts a skewed angle and remains outside to signify something is going wrong in the diner.

A Sense of Confusion: "Negative Existentialism"

Camera work allows Siodmak to express the sense of confusion signified by "objective correlates" in the short story — external details (symbols, images) reflecting the subjective state of mind of the characters.[25] A series of details conjure up the loss of usual landmarks in George's diner, which is called Henry's, and where time runs twenty minutes too fast. Both the clock and the diner's name become signs of disruption, which in the film's narrative "can serve as the site of a kind of reversibility of meaning,"[26] as Dana Polan puts it in *Power and Paranoia*. Indeed the clock is only ten minutes fast in the film, showing that "escape means only a temporary respite before things catch up."[27] In other words, Swede is ensnared by a past that the film then unveils through a maze of flashbacks disclosing his former life. Also suggestive is the clock ticking in the background, pounding like a heartbeat as the tension reaches its climax when one of the gangsters takes the cook and Nick Adams into the back kitchen. What happens there is kept out of sight, which heightens the feeling of unease. The soundtrack conveys a sense of the inescapability of time, suggesting as Foster Hirsch remarks that Siodmak's "characters are boxed into corners."[28] The ticking clock seems to slow down time, making past and present join in the negative existentialism that also partakes of Hemingway's fiction.

Dana Polan defines "negative existentialism" as a characteristic of the forties films in which "environments [...] don't reflect back to a character his/her personality or values — that is, his/her freedom to shape externality according to individual desire — but quite the contrary, rather demonstrate the radical externality and even resistance of environment to the imprinting of a self upon environment."[29] This impossibility is illustrated in both the short story and the film, which negate the individual's power to shape his life while highlighting the dysfunction of language. The value of the spoken word is all the more excessive as it expresses no intention but voices an abstraction. For example the two killers emphatically explain they hold no personal grudge against the Swede, thus revealing an abstract link between their intention to kill the man and death itself ("We're going to kill a Swede. [...] He never had a chance to do anything to us. He never even seen us"). The Swede's life is enshrouded in lies that have estranged him from his own speech and from the other characters; he is therefore unable to react physically and verbally when Nick informs him about the arrival of the hitmen ("He's been in his room all day," explains Mrs. Bell, who is working at Mrs. Hirsch's rooming house). The man answers but keeps staring at the wall as though he were already dead, crushed by the weight of words sealing his fate ("Ole Anderson rolled over to the wall. [...] He said, talking toward the wall. [...] He looked at the wall. [...] As he shut the door he saw Ole Anderson with all his clothes on, lying on the bed looking at the wall"). At the same time this position makes him able to shun his humiliation and his state of near-paralysis into a cool detachment. His speech underpins this pose as it is fraught with negations that erect a barrier between himself and Nick whose position as the spectator of a man waiting for his death is made all more acute ("There isn't anything I can do about it"; "I don't want to know what they were like"; "That wouldn't do any good"; "No, there ain't anything to do"; "No. It ain't just a bluff"; "There ain't anything to do now").

It is worth noting that in the film the Swede's face remains in the dark while his soft, cool voice becomes detached from his body, expressing the void in his life and dramatizing his non-existence. On hearing the gangsters walking up the stairs outside, he sits up and stares at the door as though he wanted to put on a brave face. Being no coward he displays a hard-boiled front showing he is determined not to flee but to look in the face of the gangsters who are to kill him. Yet he is also swathed in the darkness of his room and the flashes of a few gunshots show that his courage and bravery are but useless bravado. The man simply states "Once I did something wrong" to account for his attitude,[30] but the film provides another explanation through the flashbacks which elucidate his personality while underscoring the dichotomy that undermines his sense of identity. Both Hemingway and Siodmak decode the masquerade of maleness while drawing the portrait of men who try to perform their masculinity, turning their life into a spectacle.

Masquerading Masculinity

Reardon's investigation leads us from one testimony to another with the flashbacks visualizing their memories and shedding a new light on Swede's character. Even though the past imagined by the screenwriters was not devised by Hemingway himself, it recalls other short stories of the collection, including some decisive aspects in the characterization of his male and female figures. Siodmak uses a silk handkerchief printed with three-leaf clovers around a large golden harp as a symbol for Swede's obsession with a woman whose name "Kitty" may refer to the female character of *A Cat in the Rain*— another short story of the same collection telling the frustration a woman voices at having short hair, wishing to grow long hair that would give her a more feminine appearance. As she is fascinated with a cat lying below her window, her husband wants to get it for her, but she refuses to let him go and takes matters into her own hands, thereby performing a masculine role that estranges her from him. Hemingway dramatizes the notion of gender roles in stories that explore concepts of manhood just as *films noirs* are about the crisis in masculinity following World War II.[31] In *The Killers*, both the writer and the director use the codes of the gangster film as a backdrop to deconstruct masculinity.

In *The Killers*, Mrs. Bell mentions her admiration for the ex-prizefighter Swede is supposed to be, yet she also points out a disturbing discrepancy between his nature and his boxing career ("He's an awfully nice man. He was in the ring, you know"). By exposing this dichotomy between the image of the tough guy and his secret weaknesses, the film lays bare the gender politics of Hemingway's writings and of film noir. Both stage masculinity to expose the codes of a theatrical representation, which Thomas Strychacz explains as follows: "The codes of manhood to which Hemingway's male characters look for psychological sustenance are themselves staged, and conducive to role-playing rather than to settled identities."[32]

This role-playing is further evidenced by the scene showing Swede's last match as a prizefighter. As the camera adopts the point of view of the spectators watching the match, it enhances the ring to look like a stage on which Swede exhibits his toughness, dramatizing his fight into a performance of manhood in front of an excited audience. The whole scene comprises a series of actions framed by glances that turn the fighters into reified bodies: being looked at defines their sense of identity. The medium-close shots dwell on the Swede's inability to strike back while his blank face lets no sign of suffering seep through. Recalling "The Battler" when he fails to perform the expected role and falls unconscious, Swede demonstrates self-destructive courage since he is bound to lose with a broken fist that puts an end to his career. Boxing is part of a masquerade that encodes masculinity and his failure strips him of his sense of identity. Not only does his silence imply an emotional restraint that defines masculine bravery in Hemingway's writing, but it also signifies his life is devoid of meaning if there is no audience to give a round of applause that heightens his sense of self.

Swede's tough pose masks a deep fragility, which comes to the fore when he first sees Kitty who may well embody his female counterpart. It is no surprise in these circumstances that he is so strongly attracted and seduced by this woman who takes part in a similar masquerade when singing at a party at Big Jim Colfax's. Kitty dramatizes herself as a she poses in the gazes of men, leaning over the piano and humming a tune which drives Swede away from his girlfriend whose admiring gaze he no longer values. Kitty's extravagant femininity balances Swede's visible masculinity, and Siodmak stylizes these theatricalized behaviors that bespeak the same structure of narcissistic performance.[33]

The film records a series of disruptions to the representation of gender, unveiling the artificiality of the codes that lie behind them. Kitty's highly sexualized iconography hides a deep-rooted frustration at playing a female role. Exercising her female power on the Swede's gaze, she is able to urge him to take the blame when she is about to be arrested for wearing a stolen brooch. Her wish for freedom accounts for her corruption and perversity, for Kitty acts like a man when she double-crosses the Swede, showing she is at heart animated by the same ambition that drives all the gangsters up the crooked ladder of organized crime. When in jail, he broods over her, acknowledging a tenderness that does not fit his hard-boiled front, exposing the limits of his role playing. Foster Hirsch deems Siodmak's characters to be "nurtured by their obsessions. Their single-mindedness, their fierce grip on a hopeless love, give them a purpose and an identity; they desperately need their martyrdom to a usually lost cause."[34] This obsessive pattern produces an emptiness in the existence of the Swede who needs to be watched by an audience of spectators or of gangsters to display his maleness.

A close reading of Hemingway demonstrates that his style paved the way for the writing and the making of this film noir, for he manages to create the impression of disorder and confusion which characterized the genre by portraying Swede as a man resigned to his fate and thus questioning the definition of masculinity. In fact the short story resolves around the identity crisis undermining maleness as the individual is locked into a dead-end life. While Hemingway confines himself to describing the devastating effects of masculinity as performance through the tragic fate of the Swede, Robert Siodmak uses a multiplicity of viewpoints and flashbacks to arouse feelings of ambiguity around gender identity. Thomas Strychacz argues that "Hemingway's narrative art constantly represents masculinity as temporary and subject to abrupt changes"[35] and this confusion is highlighted by the various names taken by (the) Swede who is called either Ole Anderson or Pete Lunn in the film. His stage name (Swede) becomes the symbol for the masquerade of maleness and the failure of his constructed identity. Holed up in Brentwood where no one knows his real identity, Swede becomes a nobody who has been dying since he was deprived of his honor as a boxer after he lost his fight against Tiger Lewis. Instead of focusing on the apprentice hero played by Nick Adams as Hemingway does in the short story, Robert Siodmak's film is centered upon the Swede, thus placing the viewer in the position of an observer like Nick Adams. Although the director drops the last part of the short story, when Nick goes back to the diner and confesses he cannot face the situation ("I can't stand to think about him waiting in the room and knowing he's going to get it. It's too damned awful"), the dénouement of the film makes Swede's sacrificial life completely useless in the light of Kitty's petty calculations, leaving a bitter taste in the mouth of the viewer.

NOTES

1. Gene D. Phillips, *Hemingway and Film*, New York: Frederick Ungar, 1980, 22.

2. Hemingway was disgruntled about Stallings receiving $24,000 fees for the script he wrote from the novel because he was paid the same fee as the author of the novel. *Ibid.*

3. *A Farewell to Arms* was remade by Charles Vidor in 1957, *The Killers* by Don Siegel in 1964 and *To Have and Have Not* by Don Siegel in *The Gun Runners* in 1957 without Hemingway or his estate receiving any additional revenue.

4. Frank M. Laurence, *Hemingway and the Movies,* New York: Da Capo Press, 1981, 41.

5. *Ibid.*

6. Phillips, *Hemingway and Film*, 2. Hemingway was concerned about the lack of ambition expressed by directors like John Sturges who replaced Fred Zinneman in the making of *The Old Man and the Sea* in 1954 and relinquished shooting on location although Hemingway insisted on abiding by the rules of realism, which determined the documentary aspect of his writing. Hemingway grew more suspicious of Hollywood as John Sturges quite willingly sacrificed the concept of "documentary realism" for more comfort in the artificial, contrived settings of the studio.

7. David Lodge, "Graham Greene," *The Tablet*, 28 September 1974, 937.

8. Raymond Chandler for example was unhappy about the writing process in Hollywood: "Nearly all phases of the Hollywood writing process upset him. He not only resented the intrusions upon privacy that collaboration and an office schedule entailed, he was horrified at the fact that when a writer produced something under these difficult circumstances, a director or a producer might change or even cut it while the film was being shot." William Luhr, *Raymond Chandler and Film,* Gainesville: Florida State University Press, 1991, 6.

9. In the 1930s and 1940s, James M. Cain, Raymond Chandler, John Fante, Daniel Fuchs, Horace McCoy, Clifford Odets, Maxwell Anderson, Dorothy Parker, John Don Passos, Theodore Dreiser, Nathanael West, William Faulkner, F. Scott Fitzgerald worked in Hollywood as screenwriters and many of their novels were adapted to the screen.

10. "Ernest Hemingway's terse, brittle, vernacular prose, which was similar to that of a journalist's on-the-spot reportage, plus his economical, colloquial dialogue, impressed the writers of hard-boiled fiction; and they honed their own writing styles to achieve a similar effect." Gene D. Phillips, *Creatures of Darkness: Raymond Chandler, Detective Fiction, and Film Noir*, Lexington: University Press of Kentucky, 2000, 4.

11. John Huston was not mentioned in the credits of the film because he was under contract to Warner Bros. when he took part in devising the plot of *The Killers*.

12. Of all the films adapted from his writings, "there was only one that he liked, this *Killers*," said his wife. Oriana Fallaci, "An Interview with Mary Hemingway: My Husband, Ernest Hemingway," *Look* XXX (September 6, 1966), 65.

13. "Disequilibrium is the product of a style characterized by unbalanced and disturbing frame compositions, strong contrasts of light and dark, the prevalence of shadows and areas of darkness within the frame, the visual tension created by curious camera angles and so forth. [...] The visual dissonances that are characteristic of these films are the marks of those ideological contradictions that form the historical context out of which the films are produced." Sylvia Harvey, "Woman's Place: The Absent Family of *Film Noir*," in E. Ann Kaplan, ed., *Women in Film Noir* (1980), London: British Film Institute, 1998, 35.

14. Aldous Huxley quoted in Phillips, *Hemingway and Film*, 10.

15. "Many European filmmakers were forced to flee their homelands in the wake of the rise of Hitler; they subsequently enriched the American motion picture industry with a reservoir of new talent that had been nurtured in Europe." Gene D. Phillips, *Exiles in Hollywood, Major European Film Directors in America,* Bethlehem, PA: Lehigh University Press, 1998, 13.

16. Foster Hirsch, *The Dark Side of the Screen: Film Noir,* New York: Da Capo Press, 1982, 54. The writer comments: "These early Expressionist films, with their tormented protagonists in flight from an alien society, and their stylized urban settings, exerted a deep influence on the subject matter as well as the visual temper of the American *film noir.* Expressionist motifs filtered into *film noir,* in diluted but nonetheless significant ways, because the German style offered an appropriate iconography for the dark vision of the forties thriller and also because a number of German directors fled to Hollywood from a nightmare society bringing with them the special sensibility that permeated their early work." *Ibid.,* 57.

17. "The Killers" was first published in a magazine (*Scribner's*) before it was included in *In Our Time* (1925) and added to *Men Without Women* (1927). *The Nick Adams Stories* (1972) gathers all the short stories about Nick Adams — including "The Killers."

18. Philip Young explains: "A typical Nick Adams story is of an initiation, is the telling of an event which is violence or evil, or both, or at the very least in the description of an incident which brings the boy into contact with something that is perplexing and unpleasant." Philip Young, *Ernest Hemingway, A Reconsideration* (1956), New York: Harcourt Brace, 1966, 31.

19. *Stürme des Leidenschaft* (1931) was a turning-point in Siodmak's career. Hervé Dumont considers the film a stylistic exercise. "Siodmak y développe une maîtrise sternbergienne de l'éclairage, enveloppant les corps d'une lumière fragmentée, modelant délicatement les surfaces à demi enfouies dans la pénombre. Ailleurs, de violents clairs-obscurs, mis en valeur par une caméra souple, traduisent l'affrontement pathétique des antagonistes" ("Siodmak develops a Sternbergian mastery of lighting there, enveloping the bodies in a fragmented light, delicately sculpting surfaces half-hidden in the gloom. Elsewhere, violent high-contrast lighting, presented to advantage by flexible camera-work, translate the pathetic confrontation of the opponents," editor's translation). Hervé Dumont, *Robert Siodmak, Le maître du film noir,* Lausanne: L'Age d'Homme, 1981, 71.

20. Phillips, *Exiles in Hollywood,* 25. See also Lotte Eisner, *The Haunted Screen: Expressionism in the German Cinema,* Berkeley: University of California Press, 1994, 10.

21. Geneviève Hilly-Mane, *Le Style de Ernest Hemingway, la plume et le masque,* Paris: Presses Universitaires de France, 1983, 26.

22. Ernest Hemingway, *Death in the Afternoon,* New York: Charles Scribner's Sons, 1932, 192.

23. "L'émotion ne doit jamais être décrite de façon directe mais suggérée par des détails" ("Emotion must never be described directly, but suggested through details," editor's translation). Hilly-Mane, *Le Style de Ernest Hemingway,* 28.

24. Ernest Hemingway, "The Killers," in *The Complete Short Stories of Ernest Hemingway,* New York: Finca Vigía Edition, 1987, 215–216. The "counter" is mentioned several times during the diner scene.

25. "Il s'agit d'exprimer l'état d'esprit subjectif d'un personnage d'une façon à la fois compacte et indirecte, par un détail objectif, extérieur, sur lequel se concentre l'attention" ("The purpose is to express the subjective state of a character in a manner that is both compact and indirect, through an objective, external detail, on which the attention is focused," editor's translation). Hilly-Mane, *Le Style de Ernest Hemingway,* 28.

26. "If the project (to use the existentialists' term) is a narrative activity through which human beings work to come to terms with an environment and make it their own, forties

narratives can serve as the site of a kind of reversibility of meaning—what we might call a symbolics of narrative space—in which environment ceases to be a reflection or object of human projects and turns instead into a potential disruption, subversion, dispersion of projects. Not a symbolism in which each object is named and so has its place within a human scheme, a symbolics is the space of the object's permutability, its ability to pass through all possible functions." Dana Polan, *Power and Paranoia*, New York: Columbia University Press, 1986, 209.

27. *Ibid.*, 267.

28. Hirsch, *The Dark Side of the Screen*, 118.

29. Polan, *Power and Paranoia*, 208.

30. "Récit après récit il [Hemingway] suggère que c'est le langage, plus encore qu'une tendance personnelle de l'individu, qui l'enferme dans la solitude et dans le mensonge" ("In narrative after narrative he [Hemingway] suggests that it's language, rather than a personal initiative taken by an individual, that imprisons him in solitude and lies" editor's translation). Hily-Mane, *Le Style de Ernest Hemingway*, 46.

31. Frank Krutnik, *In A Lonely Street, Film Noir, Genre, Masculinity*, New York: Chapman & Hall, 1991.

32. Thomas Strychacz, *Hemingway's Theaters of Masculinity*, Baton Rouge: Louisiana State University, 2003, 8.

33. Thomas Strychacz comments on the American wife in *A Cat in the Rain* that "her attempt to command center stage merely entangles her in culturally sanctioned images; a potential power over the gaze becomes submission to the way women and men are supposed to look." This vision may well apply to Kitty whose femininity only helps underscore the constructedness of gender. Strychacz, *Hemingway's Theaters of Masculinity*, 70.

34. Hirsch, *The Dark Side of the Screen*, 118.

35. Strychacz, *Hemingway's Theaters of Masculinity*, 8.

BIBLIOGRAPHY

Dumont, Hervé, and Robert Siodmak. *Le Maître du film noir*. Lausanne: L'Age d'Homme, 1981.

Eisner, Lotte. *The Haunted Screen: Expressionism in the German Cinema*. Berkeley: University of California Press, 1994.

Fallaci, Oriana. "An Interview with Mary Hemingway: My Husband, Ernest Hemingway." *Look* XXX (September 6, 1966).

Harvey, Sylvia. "Woman's Place: The Absent Family of Film Noir." E. Ann Kaplan, ed., *Women in Film Noir* (1980). London: British Film Institute, 1998.

Hemingway, Ernest. *The Complete Short Stories of Ernest Hemingway*. New York: Finca Vigía, 1987.

_____. *Death in the Afternoon* (1931). New York: Scribner's, 1960.

Hilly-Mane, Genviève. *Le Style de Ernest Hemingway, la plume et le masque*. Paris: Presses Universitaires de France, 1983.

Hirsch, Foster. *The Dark Side of the Screen: Film Noir*. New York: Da Capo Press, 1982.

The Killers. Robert Siodmak, dir., Anthony Veiller, scr. Mark Hellinger Productions, 1946.

Krutnik, Frank. *In A Lonely Street. Film Noir, Genre, Masculinity*. New York: Chapman & Hall, 1991.

Laurence, Frank M. *Hemingway and the Movies*. New York: Da Capo Press, 1981.

Lodge, David. "Graham Greene." *The Tablet*, 28 September 1974, 937.

Luhr, William. *Raymond Chandler and Film*. Gainesville: University Press of Florida, 1991.

Phillips, Gene D. *Creatures of Darkness, Raymond Chandler, Detective Fiction, and Film Noir*. Lexington: University Press of Kentucky, 2000.

_____. *Exiles in Hollywood, Major European Film Directors in America.* Bethlehem, PA: Lehigh University Press, 1998.

_____. *Hemingway and Film*, New York: Frederick Ungar, 1980.

Polan, Dana. *Power and Paranoia.* New York: Columbia University Press, 1986.

Strychacz, Thomas. *Hemingway's Theaters of Masculinity.* Baton Rouge: Louisiana State University Press, 2003.

Young, Philip. *Ernest Hemingway, A Reconsideration* (1956). New York: Harcourt Brace, 1966.

Three Filmic Avatars of *The Maltese Falcon*

Gilles Menegaldo

Dashiell Hammett's famous novel, *The Maltese Falcon*[1] (published in 1930), was adapted to the screen soon after in 1931 by Roy Del Ruth,[2] and again in 1936 by William Dieterle,[3] each time by Warner Bros. who bought the rights soon after the publication. Yet the only well-known version is that of John Huston[4] (1941), also by Warner Bros., which some critics claim marks the birth of the *film noir*, though it lacks some of its main recurrent features, such as narrative voice over and flash back. Interestingly, Huston's version is the one that seems to capture best the spirit of Hammett's "hard-boiled" novel. The other two versions, especially Dieterle's, take many liberties with the plot of the original novel and more specifically seem to mingle several generic conventions, crime fiction, vaudeville, screwball comedy, etc. This article aims at a comparative analysis based in particular on a close study of the opening and closing sequences of the three films in relation to the opening and closing pages of the novel. This may enable us to trace the various devices, narrative, thematic, and formal, that are used in the process of adaptation. Among these indeed we will foreground the notions of decentering, displacement and generic hybridity. Another important aspect concerns the representation of male and female characters in relation to the context of production of the films.

Title and Credit Sequence

The titles of the three films are different. Only Huston takes up the original. We know he was very fond of Hammett's novel, wished to pay tribute to the author and wrote the screenplay for what would be his first feature film. The 1931 version is called *Dangerous Female*, foregrounding indeed the role of women by means of a very explicit warning (which is a way of attracting the spectator), but leaving aside the mysterious exotic appeal of the original title.[5] Dieterle's attempt in 1936 is called *Satan met a Lady*, which sounds irrelevant, but corresponds in fact to Spade's description in the book as a "a blond Satan." Again, the female sex is foregrounded in the title, but with another connotation, "female" being replaced by "Lady," a more innocuous and less sexually connoted word. In fact the main male protagonist called Ted Shane (Warren William) is confronted with many different kinds of "Ladies"; thus the title can also be seen as ironical.

The credit sequences are quite contrasted too and they offer a different type of entrance in the fiction. The novel starts *in medias res* with a celebrated portrait of Spade: "Samuel Spade's was long and bony, his chin jutting V under the more flexible V of his mouth. His nostrils curved back to make another smaller V. His yellow grey eyes were horizontal."[6] The 1931 film proposes a very simple sober credit sequence typical of the Warner films of the thirties with a musical score that is more on the comedic side. The 1936 version is a little more sophisticated as it features throughout a drawing of a Mephistophelian stage character, complete with top hat and black cape, as an echo to the title. The cape enfolds a woman's figure whose face only is visible. The musical score is even more comedic, close to musical comedy.

Huston's credit sequence is much more elaborate, using elements that are not in the novel but which already convey a specific kind of mood. First of all the spectator is shown in close up a statuette of the black bird we assume is the falcon. Contrary to the reader, he is given a clue from the outset. The sequence is composed of close-up shots on which the credits appear, swirl onto the screen and suddenly dissolve. This swirling takes place against the stable image of the statuette and offers some kind of elusive counterpoint. This could refer to the way the narrative develops, shifting from one mystery to the next, leading the spectator to construct a hypothesis and question it the next moment as Spade does, especially after the unexpected murder of his partner, which leaves him in the dark. This is what Marc Vernet calls the "*pot au noir*."[7] The rather complex musical score adds to the mood of mystery as it combines several motifs. The one we first hear, a solo clarinet, is repeated in various keys and is associated later in the film with the falcon. Then the music shifts to a more solemn tune with brass instruments, but the piano and the harp are present to introduce a more lyrical, even romantic mood (this fits with the trailer which foregrounds both the criminal story and the love story and aims at establishing a new image of Bogart after the success of *High Sierra* (January 1941) where he plays the part of Roy Earle, an ageing and nostalgic gangster, a congenial character however, contrasting with his usual "villain" parts such as that of the shyster lawyer in *Angels with Dirty Faces* (1938) or those of violent, psychopathic hoodlums in *The Petrified Forest* (1936) or *Dead End* (1937). The last element of the credit sequence was requested by Jack Warner, who wanted the audience to have some clues, and is probably an unfortunate choice. Indeed a title-card unrolls on the screen following the opening credits, informing us about the historical context relating to the falcon. This background is given in the novel by Casper Gutman, the leader of the small gang, but only in Chapter 13. As Hammett recalls: "Somewhere I had read of the peculiar rental agreement between Charles V [of Spain] and the Order of the Hospital of St. John of Jerusalem [the Knights of Malta]."[8] In the film, after reading this account of the myth, we know what the statuette is, why it was made, and that it is missing. This information provides us with more than we know after reading the first chapter of the novel, but suspense lies in the way the falcon may relate to the character of Miss Wonderly, who is introduced just after in the actual opening scene.

Comparative Analysis of the Opening Scene in the Three Films

In the incipit of the novel, we get a portrait of Sam Spade with an emphasis on his physical bulk, but also his irony and cynicism and the prevailing Satan image. We also have a portrait of Effie Perrine which foregrounds positive features, but also boyishness, while an erotic touch is added with the dress clinging to her with an "effect of dampness." Miss Wonderly is characterized ambivalently as shy, unsure of herself, hesitating ("tentative steps") and predatory ("probing eyes"). Coldness is emphasized by her "cobalt blue eyes" and her erotic power is signified by the darkly red hair, and the full brightly red lips. A vampire metaphor is suggested by the association of the red mouth with her white glistening teeth. The way she tells the story is meant to make her suspicious in the eyes of Spade, in particular because her account relies on a lot of clichés, especially when she refers to Floyd Thursby the villain as having "thick eyebrows" and a "loud blustery" voice. Lastly we may point out the negative characterization of Archer as both dumb and coarse, obviously unable to compete with Spade (though he tries). Thus the opening chapter of the novel already emphasizes Miss Wonderly's duplicity and foregrounds the erotic and male competition beside the criminal plot and the notion of contract that is so typical of the "hard boiled" novel. We may also note the prominence of dialogue, which makes it easy to adapt to the screen.

The three filmic adaptations propose very different transpositions of this opening scene. The Huston version is the closest to the textual source. It does follow the text rather strictly except for the first four establishing shots of San Francisco (long shots with the camera panning movement followed by a shot on the Golden Gate bridge, then on a building) which are added and lead us gradually by means of dissolves inside Spade and Archer's office through the window and the famous shot on the glass-pane where the two detective names are inscribed in inverted lettering. This shot points ominously to a "partnership" that will be broken soon. The same characters (with the same names) are kept, in a similar situation. Archer barges in exactly at the same moment as in the novel. The dialogues follow the text which is quoted almost verbatim except for a few deletions and a few lexical changes. It's interesting to note that the opening lines play down the hesitating tone of the novel. To the broken uncertain syntax of Miss Wonderly ("Could you–? I thought — I — that is–"),[9] the film script substitutes a rather assertive sentence: "I inquired at the hotel for the name of a reliable private detective and they mentioned yours." On the whole the film sequence seeks to eliminate uncertainties and facilitate the understanding of the audience. For example the literary text states "I don't know where she met him" without identifying "her" and "him" while the film introduces the sister right away : "I am trying to find my sister." Some minor changes can be explained. For instance, Honolulu was chosen instead of Europe as the film was released during World War Two and Europe was not a safe place for traveling. More interesting is the suppression of some phrases like Spade's remark to Archer "You'll play hell with her, you will,"[10] probably due to censorship requirements. Many other references to "hell" and being "damned" throughout the novel are systematically cut from the script.

The presentation of the characters is also significant. As was pointed out by James Naremore, the Bogart character is the "visual opposite" of Hammett's Spade and is indeed quite remote from the textual one in many respects. Spade is tall, strongly built and when he takes off his shirt, "the sag of his big rounded shoulders" makes him resemble "a bear." Bogart is small and slim. Spade is blond, Bogart is dark-haired and swarthy. However the filmic Spade is made quite convincing by Bogart's performance,[11] his swift delivery, the way he moves, and his gestures and facial expressions where irony can be felt. His frequent smiles (or grins) off screen (and towards the camera) establish an ironic complicity with the spectator. With Mary Astor, an already mature actress, Miss Wonderly loses some of the youthfulness of the literary character and also some of her ambiguity, but she gives also more sophistication to the part. To compensate for dropping the broken fragmented lines, Mary Astor's slightly breathless, speeded up delivery suggests her nervousness. Effie Perrine becomes a bit matron-like and loses her boyishness and erotic appeal. As the film shows, she is more a kind of mother substitute than a potential sexual partner, while the other two films play upon that eroticization of the part. Lastly, Miles Archer (Jerome Cowan) is rather close physically and psychologically to his textual counterpart and he speaks most of his own lines.

The *mise en scène* is rather classical, but some features may be outlined. The shots of the characters in the office vary from close-up to long shot. The long shots introduce them as they enter Spade's office and meet him. The close-ups and medium close-ups focus on their reactions to each other as they speak. The editing of the medium close-up and close-up shots move from a character's reaction to another in a shot/reverse-shot pattern that is typical for depicting conversation. However there are some interesting variations, especially in the way a sense of intimacy is created by the close ups alternating Wonderly's face and Spade's while Archer is not filmed in close up and is usually relegated to the margins of the screen, only forcing his way into it by conspicuous tilting movement of his body when he asserts his presence and poses as a competitor for Spade as when he states with a large grin: "I'll look after it myself."

We may also note the theatricality of the whole scene and the idea that all the characters, not only Miss Wonderly, are playing a part. She is obviously the most theatrical, but Spade also pretends to believe the deceitful story while we realize he is not convinced. Archer overdoes his own character of would-be "lady-killer" with emphatic gestures and exaggerated, artificial smiles.

The low-key lighting produces strong contrasts between the light and dark areas. This style of lighting is usually associated with the dim, sinister world of murder mysteries and detective stories. It will become a major stylistic feature in the *films noirs* of the forties and fifties. As several film critics have noted, Huston's *The Maltese Falcon* marks a starting point for this new trend or genre[12] even though it is already anticipated in a little known film, *Stranger on the Third Floor* (1940) by Boris Ingster, starring Peter Lorre as serial killer (as in *M* by Fritz Lang). There are some features of the *film noir* in the opening sequence of Huston's film, though a certain staginess prevails and though the scene is rather light in tone (until Archer's murder). As has been suggested in a recent study,[13] the animation of the credit sequence can suggest cigarette smoke (thus uncertainty, elusiveness) and urban fog, two motifs typical of *noir*. The shadowy lighting and the music create a dark mood that fits a detective story, but the opening scene also has a lighter comedic tone that here is played down, but was more prominent in the earlier adaptations.

Indeed, Del Ruth's version, though it starts with the same kinds of establishing shots as in the Huston film (including a superimposed blurry "San

Francisco") departs very early from the novel both in content and mood, even
if the outline of the main story (the dialogue between Spade and Miss Wonderly) remains. The first diegetic shot after the introduction to the urban setting features an anonymous finger pointing at the lettered indication: "Spade
and Archer private detectives." The shot dissolves into the image of a closely-
knit couple embracing, silhouetted as two shadows behind a window pane
which constitutes a frame within the frame and draws the spectator's attention.
A close up on the opening door reveals the lower part of a woman's body. Her
hands enter the frame from above to adjust her stockings, suggesting she had
taken them off previously. The man's legs are barely visible behind. The next
shot finally reveals the man in profile as he kisses the lady's hand, the rest of
her body is already off screen and we never see her face. The use of these
metonymical shots prevents the identification of the woman and we may wonder if she is the one whose finger we saw first. This little scene added by the
script sets the tone and defines Spade (Ricardo Cortez) as a "lady killer." His
relationship with his secretary, Effie, younger and more attractive, is part of
his seduction game. He kisses her on the neck and watches her intently as she
walks off screen. When he returns to his office and puts in order the disturbed
furniture and cushions, the spectator is aware that some erotic game must
indeed have taken place.

Thus the book's opening scene is startlingly delayed, decentered and per-
turbed. Effie and Spade exchange looks while Miss Wonderly (Bebe Daniels)
is seated, suggesting she is used to her boss having love affairs with customers.
Interestingly, the script keeps Wonderly's uncertain, broken opening lines that
were cut by Huston. The scene is interrupted by an added phone call. We cut
from Spade's office to Effie's as she takes up the receiver, then we have a
medium shot of the reclining body of an elegantly dressed and rather attractive
woman, Iva Archer. Thus the spectator knows from the outset that Iva is
Spade's mistress, whereas in Huston's film, this revelation is delayed. Apart
from this information, this phone call triggers a form of decentering as we
are more concerned with potential immediate conflict than with the story
told by Miss Wonderly. Indeed, while the phone conversation takes place, we
may suppose she's still telling Spade her story. In the same way, the conversation between Spade and Iva is cut off abruptly by the unexpected return of
Archer who appears here as an older man, betrayed by a much younger wife.
Archer's attention is caught by Effie's gesture when she puts the receiver down
(with a close up on her hand). He uses a pretext to get her out of the way so
as to listen to the conversation, already suspecting it may be his wife on the
phone. The editing alternates shots of Spade and Iva speaking with shots of
Archer's grim face. Thus the spectator is led to expect some kind of conflict

between Spade and Archer. Spade in turn lies to Miss Wonderly, referring to a non-existing case of a woman looking for a lost dog (this is echoed in the 1936 film with a missing poodle). Thus, Archer's abrupt intrusion in the room is rather deliberate, but it does not interrupt Wonderly's story, which has barely started. Contrary to the reader's expectations, nothing happens and Archer pretends to believe Spade's assertions. The main narrative is delayed and decentered and only comes to the foreground in the last part of the scene. We can clearly see a mingling of genres and tones here. The detective story scene is contaminated by a vaudeville-like situation. Spade then summarizes for Archer what we haven't heard (contrary to the Huston version). The competition between Spade and Archer is toned down whereas the adultery is foregrounded. Moreover, Archer's murder is not staged in this version. We cut directly from Spade's office to the nightly call that announces his partner's death.

Thus the opening scene is made richer by its staging of Spade's relationship with several women. Allusions and hints to erotic situations abound throughout the film, which was released before the reinforcement of the Hays Code in 1934 with Joseph Breen and the Production Code Administration (PCA). For instance, when Iva breaks into Spade's apartment and sees Miss Wonderly, she exclaims: "What's that dame wearing my kimono?" This suggests that both Iva and Miss Wonderly are having an affair with Spade. Significantly, the film stages a scene from the book which was cut from Huston's version, the scene when Spade asks Miss Wonderly to take her clothes off because he suspects her of having stolen the money. The vision, even fleeting, of the naked body of Miss Wonderly would have been impossible a few years later.

In the opening scene of Dieterle's film, there is no presentation of the San Francisco setting, nor do we see Spade's office. The scene takes place in a train station and has nothing to do with the incipit of the book. It features a man being driven out of town by cops (we learn later he is a private detective) and in a parallel scene, the mother of sextuplets being celebrated by a crowd of journalists. Instead of the big city, the film is set in a small town which appears rather strict in terms of morals, and the Spade character called Shane (Warren Williams) is seen as a kind of "lovable rake" as Jean Loup Bourget[14] puts it. The character is closer to the detective impersonated by William Powell in the *Thin Man* series directed by Woody S. Van Dyke. Very clearly the scene mingles the conventions of the mystery story and those of the screwball comedy and even the burlesque. The next scene on the train is reminiscent of Agatha Christie's novels. Shane encounters two mysterious women, one he talks to, a rich old lady, and another one (Bette Davis, still anonymous) who spies upon him from behind, her eyes hidden by sun glasses. The latter will reappear later, and she is the film equivalent of Miss Wonderly (named here

Valerie Purvis). We have to wait several minutes to get the actual opening scene of the novel, which is thus once again decentered and transformed by the mingling of generic conventions. Indeed, the original dialogue is cut to a minimum and the story is changed; it now concerns a betrayal of love. Miss Purvis is already seated in Ames's (Shane's partner) office. Shane barges in and Ames sums up the story while we only see the client from the back. However the reverse shot soon reveals the lady we saw in the train. The murder scene is staged, but in a different setting, as Ames is killed (appropriately) in a graveyard. Meanwhile Shane is dining with Ames's secretary, but also trying to seduce a ballet dancer, and we witness part of the stage show.

Thus the original scene is delayed, altered and fragmented by several inserted scenes which mingle different moods. As in the previous film, Shane's seductive power is emphasized. This iconoclastic approach is carried out throughout the film. The falcon is replaced by the legendary horn of Roland, supposedly filled with jewels. The secretary, rather young and silly, is called Miss Murgatroyd, a rather obvious reference to Christie's novel, *A Murder Is Announced*. More importantly, the trio of gangsters is changed. Huston's fat man, only slightly altered in the 1931 version, here becomes a fat woman, Mrs. Barabbas (the "Agatha Christian stout lady" we met on the train). The "boy" Wilmer, a rather slim and nervous fellow in both Huston and del Ruth (interpreted in the 1931 film by Dwight Frye, famous for his role of Renfield in Browning's *Dracula* and that of Fritz, Frankenstein's assistant in James Whale's *Frankenstein* [1931] and by Elisha Cook Jr. in Huston's film), becomes here a chubby ludicrous pychopath with a beret, verging on the grotesque, but also supposed to be "like a son" for Mrs. Barrabas. As to the Joel Cairo character, he loses all the homosexual connotations given to the part in the book (Cairo is called a "fairy," wears various jewels, and eats Violet sweets) and in the Huston version with the subtle interpretation of Peter Lorre. He simply becomes a tall, slightly affected, and eccentric Englishman, closer to a Phileas Fogg than to the original Hammett character. Many scenes are altered in terms of setting. For example the famous "fall guy" scene does not take place in Spade's apartment, but in the harbor, close to the docks, under a heavy rain. On the other hand, this version takes up some overlooked episodes such as the reference to Miss Murgatroyd's uncle, an archaeologist who can give information on the famous horn.

Closing Sequences

Hammett's closing scene takes place after Wonderly's arrest and in Spade's office where Spade tells Effie about Archer's murderess. The book ends on the following sentence (after Effie's announcement "Iva is here"): " Spade, looking at his desk, nodded almost imperceptibly. 'Yes' he said, and shivered. 'Well send her in.'"[15] This illustrates the kind of circle in which Spade is caught and it calls to mind one of Spade's stories that is completely absent from the films, that of Flitcraft, a character who wished to change his life (after being almost killed by a falling beam) and disappeared one day only to reproduce the same kind of life with a similar job and a similar wife elsewhere. To some extent, Spade seems to be condemned to the same kind of relationship with Iva. The films are quite different. In Huston's version, the story does end on the scene of arrest and the famous shot of Mary Astor going down the elevator, framed behind the railings as if she were behind prison bars. The actual final shot frames Spade holding the falcon after his famous Shakespearian answer to his cop friend, "It's the stuff dreams are made of," one of the few meaningful sentences added in the script. The end of that version stresses both the fated and impossible love relationship and Spade's honesty and authenticity.

In the 1931 version, this narrative resolution is taken up, but is less central. Several things are added, in particular three different shots of newspaper clippings, a headline announcing that the three murders have been solved along with a photograph of Ruth Wonderly, a close shot of the photograph, and finally a close up on a section of an article referring to Spade producing of the sole witness to the murder, a Chinese merchant. This interest in the resolution of the plot is closer to the "whodunit" type of crime fiction than it is to the "hard boiled." The film does not end there however and the romance is reintroduced by Spade's visit to Wonderly in jail, which combines an element of pathos through the prisoner's degradation and psychological collapse, some romance because of Spade's wistfulness and a touch of comedy in the last exchange between Spade and the woman guardian.

The ending of Dieterle's film is as eccentric and remote from the novel as the rest. It is based on a series of incidents. First, Purvis/Wonderly escapes from the police by catching a train and is joined by Spade/Shane who makes her confess her crime. However, Shane pretends not to care while he sets a trap. Cops are waiting for them at the arrival of the train. Purvis hides but is finally turned in by a black employee who refuses to be bribed. The most interesting moment is Purvis's provocative and almost feminist speech while she is taken away: "You'll always remember me. [...] The one woman who handled you, double-crossed you and double-crossed right up to the end. Now you found that a woman can be as smart as you are. Someday you'll find one who will be smarter. She'll marry you." This last phrase ties up with the opening of the film which ends, as an ironic illustration of Purvis's words, with a potential new love affair between Shane and his secretary; however, there is no romantic touch, simply the promise of "lots of fun"!

Contrary to what often happens, the latest version of *The Maltese Falcon* is the closest to the original text. Only Huston manages to fully capture Hammett's hard-boiled fiction because it tries and maintains a unified tone, despite some comic touches which are also present in the novel. The 1931 version starts in a more comedic mood, stressing the erotic aspect, and then adheres more closely to the novel, but Ricardo Cortez's interpretation is a bit shallow compared to Bogart's intensity and control. The 1936 version is explicitly parodic; it is a spoof that mingles several genres more openly, with the underlying filmic model of the *Thin Man* series, but in a less subtle way, while also keeping in mind the work of Agatha Christie through the motif of the train, of shifting identities, etc. The 1941 version is the purest, the least intertextual, but also the best directed and acted. No wonder it has become a landmark in film history while paying tribute to Hammett's masterpiece.

NOTES

1. Dashiell Hammett, *The Maltese Falcon* (1930), London: Pan Books, 1975.
2. *The Maltese Falcon* (*Dangerous Female*), Roy Del Ruth, dir., Maude Fulton, scr., Warner Bros., 1931.
3. *Satan Met a Lady*, William Dieterle, dir., Brown Holmes, scr., Warner Bros., 1936.
4. *The Maltese Falcon*, John Huston, dir., scr., Warner Bros., 1941.
5. The title was later changed back for video distribution.
6. Hammett, *The Maltese Falcon*, 5.
7. Marc Vernet, "La transaction filmique," *Le Cinéma américain, analyses de film*, vol. 2, Raymond Bellour, ed., Paris: Flammarion, 1980.
8. Quoted in Rudy Behlmer's article, "The Stuff that Dreams are Made of: *The Maltese Falcon*," in *The Maltese Falcon: John Huston, Director*, William Luhr, ed., New Brunswick: Rutgers University Press, 1995, 120.
9. Hammett, *The Maltese Falcon*, 6.
10. *Ibid.*, 11.
11. Nonetheless, he was not the first choice for the studio. George Raft declined the part, then Paul Muni.
12. There is a critical controversy on that matter.
13. John M. Desmond and Peter Hawkes, *Adaptation, Studying Film and Literature*, Boston: McGraw Hill, 2006, 77.
14. See his excellent article signed Jacques Segond: "Sur la piste de Dashiell Hammett (les trois versions du *Faucon Maltais*)," *Positif* 171–172 July 1975 13.
15. Hammett, *The Maltese Falcon*, 201.

BIBLIOGRAPHY

Behlmer, Rudy. "The Stuff That Dreams Are Made Of: *The Maltese Falcon*." *The Maltese Falcon: John Huston, Director*, William Luhr, ed. New Brunswick: Rutgers University Press, 1995.
Hammett, Dashiell. *The Maltese Falcon* (1930). London: Pan Books, 1975.

The Maltese Falcon (*Dangerous Female*). Roy Del Ruth, dir., Maude Fulton, scr. Warner Bros., 1931.

The Maltese Falcon. John Huston, dir., scr. Warner Bros., 1941.

Satan Met a Lady. William Dieterle, dir., Brown Holmes, scr. Warner Bros., 1936.

Segond, Jacques. "Sur la piste de Dashiell Hammett (les trois versions du Faucon Maltais)." *Positif* 171–172 (July 1975).

Vernet, Marc. "La transaction filmique." *Le Cinéma américain: analyses de film,* vol. 2, Raymond Bellour, ed. Paris: Flammarion, 1980.

The Aesthetic of Epic in Kenneth Branagh's *Hamlet*

Sarah Hatchuel

In theatre studies, the word "epic" refers to a drama which is composed of several episodes generally linked by the narration of an alienating, metatheatrical "Chorus." The dramatic events are presented without respecting the rules of Aristotle's poetics, and exclude identification and sympathy with the characters portrayed on stage. In film studies, "epic" usually characterizes a story of a vast historical sweep, full of extraordinary and/or legendary events, in which the hero fights against huge, contrary forces, and eventually comes out winning. A distinction can be thus made between an epic *genre* in the theatre (as opposed to tragedy, for example) and an epic *feeling* in the cinema. So much as epic theatre is designed to appeal to the audience's reason, epic movies are meant to create emotions. Yet, this paper aims at showing that, in Branagh's 1996 screen adaptation of *Hamlet*, the epic feeling works hand in hand with a certain kind of epic genre. In order to create "big" emotions, the director generates narrative and metacinematic effects that are reminiscent of the alienating devices of Brechtian theatre.

In works of epic feelings, the hero's actions always seem to be able to modify the course of the story. The future is not set up in advance by fate. Epic then goes with inner certainties. As Anne Souriau writes in *Vocabulaire d'esthétique*, "the epic hero has a confidence without anxieties or agonies of the soul. He or she faces obstacles, not inner wrenches."[1] In Branagh's *Hamlet*, interpolated scenes present the prince as an active and aggressive hero. For example, in Act Three Scene Three, an interpolation makes us dive into Hamlet's criminal thoughts. Contrary to Shakespeare's Hamlet who hesitates to kill Claudius at prayer and finally refrains from doing so, Branagh's Hamlet decides to stab his enemy. In a quasi-subliminal depiction, the spectators see the dagger being plunged into Claudius' ear — only to be jolted back into reality. By showing what only remains a verbal dilemma in Shakespeare's scene, Branagh gives greater importance to action and will. For a short instant, the audience can believe that Hamlet has committed his killing at last. All through the film, the prince is thus portrayed as a dauntless avenger, defying the odds. Some of his soliloquies are even turned into war exhortations. In the tradition of epics, Hamlet starts a fight against opposite, gigantic forces, from which he somehow winds up as the "winner" resplendent through glorious death.

Epic movies are also characterized by dynamism and expansion. According to Souriau, "epic is a realizing movement; this dynamism of epic exalts the hero as an individualized person."[2] Contrary to tragic feeling which works in concentration, epic feeling operates in centrifugal dilation.

In *Hamlet*, Branagh certainly plays on magnitude, first by presenting the entire, conflated text without any cuts, and by stressing the military dynamics of the play. A world of war, discipline, hierarchy, violence and indifference towards suffering is discovered. The gleaming rooms of Elsinore as well as the characters' martial uniforms participate in a military aesthetic in which an excess of order rules. This context conditions the interpretation of characters and key scenes in the play. The ghost of Old Hamlet appears as a warrior in armor, an interpretation which clashes with the recent theatrical tradition. Fortinbras takes hold of Elsinore as a conquering, threatening soldier. Ophelia becomes a deserted mistress who suffers from the indifference, imprisonment and bad treatment, which are typical of a militarized nation.

Branagh's *Hamlet* does not only use epic themes, but also appropriates an epic aesthetic, based on big effects, on dilating, expanding devices. Branagh's filmic works are generally characterized by an intense energy conveyed through the actors' gestures, but also through music, editing and camera movements. This fascination for energetic movement denies any fixedness. There is no long, steady shot that simply records the Shakespearean text like in the theatre. Nevertheless, if Branagh's movies in general avoid static "staginess," they present "theatrical" effects in the sense of a big, operatic amplification of the form. Examples are numerous — the extremely long traveling shot during the *Non Nobis* song at the end of *Henry V*, the Overture in slow-motion at the start of *Much Ado About Nothing*, or the sequence which ends the first part of *Hamlet* with its backward movement and its distorted sound perspective. The character's voice is rising while his body is disappearing in the distance. In all cases, the effect is huge, relying on its impulse and momentum, on its strength and evidence.[3]

Through flashbacks, but also through slow motion and ellipsis, Branagh's movies play with the double temporality of narrative — that is with the time of the narration and of diegesis. In *Hamlet*, the time of narration and that of diegesis are both dilated. The time of narration is expanded with the insertion of flashbacks and slow-motion, which influence the narrative organization, and the speed of the events unfolding. The love story with Ophelia is developed through several flashbacks which punctuate the film with the mode of the straight cut. But when Hamlet holds Yorick's skull and starts to remember the past, the flashback is introduced with the mode of the dissolve to evoke the effort of memory. Yorick's skull regains the living flesh of the Jester (memorially embodied through the comedian, Ken Dodd): we shift to another time dimension while the object itself— the skull — remains the same.

Even before the stage of editing, it is possible to introduce a gap between the length of the diegesis and that of narration, especially through slow motion. Slow motion produces an effect of contemplation, of emotional and lyrical emphasis. In *Hamlet*, this technique of time expansion is used to emphasize violence and to create a kind of eerie, dreamlike effect, respectively in Laertes and Hamlet's duel and in the flashbacks showing the murder of Old Hamlet.

In *Hamlet*, the duration of the diegesis, like that of narration, is expanded by elliptical cuts which simulate the passing of time. In the *ellipsis*, a period of time is entirely suppressed between two different actions: the time of narration is "infinitely" shorter than diegetic time.[4] Branagh frequently creates elliptical effects in a scene meant to remain isochronic in Shakespeare's original play, meaning that the time of performance is the same as the time of the story. In Branagh's *Hamlet*, when Barnardo, Horatio and Marcellus come to warn the Prince of the apparition, the discussion begins in the palace hall, but ends up in Hamlet's private room, as if a couple of minutes had passed by. This elliptical effect occurs when Hamlet encourages his companions to further deliver a discreet, detailed report of the event.

At that point, Branagh modifies both the time of narration and the time of the story. The rhythm of narrative displays a temporal reduction, as the action which happened during that virtual time is not revealed to the audience. But the ellipsis also creates the impression of time passing by, a time which does not exist in Shakespeare's play, and thus introduces an effect of diegetic dilation.

In Branagh's cinema, the interpretation of the main characters as Christ-like heroes left to themselves, carrying the world's sufferings on their shoulders, is often conveyed through an aesthetic that favors loneliness. Characters are generally isolated in vast sets or infinite landscapes. The movies, therefore, often need to create an impression of magnitude and immensity in order to emphasize the hero's isolation among all this vastness. They insist upon expansion through the use of backward movements of the camera, specific film format, editing, and allusions to other films. Space, like time, is also dilated.

The movie *In The Bleak Midwinter*, which Branagh directed in 1995, explicitly refers to this idea of people lost in space. When Fadge, the designer of the amateur production of *Hamlet*, unveils her concept for the theatre set, she says: "You see, we must make the design all about Space. People in space, things in space, women in space, men in space."[5] In *Mary Shelley's Frankenstein*, which Branagh directed in 1994, man is lost in infinite spaces of white and grey. This vision is renewed all through the film with images of ice and snow. The characters are turned into small silhouettes, immersed in an ocean of whiteness, as when the Creature walks steadily in the mountains towards Geneva. When Victor Frankenstein leaves to meet the Creature in the Sea of Ice, Branagh starts by filming the character in close-up as he sticks his ice axe into the rocks. Then, as the music stirs, the camera progressively goes backward. At the end of the shot, Victor becomes a mere dot, lost in the gigantic glacier. For such *tableaux*, Branagh has been clearly inspired by the aesthetic of the German Romantic paintings, notably *Wanderer Above the Sea of Fog* (1818) by David Caspar Friedrich.[6]

In *Hamlet*, a similar sequence can be found. In the scene which ends the first part of the film, an extreme backward move loses Hamlet in a snowy landscape while he delivers his second Quarto-only soliloquy "How all occasions do inform against me." Hamlet, like Victor, is turned into an insignificant black dot, melting into powerful nature.

The impression of vastness is also enhanced by the film format. *Hamlet* was filmed using a 70mm photographic film format instead of the common 35. This means a negative that is four times bigger than usual, a film which is composed of a series of photogrammes as big as postcards. The extreme definition of the picture allows for shots with great depth of focus. It thus makes possible to develop a centrifugal world, and to film infinite landscapes where vast ranks of marching soldiers can be spotted in the distance. Every emotional detail on faces can also be caught in extreme close-ups, as the entire field is sometimes filled by an ear, an eye or a mouth. It is as if faces become landscapes. Intimacy itself is turned into epic.

Representing the character inside a macrocosm is not only a way to express the hero's loneliness and human vanity; it also allows Branagh to emphasize Hamlet's determination, to extend its symbolic realm and to glorify its heroic stature. In Branagh's *Hamlet*, backward movements serve to open spaces for the prince to realize he is either a "king of infinite space" or some mere "quintessence of dust." For the soliloquy of "How all occasions," Branagh borrows a movement chosen by Laurence Olivier to film the speeches of war exhortation in his 1944 adaptation of *Henry V*. Olivier thought that the camera had to be far from the character when the vocal delivery reached its peak at the end of a speech. Olivier therefore applied the backward movement not to a meditating character, but to a character haranguing his troops. By using such a camera motion, Branagh insists upon the warlike aspects of the soliloquy and on Hamlet's "bloody thoughts." In fact, various scholars and film critics have seen this sequence as an allusion to the oratorical style of King Henry V before the battle of Agincourt. According to Lawrence Toppman, "He [Branagh] shouts some of the thoughtful monologues like Henry V stirring the weary troops at Agincourt"[7]; for James Verniere, "Branagh tries to turn this 'moment' [...] into a repeat of the St. Crispin's day speech"[8]; and, according to Robert F. Willson, "we see him [Hamlet] standing as if he is leading these troops! I immediately thought of Hal's exhortation to his troops before the battle of Agincourt in Branagh's Henry V."[9] Therefore, the scene of "How all occasions" presents an intertext which introduces into the tragedy the echo of a film which depicts its hero as an enterprising warrior.

The dilation of space can also be achieved through cross-cutting, a technique which allows the audience to follow two narrative lines happening in totally different places simultaneously. In Branagh's *Hamlet*, the speech in which the eponymous hero apologizes to Laertes before the final duel is punctuated with synchronic inserts where Fortinbras' army invades the Palace of Elsinore. Thus, the film's end presents a centrifugal development of the original play. It links a private duel inside to a national crisis outside. The centrifugal experience is enhanced by frequent shots of the façade of Elsinore throughout the film. These frequent, exterior images are reminiscent of the Hollywoodian epic movies.

So are the images of the sky, which appears as early as the first sequence. Branagh illustrates Barnardo's words, "When yon same star that's westward from the pole" (1.1.36) with a shot of the sky, and those of Horatio ("But look, the morn [...]/ walks o'er the dew," 1.1.148–149) with a shot of the rising sun.

At first, these illustrations can be considered superfluous and redundant. They seem naïvely and pointlessly to reduplicate what is already signified by the text. These images, however, do not work like mere illustrations of the word "sky." They can play an important part in the global vision that is offered by the movie. They contribute to importing into the film some elements which go beyond simple denotation. In fact, they carry a series of connotations — that is a set of emotional values linked to the perception of the sky at this exact moment in the movie. For a moment, the film frees itself from the interior space of Elsinore to show the horizon and the stars. The actions of men are thus presented under a cosmic sign. They are replaced in the infinite of the universe, in order to underline their vanity. In the same way as this shot minimizes the past events in comparison with nature's greatness, the celestial images in *Hamlet* put the importance of human actions into perspective as soon as the film starts. They appear as a means to make the film "breathe," to carry the story as well as the spectator's gaze, towards some limitless exterior. In the same 1998 interview, Branagh said that he borrowed this technique from David Lean, who directed such epic movies as *The Bridge on the River Kwaï* (1957), *Lawrence of Arabia* (1962) or *Doctor Zhivago* (1965):

> It is obvious that I've been influenced by Lean. His epic movies are built around six or seven long shots of immense landscapes, but also on close-ups. Which had a direct effect on [my films of] *Hamlet* and *Henry V*. In fact, we can convince the audience that they are watching a film much bigger than it really is. You have to choose the right moment to show the grandiose shot.[10]

Therefore, the celestial shots, which at first can seem trivial, stand to introduce epic effects in the film. Literal illustration can thus contribute to root the film into a specific, cinematic genre, to link it to well-known movies which already ring in the public's collective imagination.

By using film codes which we associate with a particular genre (such as war movies, westerns, or, in this case, epic movies), Branagh creates an intertext, as each adaptation contains in itself a series of movies which belong to the same genre. Familiar effects become aesthetic as well as cultural marks of enunciation; they tend to reveal the film as a film by creating a line of films within the film thanks to a *mise en abyme* of the *mise en scène* specific to each cinematic genre.

Branagh's *Hamlet* is set within the tradition of the Hollywood epic by its cast, its length, its landscapes, its extras, and even its intermission. It is easy to establish a parallel between the scene of "My thoughts be bloody or be nothing worth" and the sequence in *Gone with the Wind* (1939) in which Scarlett O'Hara asserts her new resolution ("As God is my witness, I'll never be hungry again!").

The camera moves backward in a similar manner until it shows the character lost in an infinite space, Scarlett under the tree at Tara, Hamlet in a snowy landscape. With its shots of Fortinbras's army marching in the snowy plain, the film also recalls David Lean's epics. The charge of Fortinbras's army towards Elsinore looks like a direct quote from *Doctor Zhivago* (1965) when the cavalry advances through the plains of Russia. To make this allusion more obvious, Branagh cast Julie Christie (who played Lara) as Gertrude. By importing well-known actors such as Christie, Billy Crystal, Charlton Heston and Robin Williams, Branagh hopes to achieve a popular success for the movie, but these stars also bring with them the echo of movies which are very familiar to the spectators. According to Christian Metz, "A well-known actor will bring to his character instability, multiplicity and virtuality."[11] Again, the "stars" who are cast as cameos participate in the creation of an intertext which can reveal the film as a cinematographic product.

With the use of a specific film format, camera moves, editing and allusions to other films, the director thus dilates the time and space of diegesis, insists upon action, diminishes the feeling of doom, and turns a tragic play into a Hollywood-like epic movie. The characters are endowed with memories and thoughts thanks to images from the past and from the mind. These images, such as flashbacks, always expand the narrative. But these devices that mean to generate epic feelings can also bend towards alienation. While allusions to other movies bring about a *mise en abyme* of the diegesis, flashbacks and interpolations can be seen as films within the film. According to Anny Crunelle-Vanrigh in her 1997 article "All the world's a screen: Transcoding in Branagh's *Hamlet*," they are Branagh's cinematic equivalent of Shakespeare's dramatic inserts.[12] The same kind of *mise en abyme* can be found in the repetition of images throughout the movie. The sequence which starts the second half (after the "Intermission") is a flashback made of images already seen in the first half. Claudius' speech about the succession of "sorrows" is, in fact, visually accompanied by a kind of summary of the previous episodes. This adaptation of *Hamlet* therefore presents a powerful reflexiveness as the flow of images ends up "feeding" on itself.

Yet, when Branagh adds flashbacks or reminders in his movie, the reflexiveness born from such devices does not jeopardize diegesis, but participates in its development, helping to clarify the story line. Even the emphatic camera moves participate in the narration. Branagh's metacinematic registers are numerous, but they eventually melt into the story. Branagh's *Hamlet* thus oscillates between the creation of a realistic diegesis, following the Hollywood aesthetic which favors logical links and nostalgic reminders, and the powerful exhibition of interpolation and narrative device, which almost discloses film enunciation. This ambivalence is at the root of two kinds of reproaches which are often made against Branagh's film. Some critics accuse the director of making Shakespeare's metadrama disappear into a naturalistic universe which presents no effects of alienation. In his article "Le théâtre apprivoisé," published in *Les Cahiers du Cinéma* in 1991 on Branagh's *Henry V*, Nicolas Saada considers that "the audience, in front of this display of means, extras, sets and sound effects, can only smile at the Chorus's initial warning 'For 'tis your thoughts that now must deck our kings...,' which is very quickly put back by this spectacular show."[13] On the contrary, other critics accuse Branagh of not respecting the realism of film diegesis, of favoring big effects over plausibility and verisimilitude. For example, H.R. Coursen underlines the various inconsistencies of Branagh's *Hamlet*: "In this wintry landscape, nettles would be the only available foliage. Crow-flowers, long purples and daisies cannot be growing nearby."[14] These critics prefer a coherent diegesis, and consider as illogical the contrast between the text and the diegetic environment. Fewer scholars, however, like Jacek Fabiszak, see in this divergence an alienating shock: "One may also wonder why Branagh chose winter (which clashes with the text), but this seems to be concordant with the epic grandiosity and distancing devices employed in the film."[15] Branagh places his movie in an in-between. He favors the creation of a realistic and coherent diegesis, but on some occasions he does not hesitate to subordinate the text to a general vision: *Hamlet* as a wintry epic à la *Doctor Zhivago*. Branagh inserts the play into a specific cinematographic genre in order to offer an original and personal artistic vision, whatever the consequences may be on the filmic world. The diegesis is therefore turned into a kind of fairy tale in which anything can happen if the situation requires it. Flowers can grow in winter, Hamlet's father can rest in a snowy orchard, and Ophelia can drown herself in a frozen river. By producing a clash with the meaning of the text, the big effects of genre give rise to effects which are not necessarily alienating but surely strange and unusual. The epic feeling can co-habit with a certain kind of the epic genre.

Branagh's filmic approach keeps mixing realism and artifice. On the one hand, the film is set in a real, often exterior environment. Bleinheim Palace was thus appropriated as Elsinore. This setting gives rise to centrifugal interpolations, and is meant to bring credibility to the plots of the plays, thus winning the spectators' adherence more easily. On the other hand, the movie displays numerous visual metaphors as well as noticeable filmic effects, such as emphasized camera movements, feverish editing, slow-motion and saturated colors. Branagh shot many sequences in a studio in order to adapt the set precisely to the vision he wanted to offer, and to control the lighting and the camera effects even more. The stylistic expression can thus be intensified. In *Hamlet*, the throne room becomes a bright and vast set where the camera moves as if in a maze. Branagh therefore combines two approaches. One aims at giving the film an appearance of historical reality so that the characters' actions seem to step out of a document from the period. The other uses expressive, symbolic and artificial means to accentuate this reality. Lighting, framing, editing and music add a specific connotation which goes beyond the simple showing of characters and objects. Branagh adapts Shakespeare plays to a universe which is at the same time firmly rooted in reality, and highly stylized. As emphatic and often unbridled as it may seem, Branagh's style can bend towards artifice and disclose the film as a piece of cinematic, fictive work. But this artifice is also mainly used to intensify the impression of reality. The specificity of Branagh's cinema therefore appears in all its paradoxes. It is through processes meant to create credibility and verisimilitude that the work of art sometimes points out its nature of filmic illusion.

Nevertheless, Branagh does not introduce intertext and *mise en abyme* to produce an irony which would work against the film. While recalling our knowledge of previous films, it is meant to work in the first level, for the emotional effect it generates. Paradoxically, the *mise en abyme* is not used as an alienating device. Branagh develops an elaborated narrative tendency — very much in line with the Hollywoodian film style — which makes the story more logical and the situations more explicit. Sometimes, enunciation pierces through narration with ostentatious camera moves or reflexive images, but it finds itself swallowed by the diegesis in the end, until the plot seems — even though it can only ever be an appearance — to prevail over discourse.

NOTES

1. Anne Souriau, "Epique," in *Vocabulaire d'Esthétique*, Etienne Souriau, ed., Paris: Presses Universitaires de France, 1990, 673. Author's translation.

2. *Ibid.*

3. See Sarah Hatchuel and Pierre Berthomieu, "Kenneth Branagh ou l'art de la clarté," in *Shakespeare et le cinéma, Actes du Congrès 1998 de la Société Française Shakespeare*, Patricia Dorval and Jean-Marie Maguin, eds., Paris: ENS, 1998, 131–140.

4. Gérard Genette, *Figures III*, Paris: Seuil, 1972, 139–141.

5. Kenneth Branagh, *In The Bleak Midwinter: The Screenplay*, London: Nick Hern Books, 1995, 17.

6. Hambourg, Kunsthalie, 74.8 × 94.8 cm.

7. Lawrence Toppman, "Nothing rotten in Branagh's big, bodacious *Hamlet*," *Charlotte Observer*, 24 January 1997, 5E.

8. James Verniere, "*Hamlet*," *Boston Herald*, 24 January 1997, S10.

9. Robert F. Willson, "Kenneth Branagh's *Hamlet*, or The Revenge of Fortinbras," *The Shakespeare Newsletter* 47.1 (Spring 1997), 7.

10. Quoted by Hatchuel and Berthomieu, "Kenneth Branagh ou l'art de la clarté," 196.

11. Christian Metz, *L'énonciation impersonnelle, ou le site du film*, Paris: Klincksieck, 1991, 90. Author's translation.

12. See Anny Crunelle-Vanrigh, "All the world's a screen: Transcoding in Branagh's *Hamlet*," *Shakespeare Yearbook*, 1997, 360.

13. Nicolas Saada, "Le théâtre apprivoisé," *Les Cahiers du Cinéma*, January 1991, 66. Author's translation.

14. H.R. Coursen, "Words, words, words: Searching for *Hamlet*," *Shakespeare Yearbook*, 1997, 320.

15. Jacek Fabiszak, "Branagh's Use of Elizabethan Stage Conventions in His Production of *Hamlet*," paper given at the conference "Shakespeare on Screen" organized by the University of Malaga, Benalmadena (Spain), 21–24, September 1999.

BIBLIOGRAPHY

Branagh, Kenneth. *In the Bleak Midwinter: The Screenplay*. London: Nick Hern Books, 1995.

Coursen, H.R. "Words, words, words: Searching for Hamlet." *Shakespeare Yearbook*, 1997, 306–324.

Crunelle-Vanrigh, Anny. "All the world's a screen: Transcoding in Branagh's *Hamlet*." *Shakespeare Yearbook*, 1997, 349–369.

Fabiszak, Jacek. "Branagh's Use of Elizabethan Stage Conventions in His Production of *Hamlet*." Paper given at the conference "Shakespeare on Screen" organized by the University of Malaga, Benalmadena (Spain), 21–24, September 1999.

Genette, Gérard. *Figures III*. Paris: Seuil, 1972.

Hatchuel, Sarah, and Pierre Berthomieu. "Kenneth Branagh ou l'art de la clarté." *Shakespeare et le cinéma, Actes du Congrés 1998 de la Société Française Shakespeare*, eds. Patricia Dorval and Jean-Marie Maguin. Paris: ENS, 1998, 131–140.

Metz, Christian. *L'énonciation impersonnelle, ou le site du film*. Paris: Klincksieck, 1991.

Saada, Nicolas. "Le théâtre apprivoisé." *Les Cahiers du Cinéma*, January 1991, 65–66.

Souriau, Anne. "Epique." *Vocabulaire d'Esthétique*, Etienne Souriau, ed. Paris: Presses Universitaires de France, 1990.

Toppman, Lawrence. "Nothing rotten in Branagh's big, bodacious *Hamlet*." *Charlotte Observer*, 24 January 1997, 5E.

Verniere, James. "*Hamlet*." *Boston Herald*, 24 January 1997, S10.

Willson, Robert F. "Kenneth Branagh's *Hamlet*, or The Revenge of Fortinbras." *The Shakespeare Newsletter* 47.1 (Spring 1997), 7–8.

White Lies, *Noir* Lighting, Dark Others

Joyce Goggin

In her brilliant essay entitled "Literary Film Adaptation and the Form/
Content Dilemma," Kamilla Elliott reads various adaptations of Emily
Brontë's *Wuthering Heights* as allegorical renderings of various concepts of
film adaptation. In the process, Elliott identifies six concepts that characterize
film adaptation studies to date, namely "the psychic," "the ventriloquist," "the
genetic," "the de(re)composing," "the incarnational" and finally, "the trumping
concept." Almost anyone will immediately recognize the aptness of Brontë's
gothic novel, featuring hauntings, reincarnation and necrophilia, as an exem-
plum for Elliott's study. Moreover, that *Wuthering Heights* has been adapted
in pop songs, television productions and a number of films by everyone from
William Wyler to Kate Bush makes it an exceptionally good test case for adaptation studies. This is because the many adaptations of *Wuthering Heights* perform the various ways in which adaptation has been conceptualized as
appropriation, reconfiguration or decomposition and recomposition of the
"spirit" of the dead author, or of some more obscure quality located in the
text and its aura.[1]

In what follows I will have occasion to draw on three of Elliott's concepts
of adaptation, the first being the "psychic" concept of adaptation. In her construction of this concept, Elliott borrows Catherine Earnshaw's claim that
"whatever souls are made of, [Heathcliff's] and mine are the same," and
Heathcliff's declaration that he "cannot live without [his] soul" after her
death.[2] In other words, the idea that two entities could share the same soul
informs adaptation theories that posit an innate communication between the
dead text and the film that brings it to life on the screen. In this scenario, the
director's job is to preserve the so-called "spirit" of the literary work it adapts

and, as a consequence, "[t]he psychic concept of adaptation [ultimately] argues that to be true to the spirit of a text adaptation has to leave behind the literary corpse."[3] However, in intuiting and reproducing the spirit *Wuthering Heights*, the filmmaker must leave out much of the detail of this expansive 19th-century novel. More specifically, in the case of William Wyler's film adaptation, the stakes reside in the "spirit" that he and his viewers might have attributed to Brontë's novel in 1939, as well as in which elements of the text's supposed "spirit" that Wyler chose to bring to the screen and how.

I will also have occasion to cite Elliott's "ventriloquist concept" wherein the adaptation, "like a ventriloquist, props up the dead novel, throwing its voice onto the silent corpse."[4] This concept, of course, has its parallel in *Wuthering Heights* when Heathcliff frenziedly digs up Catherine's body and insists that she is merely sleeping, thereby projecting the fervor of his passion onto her rigid corpse. In my reading of the film then, I will endeavor to identify, however tentatively, some aspects of Wyler's voice in the film, in order to shed light on what he and his contemporaries may have projected onto *Wuthering Heights* in their own ardor for the text.

Heathcliff's impassioned necrophilia, including his desire to decompose alongside Catherine in the grave, is likewise illustrative of Elliott's de(re)composing concept of adaptation. Elliott defines this notion of "adaptation [as] a (de)composition of textual and filmic signs merging in audience consciousness together with other cultural narratives."[5] Significantly, in the ensuing process of recomposition, films are often truncated "by detaching parts of the novel and representing them as the whole in defiance of the novel's whole."[6] As she points out, however, when this process is read both ways, we often uncover uncanny details in the filmmaker's recomposition that seem to directly reference some aspect of the text as an afterthought, which in its new filmic context becomes a salient feature of the re-reading. In my paper then, I will look specifically at where Wyler truncates the novel and how he then recomposes the film to represent the desires of Hollywood in the 1930s.

In order to analyze what, in my view, is the "spirit" that Wyler decomposed from *Wuthering Heights* and recomposed for the screen, I would like to revisit Brontë's novel by focusing on an aspect of the plot that is always ignored in adaptation. The *fabula* at the centre of this complex narrative begins in 1771, when Mr. Earnshaw of Wuthering Heights returns from Liverpool with a stray child, "dark almost as if it came from the devil," that he found wandering the streets.[7] This "dirty, ragged [and] black-haired" child, later christened simply Heathcliff, speaks to his adopted family "in some gibberish that nobody could understand."[8] Clearly, he is not English and later it is surmised that he is a gipsy, "a little Lascar, or an American or Spanish castaway," and indeed in the first chapter we are told that "Mr. Heathcliff forms a singular contrast to his abode and style of living. He is a dark-skinned gipsy in aspect."[9] Moreover, given Heathcliff's own confession that he wishes he had "light hair and a fair skin" as well as the constant references to him as "black" and "dark" throughout the text, it seems reasonable to conclude that Heathcliff is ethnically inflected as "other," and set off against the white characters in the novel.[10]

The blackness of Emily Brontë's strange protagonist startled and repulsed Victorian readers so fiercely that in a preface to an edition of *Wuthering Heights* published after Emily's death, her sister Charlotte asked "[w]hether it is truly right or advisable to create beings like Heathcliff," only to conclude, "I scarcely think it is."[11] Although readers were obviously also shocked by the novel's celebration of necrophilia as romantic passion, Maja-Lisa von Sneidern argues that a good deal of what made this novel so unacceptable was Heathcliff's ethnicity, on which point Brontë was insistent.[12] To further exacerbate matters for the nineteenth century reader, we are told that Catherine shares a bed with Heathcliff throughout her childhood, which raises the uncomfortable possibility of interracial relations at a moment in history when discourses on the odiousness and danger of miscegenation were uppermost in Victorian minds.[13] Although readers were no doubt scandalized that a novelist could imagine an intimate relationship that ignored racial boundaries, von Sneidern suggests that the isolated world of the text more accurately reproduces a remote, chivalric England of the past, so that "we are predisposed to minimize Heathcliff's racial otherness," against constant admonition in the text to do otherwise.[14] In so doing, we then "ignore the possibility that [Heathcliff] is a product of the Liverpool slave trade," and with it the possibility of reading him as anything but white.[15] This said, however, von Sneidern goes on to argue that Brontë wrote enough recognizable signs of the master–slave relationship into Catherine and Heathcliff's romance to make it somewhat more understandable and acceptable to English readers in 1847, the year of its publication.[16]

The desire to minimalize Heathcliff's "racial otherness" seems to be a constant in film and television adaptations of the novel right up to the present, and directors continue to cast white actors such as Ralph Fiennes to play Heathcliff, even though a black actor in the role would hardly come as a shock to the contemporary spectator. Ironically enough, therefore, what every adaptation of *Wuthering Heights* so far has done, is to reproduce Nelly Dean's gesture in the text when she wonders if Heathcliff is "ghoul, or vampire," and sets to imagining "some fit parentage for him."[17] As narrator and servant Nelly unsuccessfully attempts to invent an ethnic heritage for "the little dark thing" that would not disrupt and contaminate the lives of the inhabitants of Wuthering Heights and the neighboring Thrushcross Grange, as the nineteenth century reader would have feared.[18] But where Nelly Dean fails, film makers have at least partially succeeded by ignoring Brontë's constant descriptions of Heathcliff's "blackness," casting white actors in the role, and then creating ethnic "effects" with lighting and make-up.

The 1939 adaptation of *Wuthering Heights* invites viewers to project "blackness" onto an otherwise white Lawrence Olivier through his constant positioning in shadowy recesses and his association with an enormous black dog, which produces ethnicity by metonymy. Likewise, Olivier is underlit through most of the film, while constantly juxtaposed against a remarkably "white" female lead.

Hence, without actually casting a black actor in the part, which in 1939 would have presented many problems, Wyler suggests Olivier's "blackness" through the use of high-contrast lighting and by setting him off against Merle Oberon whose intense "whiteness" is created with pancake makeup, elaborate white dresses and hats.

At a more textual level, Nelly Dean's admonition to Heathcliff in the novel to not be "a regular black" and to "frame high notions of [his] birth" is delivered in the film by Catherine who tells him, "Who knows but that your father was Emperor of China and your mother an Indian queen."[19] This last line is rendered both uncanny and particularly ironic in the film because it is not spoken by Nelly Dean as it is in the novel, but is instead delivered by Sarita Wooten, playing Catherine Earnshaw as a child, and later reiterated by Merle Oberon. The irony here lies in the decision to shift a line about re-inventing one's ethnic background to Oberon and, although the decision almost certainly had to do with expediency and the need to condense a number of scenes into one another in order to produce a film of reasonable length, this detail bears closer scrutiny.

Oberon's Origins

In the introduction to Higham and Moseley's bibliography of Merle Oberon, we are immediately told the one thing about the actress that remains the most obscure, namely, her heritage. Here we read that:

> this mysterious, radiant and joyous figure, exuding womanly wisdom and honesty and kindness, was ironically forced to live her life as a lie, a lie caused by the racism and snobbery of the era in which she was raised. Because no woman of "coloured" blood could become a star of the screen in those days, because the idea of suggested miscegenation was repellent to the powerful women's clubs and

religious groups that controlled the audience, she had to pretend, on studio instructions, to be white.[20]

Oberon's masquerade as a white, upper-class, English woman began when she was a teenager and moved from Bombay, where she was born, to Calcutta. Here she began frequenting a businessmen's club known as Firpo's, "the only place in Calcutta," we are told, "where young Eurasian women could meet the kind of men who could help them up the social ladder."[21] According to Oberon's biographers, it was here that "she caught all eyes as she swayed across the floor in a backless dress, her dark body powdered to create an impression of whiteness."[22] At some point in her clubbing years Oberon dated Colonel Ben Finney, a former actor in the budding film industry, who was "horrified" enough to drop her when Oberon could no longer prevent him from meeting her mother whose skin looked "very dark against her white robe."[23] Fortunately, before he left her, Finney suggested that she contact Rex Ingram, the director of Victorine Studios in Nice, who reportedly had a "fondness for the oriental and the exotic."[24] It was here that she played her first small role in Ingram's 1929 film *The Three Passions*, a story of "money, religion and love."[25]

From there Oberon moved on to England, a country to which she was "devoted as only a colonial could be, in love with visions of empire."[26] It was here that she became "fascinated by cameraman [Gregg Toland]" who "she realised was her saviour."[27] This is because Toland knew how to make Oberon look white:

> He photographed her with a special technique that involved pouring the whitest and most blazing archlights directly onto her face. The result of this treatment was to make her look almost transparently fair. [...] Toland removed any hint of her Indian skin texture.[28]

Toland was with her again on *Wuthering Heights*, a picture for which, according to Higham and Moseley, "it took all of Merle's charm to persuade Goldwyn to hire her."[29] Oberon's efforts here matched those it would take to play a white, English country girl and only Toland, whose method for "decorating [...] her face with the intense whiteness that removed the hint of dark colour, of pigment in the skin" could help her to carry it off.[30]

This brief sally into Oberon's personal history, as fascinating as her life must have been, was undertaken with the goal of explaining what I see as two major ironies. First, as I have been arguing, readers of *Wuthering Heights* tend to ignore all the clues in the text that Heathcliff was not white and probably entered Liverpool, the largest slaving port in Britain for most of the 18th century, through the slave trade. Von Sneidern argues that there are clear signals in the text to this effect, not the least of which being that Heathcliff is "given" to Cathy and Hindley Earnshaw, to their great disappointment, instead of the fiddle and whip they had requested. As she goes on to explain, these are "objects emblematic of the cruelty and indolence nurtured by institutionalized slavery" that Victorian readers recognized, as well as of the kind of fetishistic and addictive relationship that often formed between masters and slaves.[31] In other words, the novel's contemporary readers would have had to repress the notion that Cathy — who had wanted a whip instead of Heathcliff, and who consistently refers to him as her possession thereafter — could enter into a relationship based on erotic desire with someone who was her social inferior and at least symbolically her slave. As I suggested earlier, this operation of constantly reading against the grain of the text would have been undertaken in the context of rising discourses on blood, race, miscegenation and paranoid accounts of the deleterious effects of hybridity.[32]

By the time that William Wyler made his *Wuthering Heights* then, it would seem that the received reading of the text included the notion that Heathcliff was white but tenebrous and brooding.[33] This said, however, a little ethnicity went a long way in Hollywood in 1939, and Oberon's biographers tell us that Sam Goldwyn complained that Wyler had gone too far in making Olivier "filthy and intent as was proper, for a creature of the moors."[34] Of course, whether or not these biographers intended to exploit the polysemous potential of the word "moor" here is doubtful, yet once again it points to the suppression of otherness that casting Olivier involved, coupled with the return of that same suppressed otherness as metaphorical projection through lighting, costume and make-up. In other words, in the vocabulary of Kamilla Elliott, the makers of the 1939 film subscribed to the ventriloquist concept of adaptation while claiming to follow the psychic concept. That is, while propping up the dead novel, Wyler and Goldwyn threw their voice onto the text's silent corpse in order to claim that they had preserved the spirit of Brontë's great novel.[35]

The second irony lies in Merle Oberon's having been given the line about Heathcliff's father being the Emperor of China and his mother an Indian queen, a line spoken in the text by Nelly Dean. As I explained earlier, Oberon was at pains to cultivate the impression that she was a white, upper class English-woman, whereas she was actually Anglo-Indian and born in Bombay. When she came to Hollywood she was assisted in maintaining the illusion by publicists as well as technology invented especially for her by lighting and cameramen, one of whom she married.[36] In fact, the Oberon myth was so rigorously policed that biographers and documentary film maker Maree Delofski have only recently come to something like "the truth" about her origins.

Along the way these researchers followed the official Hollywood line to Tasmania, an English colony far enough away in the 1930s that no one bothered to check if she had actually been born there or not.[37] In 1978, however, the Lord Mayor of Hobart, Tasmania invited Merle Oberon to a Welcome Home ceremony for an actress whom Tasmanians had been telling the world was their own native daughter for more than forty years. Before Oberon arrived, however, someone did bother to check and found no record of her birth, the pressure of attending the ceremony and maintaining the masquerade for an audience of admirers who were now "on to her" caused the elderly actress to break down and flee the room during her acceptance speech. Merle Oberon died almost exactly a year after her staged return to a native country in which she had never before set foot. One can only speculate as to whether or not her death was related to the demise of an image she had struggled all her life to hold on to.

More interesting still is the fact that the Tasmanian government's decision to honor Oberon brought to the surface her repressed Indian origins, along with another story that had been invented that gave her Chinese origins. It turns out that the story that most Tasmanians believed is that she was the "illegitimate daughter of a poor Australian-Chinese chambermaid from the remote north-east of the island, [...] from a family called Chintock, who had been seduced by the wealthy, married Anglo hotel manager for whom she worked."[38] In light of the Chinese version of Oberon's origins, and her supposedly authentic past in the dance clubs of Calcutta, the full irony of her delivering a line about "framing high notions" of one's birth and reinventing oneself as the progeny of the "Emperor of China" and "an Indian queen" acquires full force. It is also clear that, throughout Oberon's life, everyone including herself, Hollywood and a whole population of Tasmanians propagated bizarre myths concerning her race, and this for a young woman whom Ray Milland was to describe as "the most exotically beautiful creature" he had ever seen.[39]

And herein lies the crux of the issue. As writers on the topic of postcolonialism have pointed out ever since Edward Said published his groundbreaking work *Orientalism,* the mechanisms by which the appropriation and exploitation of otherness work involve both attraction and repression. Hence, while the Orient is read as beautiful and exotic, it also has to be excoriated as base, indolent and dirty so that the attraction and fascination of the Orient can be admired from a comfortably self-satisfied, false sense of superiority. In Oberon's case, her "exotic" heritage haunted her like Cathy's ghost from beneath the layers of deception, yet this repressed otherness was also circuitously celebrated in a safe, sanitized, westernized form for consumers of popular culture. In fact, whenever Hollywood needed an exotic, eastern beauty, Oberon was trotted out, her face over-lit and whited-out for the camera and the spectator, while ethnic trappings filtered through Western fantasies of the Orient were piled on.[40] This is "otherness" tamed, rendered partially familiar and pleasurable for the appropriating gaze of the West. Indeed, Oberon's otherness was subordinated and consumed through precisely the reverse operation that made a white, English Olivier acceptably "black."

De(re)composition

To return to Elliott's concepts of adaptation with which I began, I would like now to examine the de(re)composition model in the context of Wyler's *Wuthering Heights*. For the film, screenwriters Ben Hecht and Charles MacArthur decided to terminate Brontë's text at book twelve, at the close of the first half of the novel, which also marks a shift in attention from one generation to the next. At this crucial juncture in the text, Catherine Earnshaw, who has married Edgar Linton, dies giving birth to Catherine Linton, while Heathcliff repays Catherine's rejection by marrying Isabella Linton, whom he beats and incarcerates at Wuthering Heights. Isabella leaves Heathcliff and bears him a son before her death, whom she names Linton after her brother. As Heathcliff's heir, Linton goes on to serve the function of a sign in the text and points to the scandal of inter-racial relations; hence on their first meeting Heathcliff tells him "it is something to see you have not white blood."[41] As such, writes von Sneidern, he represents "the worst accidents and mistakes mixed blood could represent for mid-century England: disease, viciousness, treason, cowardice, duplicity, unmerited power, shiftlessness."[42] Linton's inherited infirmity is frequently remarked upon by other characters in the novel, like Nelly Dean, who describes him as a "pale, delicate, effeminate boy," entirely in keeping with the received 19th-century notion that mulattoes were weak, effeminate and prone to disease.[43]

Given that miscegenation was odious and threatening, and that the hybrid progeny of such a union were thought to be invariably feeble, sickly and morally reprehensible, it stands to reason that Linton Heathcliff, a "paltry creature" of a "distorted nature," dies just after he is married to Catherine Linton. The world of the text is spared, therefore, from further transgression and order is restored to the community of the Heights and the Grange once Heathcliff and his son, the sources of contamination, are removed. But what the novel takes an entire generation to purge, the film eliminates from the outset. As George Bluestone wrote, Hecht and MacArthur "cut the book in half" and "a substantial number of scenes from the novel, primarily those devoted to the suffering and redemption of the third generation" are left out of the film.[44] This has the effect of shifting "the meaning and emphasis of the novel," so that meaning is now centered in the romance of the movie thereby, according to Bluestone, missing the "spirit" of the text.[45] While I agree with Bluestone that in omitting the second half of the novel the writers "force Emily Brontë's story into a conventional Hollywood mode," I would like to add that their ending also short-circuits the threat of miscegenation and eliminates the hybrid weakling Linton, so that the very possibility of such a union is ruled out entirely.[46] Hence, the racial purification that the novel takes another nineteen chapters and a subsequent generation to accomplish is avoided altogether in the film, with the consequence that the central condemnation of miscegenation is never once challenged as it is by the novel's ambiguous and complex ending.

In Elliott's discussion of de(re)composition and adaptation, she notes that if one reads from the film back to the novel in cases where the screenwriters have drastically truncated the text, "one often finds that many supposed infidelities appear clearly in the text. Some apparently total departures from the novel by an adaptation serve to fulfill the disappointed hopes and desires of its characters."[47] One example of this, then, is the way in which the film nips hybridity in the bud before it has the chance to flourish and to create anxiety before it is stamped out and order re-established. One further example relates again to the transfer of the line about pretending to be the son of the Emperor of China and an Indian queen" to Cathy. As Bluestone points out, a preceding scene establishes a childhood game played by Cathy and Heathcliff that does not occur in the novel. In this scene Heathcliff is the winner and Cathy, in an odd reversal of their romantic bondage, declares herself his slave. He replies that she will always be his queen, as if to suggest at this early juncture in the film that whatever reversals are to interrupt the "natural" order at the Heights, the hierarchy will be restored without consequence. In the film in fact, Heathcliff the faithful slave follows Cathy obediently to the grave in complete obeyance with the "natural" order, echoing the nineteenth century sentimental cliché of the faithful servant who would rather die than live without his master. Is this then perhaps the voice of adaptation, projected onto the text as the much truncated story makes its way, almost a century later, from the moors of Northern England to be filmed on location in the San Fernando Valley?

At the Turner Classic Movie website, *Wuthering Heights* is synopsized in one brief sentence as follows: "A married noblewoman fights her lifelong attraction to a charismatic gypsy." In this paper I have followed Elliott's essay in order to argue for yet another concept of film adaptation, one which could be similarly synopsized as a concept of desire. Such a concept would understand adaptation as the desire for, and the repression and appropriation of, the other. In proposing such a concept, I have tied the race and class struggles that occur in Brontë's novel to the truncated version of these same struggles in the 1939 film as well as to the historical context in which the film was made. At the same time, I have focused my argument through Merle Oberon's own extraordinary struggle to pass for white as a sort of "real-life" example of the mechanism at work in the "desire concept of adaptation" that I am proposing. In so doing, I have offered a reading of *Wuthering Heights* based on a concept of adaptation that seeks to discern the political and historical voices of directors, producers and spectators as desire, and at the same time seeks to explain how this desire works to channel, reshape and repress ethnicity in classical Hollywood cinema.

NOTES

1. In her essay Elliott refers specifically to *Dil Diya Dard Liya*, an Indian adaptation directed by A.R. Kardar in 1966, Bunuel's *Abismos de Pasion* of 1953, Peter Kominsky's film version of 1992, William Wyler's 1939 production with which I will be concerned here, and a Westinghouse Television Theater production directed by Paul Nickell in 1950. This is by no means, however, an exhaustive list of adaptations of *Wuthering Heights*.

2. Emily Brontë, *Wuthering Heights* (1847), Richard J. Dunn, ed., New York: W.W. Norton, 2003, 62, 130.

3. Kamilla Elliott, "Literary Film Adaptation and the Form/Content Dilemma," *Narrative across Media: The Languages of Storytelling*, Marie-Laure Ryan, ed., Lincoln: University of Nebraska Press, 2004, 220–243, 224.

4. *Ibid.*, 226.

5. *Ibid.*, 233.

6. *Ibid.*, 234.

7. Brontë, *Wuthering Heights*, 29.

8. *Ibid.*

9. *Ibid.* 40, 5.

10. *Ibid.*, 45.

11. Charlotte Brontë, "Editor's Preface to *Wuthering Heights*," in Emily Brontë, *Wuthering Heights*, 316. For example, in January 1848 *Douglas Jerrold's Weekly Newspaper* proclaimed that the book displayed "brutal cruelty, and semi-savage love" and further that "the reader is shocked, disgusted, almost sickened by details of cruelty, inhumanity, and the most diabolical hate and vengeance." *Ibid.*, 284–285.

12. Maja-Lisa von Sneidern, "*Wuthering Heights* and the Liverpool Slave Trade," http://muse.jhu.edu/journals/elh/v062/62.1sneidern.html.

13. Emily Brontë, *Wuthering Heights*, 98. The word miscegenation was coined in 1864 and was intimately connected with fears of racial intermarriage and the threat of such unions producing hybrid offspring who, it was predicted, would be infirm, insipid and impotent. Hence, by the mid 19th century, a "disruption of domestic culture, and [an] increasing anxiety about racial difference and racial amalgamation [...] was apparent and an effect of colonialism and enforced migration. Both of these consequences were regarded

as negative, and a good deal of energy was expended on formulating ways in which to counter those elements that were clearly undermining the cultural stability of a more traditional, apparently organic, now irretrievably lost, society." Cf. Robert Young, particularly chapter one, "Hybridity and Diaspora," 1–91. Robert Young, *Colonial Desire: Hybridity in Theory, Culture and Race,* London: Routledge, 1995, 4.

14. von Sneidern, "*Wuthering Heights* and the Liverpool Slave Trade," 3.

15. *Ibid.* On Liverpool as a slave trading capital she writes: "At mid-century Liverpool ranked third behind London and Bristol, but by the inter-bellum period (1763–1776) she had eclipsed her competitors and was the premier slaving port in Britain" (1).

16. She cites Joan Dayan's "Race and Romance" where the author argues that the relationship of master to slave is represented in American romance and elsewhere as a kind of "twisted sentimentality," and an addictive, masochistic, obsessive love deriving from ownership and enslavement (*Ibid.*, 90). Anyone familiar with *Wuthering Heights* will readily agree that this is a fitting description of the romance central to the text.

17. Brontë, *Wuthering Heights,* 252.

18. *Ibid.*

19. *Ibid.*, 45.

20. Charles Higham and Roy Moseley, *Merle: A Biography of Merle Oberon,* London: New English Library, 1983, ix.

21. *Ibid.*, 13.

22. *Ibid.*

23. *Ibid.*

24. *Ibid.*, 16. According to the biography, Ingram "was surrounded by an entourage of African traders in turbans, giants, midgets, dwarves and Moslem [sic] women in veils," the implication of course being that Oberon fit right in.

25. *Ibid.*

26. *Ibid.*, 73. According to her biographers, London was a big step towards gentility and acceptability. Here, for example, she also began "sleeping with Hutch" a black pianist who was famous for singing Cole Porter songs and being a "legendary stud" to society women" (*Ibid.*, 21). They go on to explain that in bedding Hutch "she gigantically elevated her career" and became "a cousin to lady aristocrats — at least in one sense" (*Ibid.*). This remarkable passage clearly illustrates the twisted path from repression to desire through which Oberon's ethnicity was filtered as she negotiated a career in the movies.

27. *Ibid.*, 48.

28. *Ibid.*

29. *Ibid,* 69. Oberon's biographers make it quite clear what using all of one's charms meant in the early days of Hollywood. At a dinner party thrown by Myron Selznick, Oberon told him that he wasn't listening to what she was saying. His reply was "Merle, I'm so hard thinking about going to bed with you that I can't concentrate." Her legendary and immediate reply was "Well then, let's go upstairs so you can get it off your mind" (*Ibid.*, 53).

30. *Ibid.*

31. Maja-Lisa von Sneidern, "*Wuthering Heights* and the Liverpool Slave Trade," 2. On this point see also Joan Dayan's "Romance and Race," in *The Columbia History of the American Novel,* Emory Elliott, ed., New York: Columbia University Press, 1991, 89–109. See also note 12 above.

32. Cf. Michel Foucault's *The Will to Knowledge: The History of Sexuality Volume I,* particularly part one, "We 'Other Victorians'" and part five, "Right of Death and Power Over Life." See also Roxann Wheeler, particularly pp. 11–18. Michel Foucault, *The Will to Knowledge: The History of Sexuality Volume I* (1978), Robert Hurley, trans., New York: Vintage, 1990; Roxann Wheeler, "'My Savage,' 'My Man': Racial Multiplicity in *Robinson Crusoe,*" http://muse.jhu.edu/journals/elh/v062/62.4wheeler.html.

33. On his website, Nigam Nuggehalli claims, for example, that Olivier "looks the part in the movie: dark, brooding, and imposing." See http://www.culturevulture.net/Movies5/ WutheringHeights.htm. In other words, this is the kind of Heathcliff that viewers expected to see given the traditional reading of the text.

34. Higham and Moseley, *Merle*, 69.

35. When the film was released, Frank Nugent of the *New York Times* wrote that "Mr. Goldwyn and his troupe have fashioned a strong and somber film, poetically written as the novel not always was, *sinister and wild as it was meant to be, far more compact dramatically than Miss Brontë had made it.* And it has been brilliantly played. Laurence Olivier's Heathcliff is the man. He has Heathcliff's *broad lowering brow, his scowl, the churlishness, the wild tenderness*, the bearing, speech and manner of the demon-possessed" (my italics). http:// www.murphsplace.com/olivier/wh.html. Interestingly, von Sneidern points out Thomas Jefferson and his contemporaries believed that such "wild tenderness" was an essential characteristic of the negro slave (14).

36. Oberon's cameraman and second husband Lucien Ballard, whom her biographers stress was part Cherokee Indian, invented a special light for her that came to be known as the "Obie," and which "whitened the features even more completely than Gregg Toland's lighting had done in the 1930s" (113). Revealingly enough, Higham and Moseley insist that the "romance between Merle and Lucien was electric" and give as the first source of this electricity the "fact" that "both were of mixed blood, passionate, [and] longing for fulfillment" (*Ibid.*).

37. According to Delofski, "Tasmania in the 1930s was a conservative kind of place, resolutely British (read 'white'), and so isolated it was sometimes dropped off the map entirely. A perfect place to bury Merle's inconvenient Anglo-Indian identity. Because it was also so far from the U.S.A. and Europe the likelihood of the deception being discovered was minimal — after all it could take over six weeks for a letter to travel to Australia from the northern hemisphere in the 1930s." Maree Delofski, "Archival Footage and Storytelling in *The Trouble with Merle*," http://muse.jhu.edu/journals/the_moving_image/v006/6. 1delofski.html, 2004, 7.

38. *Ibid.*, 8. According to Higham and Moseley, "Merle was [in this story] the scion of a mining clan named the Chintocks, who were quarter-caste Chinese" (x). It is worth noting that in some countries "Chintock" is used as a racist slur and in my correspondence with Delofski, she has suggested that the name is perhaps "a corruption of a Chinese name" (email May 30, 2006). Whatever the case may be, the Tasmanian version, as Delofski has pointed out, "in a great irony, landed Merle right back in the place the studio had tried to avoid" (*The Trouble with Merle*, 3).

39. Higham and Moseley, *Merle*, 19.

40. Commenting on this same phenomenon, Delofski writes that images of Merle Oberon were "a mix of studio glamour stills and moving images" that celebrate "the range of personae the star embodied" while indicating that the distinction between her mythical ethnicity and the actress herself turn out not to be rigid. Frequent slippage occurred throughout her career as in *Over the Moon* wherein Oberon reads "his eyes smoldered with all the passion of the Orient, flicker[ing] with unsated desire" on the topic of the "Oriental set" of a fellow character's eyes.

41. Brontë, *Wuthering Heights*, 161.

42. von Sneidern, "*Wuthering Heights* and the Liverpool Slave Trade," 8.

43. Brontë, *Wuthering Heights*, 155.

44. George Bluestone, *Novels into Film: The Metamorphosis of Fiction into Cinema*, Berkeley: University of California Press, 1957, 92.

45. *Ibid.*

46. Here again it is possible to draw an uncanny parallel with Oberon's own life. While still in her 20s, Oberon "had her Fallopian tubes tied as a contraceptive measure," and

reportedly told friends that "she was afraid that if she married a title that her husband would not want to have a black child." Higham and Moseley, *Merle*, 30.

    47. Elliott, "Literary Film Adaptation and the Form/Content Dilemma," 234.

BIBLIOGRAPHY

Bluestone, George. *Novels into Film: The Metamorphosis of Fiction into Cinema.* Berkeley: University of California Press, 1957.

Brontë, Charlotte. "Editor's Preface to *Wuthering Heights.*" *Wuthering Heights*, Richard J. Dunn, ed. New York: W.W. Norton, 2003.

Brontë, Emily. *Wuthering Heights* (1847). Richard J. Dunn, ed. New York: W.W. Norton, 2003.

Dayan, Joan. "Romance and Race." *The Columbia History of the American Novel*, Emory Elliott, ed. New York: Columbia University Press, 1991, 89–109.

Delofski, Maree. "Archival Footage and Storytelling in *The Trouble with Merle.*" http://muse.jhu.edu/journals/the_moving_image/v006/6.1delofski.html, 2004.

_____. *The Trouble with Merle.* Australia, 2002.

_____. "TV Documentaries: *The Trouble With Merle.*" www.abc.net.au/tv/documentaries/stories/s657300.htm.

Elliott, Kamilla. "Literary Film Adaptation and the Form/Content Dilemma." *Narrative across Media: The Languages of Storytelling.* Marie-Laure Ryan, ed. Lincoln: University of Nebraska Press, 2004, 220–243.

Foucault, Michel. *The Will to Knowledge: The History of Sexuality Volume 1* (1978). Robert Hurley, trans. New York: Vintage, 1990.

Higham, Charles, and Roy Moseley. *Merle: A Biography of Merle Oberon.* London: New English Library, 1983.

Nuggehalli, Nigam. http://www.culturevulture.net/Movies5/WutheringHeights.htm.

Murphy, M. "Wuthering Heights (1939)." http://www.culturevulture.net/Movies5/WutheringHeights.htm.

Said, Edward. *Orientalism.* New York: Random House, 1979.

von Sneidern, Maja-Lisa. "*Wuthering Heights* and the Liverpool Slave Trade." http://muse.jhu.edu/journals/elh/v062/62.1sneidern.html. See also *ELH* 62 (1995): 171–196.

Wheeler, Roxann. "'My Savage,' 'My Man': Racial Multiplicity in *Robinson Crusoe.*" http://muse.jhu.edu/journals/elh/v062/62.4wheeler.html. See also *ELH* 62.4 (1995): 821–861.

Wuthering Heights. William Wyler, dir., Charles MacArthur, Ben Hecht, John Huston, scrs. MGM, 1939.

Wuthering Heights. Peter Kosminsky, dir., Anne Devlin, scr. Paramount, 1992.

"Wuthering Heights." Turner Classic Movies. http://tcmdb.com/title/title.jsp?stid=96324.

Young, Robert. *Colonial Desire: Hybridity in Theory, Culture and Race.* London: Routledge, 1995.

Making Red Black: Race and *The Shawshank Redemption*

Donald Ulin

The Shawshank Redemption (1994), written and directed by Frank Darabont, is one of those films that are regularly described as "better than the book," at least by those who have read or even heard of Stephen King's original "Rita Hayworth and the Shawshank Redemption," one of four novellas in a little-known collection, *Different Seasons*. One explanation given for the film's greater success is that Darabont "took a somewhat improbable, loosely structured [...] novella [...] and turned it into a work of art.[1]" Another is the superb camera work. Mark Kermode points to the "quasi-religious environment" and spiritual symbolism through which the medium of film itself assumes powerful redemptive qualities.[2] Without discounting these factors, I want to suggest here that, in adapting King's novella, Darabont turned the story he had inherited into a retelling of a much earlier work, namely Mark Twain's *Adventures of Huckleberry Finn*.

I don't mean that Darabont set out to retell Twain's story: he didn't need to, any more than the writers of *Edward Scissorhands* or *Bladerunner* set out to retell *Frankenstein*. Nevertheless, what he has done is to alter some of the details of King's story so as to situate that story within a mythic tradition originating in the story of Huck and Jim on the Mississippi. "The purpose of myth," Lévi-Strauss argues, "is to provide a logical model capable of overcoming a contradiction (an impossible achievement if, as it happens, the contradiction is real)." In such cases, "a theoretically infinite number of [iterations of the myth] will be generated, each one slightly different from the others."[3] *Huckleberry Finn* has been retold in many forms and for many purposes by literary critics, teachers, filmmakers, translators, and others — more times than any other work of American literature.

The "Hyper-Canonicity" of Huckleberry Finn

For a variety of reasons too complicated to get into here, *Huckleberry Finn* has achieved the status of what Jonathan Arac calls "hyper-canonicity" as the ultimate emblem, or fetish (if you prefer), of American literature and national identity. Hemingway once wrote that "all modern American literature comes from one book by Mark Twain called *Huckleberry Finn.*"[4] The English scholar V.S. Pritchett declared that Mark Twain "has become the channel of the generic emotion which floods all really American literature."[5] Lionel Trilling called the book's style "not less than definitive in American literature."[6] Shelley Fisher Fishkin founds her work on the notion of "Huck as the representative American, and his book as the exemplary great American book."[7] What makes the controversies over *Huckleberry Finn* so much more bitter and painful than similar controversies over other books is its "identification not just with a nation, but with the *goodness* of the nation."[8] It raises spectral figures of our deepest national problems, and it tries, unsuccessfully, to bring those problems to some sort of satisfactory resolution. As Leo Marx has written, Twain "had taken hold of a situation in which a partial defeat was inevitable, but he was unable to — or unaware of the need to — give imaginative substance to the fact."[9] Where defeat is inevitable but unacceptable, we find ourselves caught in a perpetual retelling of the story, hoping each time to "get it right," to "fix" those problems that leave us uncomfortable.

At its deepest and most general level, the contradiction troubling *Huckleberry Finn* involves the profoundly American conflict between the ideals of romantic individualism and the moral imperatives rooted in Puritanism. Numerous critics have, quite reasonably I would say, read *Huckleberry Finn* as a powerfully moral and ethical work.[10] And yet its conclusion, with Huck "lighting out for the territory" because he can't stand to be civilized, rejects the ethics of civic responsibility in favor of the romantic and equally American myth of radical individualism. The contradiction is real and thus, as Lévi-Strauss argues, destined to perpetual reiteration.

More specifically, within the Huck Finn myth (and all its reiterations), this conflict between commitment and individualism becomes the medium through which the great American problem of race is explored, refracted, and ultimately mystified. Lionel Trilling, one of the great advocates for a moral reading of *Huckleberry Finn*, writes that "no one who reads thoughtfully the dialectic of Huck's great moral crisis will ever again be wholly able to accept without some questions and some irony the assumptions of the respectable morality by which he lives."[11] Trilling is referring, of course, to Huck's famous decision to go to Hell rather than take what he has been taught is the ethically correct course of turning Jim over to the authorities. Twain himself associated Huck's crisis with that classically Romantic antithesis between the individual and society when he described the novel as one "in which a sound heart & a deformed conscience come into collision, and conscience suffers defeat" (1895 lecture). Certainly, however, the novel has succeeded less by forcing generations of readers to question the morality by which they live than by allowing them to feel good about the soundness their own hearts. Twain's contemporary northern reader would have found far more occasion for self-congratulation than self-critique: he was not one of those Sheperdsons or Grangerfords after all, or even a sanctimonious Aunt Polly; he was a northern liberal, made confident in his principles by the recent defeat of the South. In fact the real, social issue of race is mystified altogether insofar as Huck's decision becomes "a miracle of the human heart,"[12] utterly unconnected to the very active public discourse on slavery and racism that was going on even in the southern states.

With the rise of the civil rights movement in the twentieth century, while some authorities denounced the novel as "racist trash,"[13] others elevated its moral mission to new heights, calling it "a weapon in the battle against racism that we can't afford to take out of our classrooms."[14] The polarity and vehemence of the debate are a consequence of what Arac describes as our idolatrous relationship to this novel: "Liberal white American opinion identifies with the wonderful boy Huck. Even though his society was racist, he was not, and so 'we' are not. [...] to challenge this view, is to challenge 'us,' just where 'we' feel ourselves most intimately virtuous, and it is also to challenge Mark Twain, and thereby the America he quintessentially represents."[15]

I don't want to argue that the novel itself is or is not racist — I am more interested in the politics and history of its reception. But to recognize and understand the forces of desire at work in that reception, we have to recognize the formal and ideological problems in the novel that might resist the sort of idolization I have been describing. Insofar as it is, on some level, a novel about Jim's run for freedom, it makes no sense for Huck and Jim to float down the Mississippi into the deep South. Once Huck and Jim get lost in the fog and miss the confluence with the Missouri River, which was to take them North to freedom, Twain was so lost for where to go next that he put the novel away for three years before coming back to finish it. When he returned to the novel, his writing took on a darker tone with bloody feuds, murders, tarring and feathering, and more. By the end, the worst has happened, and Jim has been captured, and yet the novel offers us a seemingly happy ending, saved by a return to romance. Tom Sawyer returns to the action and, instead of giving up his secret that Jim has actually been freed by Miss Watson on her deathbed, he draws both Jim and Huck into an absurdly orchestrated escape along the lines of his favorite boyhood romances, making a mockery, not just of Jim himself but of every slave's longing for freedom and of every African American's desire to be treated with common decency.

T.S. Eliot argued that "it is right that the mood of the end of the book should bring us back to that of the beginning. Or, if this was not the right ending for the book, what ending would have been right?"[16] Most critics, however, even many of the most favorable, have been troubled both by the cruel frivolity of the boys' charades and the farcical *Deus ex machina* liberation of Jim, seeing such a conclusion as an affront to the novel's artistic integrity, to Jim's humanity, or both.

Indeed, Twain's inability to resolve the book's formal problems on their own terms is consistent with America's inability to resolve its racial problems. David Smith, a great defender of the novel, argues that its value as social critique lies precisely in its own aesthetic problems, that in *trying* to bring a satisfactory resolution to a narrative enmeshed in the discourse of racism, Twain *must* fail because America was not and is still not ready for an honest confrontation with its own racism. In founding its hope for redemption on the myth of the romantic individual, Twain effectively shuts out the public discourse that surrounded the issue of slavery and thus unwittingly exposes the complicity of the liberal tradition in the continuation of racism. "If we, a century later, continue to be confused about *Adventures of Huckleberry Finn*, perhaps it is because we remain more deeply committed to both racial discourse and a self-deluding optimism than we care to admit."[17]

Huckleberry Finn *on Screen*

Huckleberry Finn's original illustrations by Edward W. Kemble depicted Jim as a buffoon, calling attention to his superstitiousness, foolishness, and servility. The first film version in 1920 reproduces those stereotypes and was even based visually on Kemble's illustrations.[18] What these images illustrate is that for at least 35 years after the novel's publication, readers were apparently able to pride themselves on their recognition of Huck's sound heart without pausing to consider the damaging stereotypes applied to his friend Jim: indeed, believing complacently in the soundness of their own hearts, these audiences may have been *more* comfortable laughing at Jim's antics even as he is re-enslaved for the sake of Tom Sawyer's romantic games. One significant innovation in this 1920 adaptation suggests an effort, at least, to deal with the contradictions between individualism and commitment: instead of "lighting out for the territory," as he does in the novel, this Huck returns to "sivilization" and the widow Douglas.

In MGM's 1939 production, Mickey Rooney's Huck "metamorphoses into an abolitionist who convinces the Widow Douglas to free Jim,"[19] tempering the romantic individualism of Twain's ending with at least a gesture toward social realism. In 1960, with the growth of a civil rights movement, MGM made a second attempt at *Huckleberry Finn*, giving us a stronger, less farcical Jim. This time boxing champion Archie Moore takes the role, playing up Jim's "warmth, humanity, and courage."[20] Taking a very different approach to the problem of race, at least two versions opted to reduce or eliminate Jim's role altogether. More recent adaptations have either shifted the focus to Huck's boyhood adventures or gone out of their way to demonstrate Jim's strength of character against the tendencies of the original novel. We have, or so we like to tell ourselves, moved courageously beyond the racism of our past, and *Huckleberry Finn* has somehow been there all along to help us prove it.

Shawshank Redemption *and* The Adventures of Huckleberry Finn

According to at least one critic, *Huckleberry Finn* has never met with a truly successful film adaptation.[21] And yet I would argue that, with his *very* successful adaptation of Stephen King's novella, Frank Darabont has done more than any literal film adaptation toward redeeming that troubled icon of American cultural identity. We have here the story of a young white man and an older black man, two outcasts thrown together by a hostile society mired in violence, greed, and corruption. As hard as prison conditions are, the security and stability of this community make a kind of raft on which they sail, relatively unscathed, through an ignorant, vicious world. Darabont emphasizes that sense of community with regular shots of the inmates socializing in the yard or laughing over a meal. The violent exceptions, the so-called "sisters," operate outside of that community: they are tolerated as an inevitable part of prison life, but we don't see them participating in any of the camaraderie with the others. Anyway, like Twain's Duke and Dauphin, they, too, get their comeuppance.

There is also, of course, the brutality and corruption of the guards, but Darabont emphasizes their affiliation to the outside world through illegal contracts, political ambitions, and money laundering. We learn, as does Huck, that "human beings *can* be awful cruel to one another,"[22] but the men there seem to understand Huck's simple statement that "what you want, above all things, on a raft, is for everybody to be satisfied, and feel right and kind towards the others."[23] In the end, Andy follows Huck's footsteps by refusing the cynical pretenses at civilization offered, not only by the prison, but by the society around it, choosing instead to "light out for the territory" of Zihuatanejo. Thus the closing shot features the two friends together, not on a raft on the Mississippi, perhaps, but working on a boat in the Pacific Ocean.

Andy Dufresne, as played by Tim Robbins, is certainly more than a boy, but he is a young man and young-looking, especially next to the older, paternal character of Red as played by Morgan Freeman. Nor—surprisingly— does Andy age very much during nearly thirty years of prison life. Like Huck and Jim on the raft, they seem to live outside of history in a kind of time warp, isolated not only from the goings-on of the outside world, but from the effects of time itself. And I will say more about this later.

To call *The Shawshank Redemption* an adaptation of *Huckleberry Finn* would be stretching the definition of "adaptation." King's novella makes clear through various biographical details that "Red" is a white man of Irish descent. Although those details are absent from the screenplay, it was nevertheless written with such a character in mind. When Morgan Freeman was suggested for the part, Darabont "was first startled, then immediately converted."[24] Regardless of Darabont's original intentions in writing the script, that casting decision makes possible an experience of the film as a reiteration, if not literally an adaptation, of America's most famous multi-racial buddy story.

In accepting that role, *The Shawshank Redemption* must, of course, offer its audience a more satisfactory account of race relations than what is left us in Twain's novel. To begin with, Red has all of Jim's noble qualities—the dependability, the loyalty, the moral clarity—without the foolish stereotypes. In the end, *he also* gets to light out for the territory to meet up with his younger friend. Far less innocent than Huck, Andy's native goodness is nevertheless assured: "On the outside," he tells us, "I was an honest man. Straight as an arrow. I had to come to prison to be a crook." Like Huck's coarseness and racist language, Andy's money laundering schemes and tax dodges for the guards are the impositions of a corrupt world on a basically sound heart. While Andy displays all of the craftiness of Huck in dealing with complicated people and situations, his maturity makes him a more productive character, one who builds a library, talks the prison guards into buying beer for the prisoners, and commandeers the warden's office to entertain the rest of the inmates with Mozart. He is also an *easier* character insofar as there is none of the irony that would require an audience to understand him better than he understands himself, to distinguish between that "deformed conscience" and "moral heart."

Tom Sawyer with his brutal disregard for reality is gone (unless somehow the selfishly manipulative "sisters" can be made to fit that bill). Whereas Twain's novel is emphatically Huck's story from beginning to end, King's story is told from Red's perspective. Darabont revised King's novella to focus more on Andy, but he retained Red's perspective with a heavy use of voiceover. Perhaps this time it is Jim's story and, most important, it's one we can all be proud of. Darabont may not have had Twain's novel in mind, but the film's narrative aims at precisely the sort of closure that readers have been trying for years to find there. As Darabont told one interviewer, "Everybody gets redeemed in the movie to some degree or another. One of the cool things about life — or drama, if not life — is that a forceful and righteous individual can really effect a lot of change."[25]

Whereas King's novella is primarily about hope, "the theme of the screenplay really seems to be about the triumph of good over evil."[26] The novella ends with Red's hopes for a reunion with Andy, but he is still sitting in his room at the Brewster hotel. "For Darabont, hope is not enough for closure. We need triumph. Which is why he adds one more scene, in Mexico, where the good guys reunite in the promised land outside Shawshank."[27] In fact, Darabont's first screenplay concluded, like the novella, with Red on the bus headed uncertainly toward Mexico. It was only at the suggestion of Liz Glotzer from Castle Rock and after the rest of the film had been shot that he wrote in the unification of Red and Andy on the beach. Even then, it was only after an enthusiastic audience response at a test screening that he was convinced of its value in "providing emotional catharsis" and "even more than that, [...] a tremendous sense of closure. By ending with that final image, we've brought the viewer on a full journey that begins in tight claustrophobia defined by walls and concludes where the horizon is limitless; the movie has traveled fully from darkness to light, from coldness to warmth, from colorlessness to a place where only color exists, from physical and spiritual imprisonment to total freedom."[28] Ninety percent of the test audience identified this concluding scene as their favorite; the scene of the convicts drinking beer on the rooftop, another triumphant scene unmarred by any negative repercussions, was the other favorite.[29]

The reason for the popularity of that ending is no doubt that it gives us permission to believe again for just an instant in that myth of "total freedom" and "limitless horizons" — that purely negative freedom associated with the severance of all social ties and obligations. To work, it has to be a brief scene because such illusions are terribly difficult to sustain. Ironically, the old boat that Andy is working on is beached at mid-tide, suggesting (though surely Darabont did not intend this suggestion) that in only a few hours the beginnings of their new freedom will be undone by powerful forces still operating beyond their control. In fact the screenplay conclusion (the part written in response to Castle Rock's request) includes two lines of dialogue omitted in the editing room. Echoing their earlier conversation, Andy (until that moment unrecognizable in a mask and goggles) looks up from his work, pulls off his mask and goggles and comments, "You look like a man who knows how to get things," to which Red replies, "I'm known to locate certain things from time to time."[30] Instead of providing the ironic juxtaposition between the limitations of prison life and the "total freedom" of their new one, where things could be gotten with relatively little difficulty, Darabont felt that these lines "trampled the clarity and emotion of the moment" and "had a cloying 'golly-gee-ain't-we-cute' quality."[31] I would suggest, however, that the greater problem with these lines is the extent to which they would have established the subordination of Red as Andy's hired handyman, dispelling the illusion of "limitless horizons" and "total freedom."

The conclusion to *Huckleberry Finn* combines an implicit declaration of triumph with an inability to deliver. Leo Marx argues that a less certain ending in which Jim's quest for freedom was "unsuccessful but not abandoned [...] would have been [more] consonant with the symbols, the characters, and the theme as Clemens had created them — and with history."[32] King leaves us with hope but also with that uncertainty, knowing the psychological and physical obstacles that stand between Red and Zihuatanejo. The film's ending offers the triumph of *Huckleberry Finn* without such compromises as the absurd cruelty of the Phelps farm chapters or the return of Jim into something not much better than slavery — having to work for a black man's wages to pay a white man's price to purchase the freedom of his own wife and children (a sum that would have amounted to anywhere upward of $2,500 depending on the size, age, and health of his family).[33]

Even this seemingly more ideologically up-to-date account of the Huck-Jim dyad reproduces in its own way those "racialized binaries of white/black and superior/inferior"[34] that have informed racial discourse at least as far back as *Huckleberry Finn*. Red is more the agent of his own success than Jim, but far less so than Andy, who "decides the location [where they are to meet], has the knowledge about how to escape from prison, and provides the money for the escape, while Red acts as his assistant."[35] Andy's power derives not just from his financial resources smuggled into the prison but from the cultural capital he exhibits in running the library or enthralling the rest of the inmates with *The Marriage of Figaro* broadcast over the prison's PA system. Andy impresses his would-be-rapist with a scientific-sounding theory about the effects of brain damage on the human facial muscles; he identifies the field where Red is to find the money as being "like something out of a Robert Frost poem." Andy's use of the posters to cover the tunnel he is digging in his cell wall demonstrates his ability to manipulate the materials, not only of high culture, for his own ends, but of the popular prison culture as well.

In contrast to King's story, which is really about Red, Darabont "takes Andy's story as the dramatic backbone, [...] simply using Red to tell the story."[36] Red is necessary to Andy, both as "a man who knows how to get things" and as the narrator of his story, but the relationship is instrumental and entirely asymmetrical: for a reasonable price, Red gets Andy a rock hammer and a picture of Rita Hayworth; Andy is Red's redeemer, who gives him his reason to go on living. Kermode goes so far as to identify Andy as a Christ-figure, "only partly of this earth, a displaced angel traipsing through the dirt of the world, untarnished by its imperfections."[37] For Kermode, the turning point of the film on top of the license-plate factory roof, where Andy delivers cold beers to the other twelve inmates, constitutes a sort of last supper, its significance accentuated when Captain Hadley holds Andy threateningly over the edge of the roof "in a deliberately Christ-like pose."[38]

But let me anticipate one objection to the case I have been making, namely that this film really is not about race at all, but rather about hope and the triumph of the human spirit over adversity. It certainly is very much about those things. In fact, the screenplay makes no reference to race in casting any of the characters, nor is race ever explicitly an issue in the novella or the film. Why should we look beyond Freeman's tremendous talent as an actor and especially his reputation for voiceover narration, which is such a big part of this screenplay? Since Darabont made no changes to the script when Freeman was cast for a part originally written only incidentally with a white Irishman in mind, one might argue that neither ethnicity nor skin color is relevant and that any connection to *Huckleberry Finn*, which takes racial difference and prejudice as its central problem, is utterly fanciful.

But Americans are not color-blind, however much some of us like to imagine it: in the semiotics of American culture, *race signifies*, however little consensus there may be on precisely *what* it signifies. Though Darabont did not intend a retelling of *Huckleberry Finn* when he wrote the screenplay, the casting of a black man in place of the white man in King's story raised various new possibilities for audience response, including an association with American literature's most famous friendship between an older black man and a younger white man.

In fact, what may be most significant is the extent to which the film *obscures* race and thereby mystifies it as an element of identity or a factor in social, political, or interpersonal relations (just as one cold-war-era television version of *Huckleberry Finn* dealt with the problem by omitting Jim altogether along with any reference to race or slavery). Perhaps to avoid reminding the audience of even the idea of racial conflict (and perhaps to avoid the sort of criticism leveled at *Huckleberry Finn*), Darabont has even omitted King's two figurative uses of the word "nigger." Sean O'Sullivan has suggested that the film might be unfairly criticized for "giving an appearance of racial equality which it in fact does not live up to," with its "predominantly white main cast and only a weakly multi-racial *mise en scène.*" Yet against that potential charge, O'Sullivan argues that Darabont's casting choice reflects a rejection of the excessively violent depictions of inmates in earlier action-adventure films featuring "racially divided prisons controlled by warring factions of 'hard-core gang members.'" Instead, O'Sullivan suggests, Darabont should be praised for trying "to circulate an alternative representation of prisoners as being worthy and capable of rehabilitation," even if that means restricting the representation of minority inmates to one exceptional individual.[39]

O'Sullivan's logic and motives are suspect insofar as he imagines the erasure of minority inmates as a step forward in prison reform, but his information is wrong as well. In fact, the percentage of African American prisoners in Shawshank is significantly greater than it was for Maine's actual inmate population during the period in which the story is set. In one shot from the *Marriage of Figaro* sequence, I count roughly 140 inmates in the yard, of whom perhaps eight (six percent) are black. Earlier shots in the same sequence, in the infirmary and woodshop, show at least three more black inmates and perhaps a dozen white, bringing the percentage even higher. By 1985 (the earliest year for which I have found data), the percentage of African American inmates in the Maine prison system stood at 1.2 percent, rising to 3.6 percent in 1997 and 6.2 percent by January 1, 2006.[40] It seems likely, then, that in 1955, when that sequence is supposed to have taken place, the percentage of African American inmates would have been close to zero. The point of these statistics is to suggest the tension between a realistic representation of a Maine state prison population and a racial balance adequate for the film's thematic requirements. Red's credibility as a narrator and focal point of the prison community required at least a few other African Americans and so the inmates were cast accordingly. That casting of extras was *not* color blind may be inferred from the much higher actual percentage of blacks and African Americans in Mansfield Ohio, where the prison scenes were shot (19.6% according to the 2000 census).

Taking Maine as its *mise en scène* (the film was actually shot in Ohio) the film provided a space in which audiences from across America could experience an idealized vision of race relations as embodied in the multi-racial friendship of two exceptional individuals. America's systemic racial inequities, from racial profiling to preferential sentencing to widely disparate socio-economic conditions cease to exist in the aura of Red and Andy's friendship. Within the walls of Shawshank, prisoners and audiences alike are isolated from the civil rights movement and the political changes that were transforming American society during precisely the years of Andy's incarceration. As Nero points out, the inmates are removed "from participation and debate in this second American revolution. Once outside of prison, they are excused from the aftermath of the movement by being relocated to a so-called place 'with no memory.'"[41] As in *Huckleberry Finn*, social movements and solutions are excluded: problems are soluble on the interpersonal level or not at all. The choice is only between the raft and "the territory," between prison and Zihuatanejo.

Marketing for King's *Different Seasons* includes a remark from a *Los Angeles Times* review that "to find the secret of his success, you have to compare King to Twain. [...] King taps the roots of myth buried in all our minds."[42] What Darabont has done is to flesh out the comparison and, in so doing, to resituate King's story within the mythic structures of the American mind. In so doing, the redemption the film aims at is nothing less than the redemption of American culture from that history even if, simultaneously and paradoxically, it makes that history more palatable by continuing the long tradition of mystification going back at least to Mark Twain's miraculously happy ending to his most famous and controversial novel.

NOTES

1. Barry Hampe, "Shawshank: Rambling Narrative to Dramatic Structure," *Creative Screenwriting* 4:2 (1997), 17–25, 17.

2. Mark Kermode, *The Shawshank Redemption*, London: British Film Institute, 2003, 14ff.

3. Claude Lévi-Strauss, *Structural Anthropology* (1955), Claire Jacobson, Brooke Grundfest Schoepf, trans., New York: Basic Books, 1963, 229.

4. Jonathan Arac, *Huckleberry Finn as Idol and Target: The Functions of Criticism in Our Time*, Madison: University of Wisconsin Press, 1997, 144.

5. V.S. Pritchett, "America's First Truly Indigenous Masterpiece," in *Huck Finn Among the Critics: A Centennial Selection*, Thomas M. Inge, ed., Frederick, MD: University Publications of America, 1985, 75–80, 77.

6. Lionel Trilling, "The Greatness of *Huckleberry Finn*," in *Huck Finn Among the Critics: A Centennial Selection*, Thomas M. Inge, ed., Frederick, MD: University Publications of America, 1985, 81–92, 90–1.

7. *Ibid.*, 184.

8. Jonathan Arac, "Why Does No One Care about the Aesthetic Value of *Huckleberry Finn?*" *New Literary History* 30, no. 4 (1999): 769–84, 781.

9. Leo Marx, "Mr. Eliot, Mr. Trilling, and *Huckleberry Finn*," in *Huck Finn Among the Critics: A Centennial Selection*, Thomas M. Inge, ed., Frederick, MD: University Publications of America, 1985, 113–130, 127.

10. Cf. Jonathan Arac, "Why Does No One Care about the Aesthetic Value of *Huckleberry Finn?*" for a critique of moral readings of *Huckleberry Finn*.

11. Trilling, "The Greatness of *Huckleberry Finn*," 88.

12. Arac, "Why Does No One Care about the Aesthetic Value of *Huckleberry Finn?*" 776.

13. John Wallace, "The Case Against *Huck Finn. Satire or Evasion?*" in *Black Perspectives on* Huckleberry Finn, J.S. Leonard et al., eds., Durham: Duke University Press, 1992, 16–24, 16.

14. Arac, "Why Does No One Care about the Aesthetic Value of *Huckleberry Finn?*" 779.

15. *Ibid.*

16. T.S. Eliot, "Mark Twain's Masterpiece," in *Huck Finn Among the Critics: A Centennial Selection*, Thomas M. Inge, ed., Frederick, MD: University Publications of America, 1985, 103–112, 110.

17. David Smith, "Huck, Jim, and Racial Discourse," in *Huck Finn Among the Critics: A Centennial Selection*, Thomas M. Inge, ed., Frederick, MD: University Publications of America, 1985, 247–265, 261.

18. Stephen Railton's website, "Mark Twain and His Times," offers excellent images and a thoughtful discussion of the illustration of *Huckleberry Finn.* http://etext.virginia.edu/railton/huckfinn/huchompg.html.

19. Perry Frank, "Adventures of *Huckleberry Finn* on Film," in *Huck Finn Among the Critics: A Centennial Selection*, Thomas M. Inge, ed., Frederick, MD: University Publications of America, 1985, 293–314, 296.

20. *Ibid.*, 298.

21. *Ibid.*, 306.

22. Mark Twain, *The Adventures of Huckleberry Finn* (1884), New York: W.W. Norton, 1999, 239.

23. *Ibid.*, 142.

24. Kermode, *The Shawshank Redemption*, 28.

25. Erik Bauer, "Stephen King's Other Half: Interview With Frank Darabont," *Creative Screenwriting* 4, no. 2: 3–16, 6.

26. Hampe, "Shawshank: Rambling Narrative to Dramatic Structure," 19.

27. *Ibid.*, 25.

28. Frank Darabont, The Shawshank Redemption*: The Shooting Script*, New York: New Market Press, 1996, 158.

29. *Ibid.*, 158.

30. *Ibid.*, 296.

31. *Ibid.*, 157.

32. Marx, "Mr. Eliot, Mr. Trilling, and *Huckleberry Finn*," 127.

33. Alfred H. Conrad and John R. Meyer, *The Economics of Slavery and Other Studies in Econometric History*, Chicago: Aldine, 1964, 86–89.

34. Charles Isidore Nero, "Diva Traffic and Male Bonding in Film: Teaching Opera, Learning Gender, Race, and Nation," *Camera Obscura* 19, no. 2 (2004): 46–73, 55.

35. *Ibid.*

36. Hampe, "Shawshank: Rambling Narrative to Dramatic Structure," 19.

37. Kermode, *The Shawshank Redemption*, 30.

38. *Ibid.*, 32.

39. Sean O'Sullivan, "Representations of Prison in Nineties Hollywood Cinema: From *Con Air* to *The Shawshank Redemption*," *The Howard Journal*, 40:4, 317–334, 326.

40. Barry Holman, *Masking the Divide: How Officially Reported Prison Statistics Distort the Racial and Ethnic Realities of Prison Growth*, Report from the National Center on Institutions and Alternatives, May 2001, 26. Data from 2006 are provided by personal e-mail from Tora Starbird-Devos of the Maine Department of Corrections, May 26, 2006.

41. Nero, "Diva Traffic and Male Bonding in Film," 68.

42. From the inside cover of Stephen King, *Different Seasons*, New York: Penguin Putnam, 1983.

BIBLIOGRAPHY

The Adventures of Huckleberry Finn. Richard Thorpe, dir., Hugo Butler, scr. Metro-Goldwyn-Mayer, 1939.

The Adventures of Huckleberry Finn. Michael Curtiz, dir., James Lee, scr. Formosa Productions, 1960.

Arac, Jonathan. *Huckleberry Finn as Idol and Target: The Functions of Criticism in our Time*. Madison: University of Wisconsin Press, 1997.

_____. "Why Does No One Care about the Aesthetic Value of *Huckleberry Finn*?" *New Literary History* 30, no. 4 (1999), 769–84.

Bauer, Erik. "Stephen King's Other Half: Interview with Frank Darabont." *Creative Screenwriting* 4, no. 2, 3–16.

Conrad, Alfred H., and John R. Meyer. *The Economics of Slavery and Other Studies in Econometric History*. Chicago: Aldine, 1964.

Darabont, Frank. The Shawshank Redemption: *The Shooting Script*. New York: New Market Press, 1996.

Eliot, T.S. "Mark Twain's Masterpiece." *Huck Finn Among the Critics: A Centennial Selection*, Thomas M. Inge, ed. Frederick, MD: University Publications of America, 1985, 103–112.

Frank, Perry. "*Adventures of Huckleberry Finn* on Film." *Huck Finn Among the Critics: A Centennial selection*, Thomas M. Inge, ed. Frederick, MD: University Publications of America, 1985, 293–314.

Hampe, Barry. "*Shawshank*: Rambling Narrative to Dramatic Structure." *Creative Screenwriting* 4:2 (1997), 17–25.

Holman, Barry. *Masking the Divide: How Officially Reported Prison Statistics Distort the Racial and Ethnic Realities of Prison Growth*. Report from the National Center on Institutions and Alternatives, May 2001.

Huckleberry Finn. William Desmond Taylor, dir., Julia Crawford Ivers, scr. Famous Players Lasky Corporation, 1920.

Kermode, Mark. *The Shawshank Redemption*. London: British Film Institute, 2003.

King, Stephen. *Different Seasons*. New York: Penguin Putnam, 1983.

Lévi-Strauss, Claude. *Structural Anthropology*. New York: Basic Books, 1963.

Marx, Leo. "Mr. Eliot, Mr. Trilling, and *Huckleberry Finn*." *Huck Finn Among the Critics: A Centennial Selection*, Thomas M. Inge, ed. Frederick, MD: University Publications of America, 1985, 113–130.

Nero, Charles Isidore. "Diva Traffic and Male Bonding in Film: Teaching Opera, Learning Gender, Race, and Nation." *Camera Obscura* 19, no. 2 5 (2004): 46–73.

O'Sullivan, Sean. "Representations of Prison in Nineties Hollywood Cinema: From *Con Air* to *The Shawshank Redemption*." *The Howard Journal*, 40:4, 317–334.

Pritchett, V.S. "America's First Truly Indigenous Masterpiece." *Huck Finn Among the Critics: A Centennial selection*, Thomas M. Inge, ed. Frederick, MD: University Publications of America, 1985, 75–80.

The Shawshank Redemption. Frank Darabont, dir., scr. Castle Rock Entertainment, 1994.

Smith, David. "Huck, Jim, and Racial Discourse." *Huck Finn Among the Critics: A Centennial selection*, Thomas M. Inge, ed. Frederick, MD: University Publications of America, 1985, 247–265.

Trilling, Lionel. "The Greatness of *Huckleberry Finn*." *Huck Finn Among the Critics: A Centennial Selection*, Thomas M. Inge, ed. Frederick, MD: University Publications of America, 1985, 81–92.

Twain, Marc. *The Adventures of Huckleberry Finn*, 3d ed. New York: W.W. Norton, 1999.
Wallace, John. "The Case Against Huck Finn. Satire or Evasion?" *Black Perspectives on Huckleberry Finn*, J.S. Leonard et al., eds. Durham: Duke University Press, 1992, 16–24.

Shaft's Political Shifts

Hélène Charlery

Today epitomized as the first film of the blaxploitation genre of the early 1970s, *Shaft* was produced with a miserable budget that did not exceed 1.5 million dollars. Released in 1971, it brought in 12 million dollars in the U.S. alone.[1] MGM, *Shaft*'s production company, had not anticipated such success. The company originally produced the movie following the unexpected popularity, among ghetto residents, of the independently-produced and politically-engaged *Sweet Sweetback's Baadasssss Song*, released months earlier. Both films cast two black ghetto heroes who challenged Hollywood's traditional black male protagonists.

Directed by African American filmmaker Gordon Parks, *Shaft* is adapted from a novel written by Ernest Tidyman. As the author wrote the scenario of the screen version, the plot remains unchanged. It relates the story of a black private detective from New York, John Shaft, who is contacted by a black drug baron in Harlem, Knocks Persons, to recapture his missing daughter. Shaft soon discovers that she was abducted by the Italian mafia whose intention is to force Persons to release the monopoly that he holds on the city's drug market, in exchange for his daughter. In a boiling interracial context, the police dread the assuredly violent confrontation that will erupt between the city's dealers. Yet, any intervention from the police in the ghetto will inevitably lead the heavily-armed black radical organizations to join the conflict, and publicly decry the police's violence against black ghetto residents. As a solitary hero, Shaft is entangled in the middle of all those groups' interests.

Tidyman's literary character is a black man, as much affected by the Vietnam War as he is by his past involvement in the underworld of Harlem. Now a private detective, he stands as a middleman between the police, gangsters and black radical militants of the ghetto. Although the literary character is somehow connected to the three of them, he does not support any. Indeed, he admonishes drug dealers and he distrusts the police as much as he scolds the ideology of black radicalism. Yet, Shaft's filmic character had been transformed so that it could meet the period's political and racial climate. The movie was released at a time when the ghetto's racial pride and desire for separatism were voiced through howls of "black power," "black is beautiful" and "power to the people." The film's character is thus further distanced from the police and brought closer to the radical organizations of the story.

In *Shaft 2000*, the first remake of a blaxploitation movie, remarkable changes were made to the literary character and his environment. Tidyman's private detective, purposely deprived of any institutional attachment, had become a black detective of the NYPD. In addition, while in the 1971 version, the racial binary opposition between the black and white communities was heightened, in the 2000 re-adaptation, Shaft's enemies and allies are racially chosen to respond to the multicultural picture of contemporary American society. This literary character, originally created by a white author, first adapted on screen for black viewers, has become a protagonist re-imagined to seduce a multicultural audience.

Thus, in 1971 and in 2000, Hollywood studios wanted to adapt the novel while responding to the racial discourses of each period, and therefore to the expectations of the audiences the movie was directed at. In 1971, Shaft was a black private, proud of living in Harlem's ghettos. In 2000, he became an African American detective who scorns the attitude of black people towards the police and evolves around multiracial protagonists. The almost neutral literary character has thus gone from racial pride to an exaltation of multiculturalism. Yet, this racial mixing found its limits, since the new Shaft does not cross intimate racial boundaries. Similarly, his treatment of suspects differs according to their racial origins. It is mostly Shaft's new position as a police detective that thus illustrates the thirty-year *evolution* of the American discourse on race relations.

Blaxploitation or the Exploitation of Black Culture

Born from the connection of "black" and the filmic meaning of "exploitation," the blaxploitation referred to a coded genre where the culture and universe of black ghettoes were valued. The most visible aspects of the films were connected to the black community. On the other hand, the production, distribution and scenario were handed over to white professionals. *Shaft* was indeed produced by MGM, was adapted by Ernest Tidyman. Yet, it starred black actor Richard Roundtree, and was directed by Gordon Parks, with an original soundtrack from black composer Isaac Hayes.

The genre put forward characters who contrasted with those Hollywood movies had long depicted as being secondary to white protagonists. In *Shaft*, the lead character was given new power which was thoroughly associated with his being black. This new filmic "black power" emerged at a moment when the concept was familiar to residents of American black ghettoes. These new heroes progressed in an environment that emphasized the ideology of separatism that organizations like the Black Panthers defended. They were no longer subordinate to white characters, but in control of their destinies, their decisions and their ways of life: hence the movie and the genre's popularity among those inhabitants. Shaft was the true hero of a period of black contestation against the government and the system in general. In other words, like *Sweet Sweetback's Baadasssss Song*, *Shaft* embodied the cultural aspect of political engagement. Gordon Parks ironically and modestly defined the movie as a Saturday night film which people watched to see a Black man win.[2]

While integration movies of the 1950s and 1960s portrayed middle class or morally acceptable black characters, blaxploitation movies focused on uneven heroes such as drug dealers (*Superfly*, 1972) and put the ghetto at the core of the filmic space. As at the beginning of the novel, the movie *Shaft* starts with Richard Roundtree walking out of the subway, strolling across the city to his office. The dialogue-free musical scene shows how Harlem is *his* universe before he has uttered a line. Every resident of the poor neighborhoods where the black detective carries on his investigation is given some importance as they all provide some information that might lead him to his point. Many professions (from the landlord to the shoe shine or the newspaper vendor) are then pointed out. The shift from long shots depicting Shaft walking in the city's streets and medium shots where he is seen interviewing ghetto residents actually suggests how the city is deeply related to its inhabitants and vice versa.

The city is given as much importance as it is given in Ernest Tidyman's novel, which starts with a precise depiction of New York. The author also portrays the everyday life of a black ghetto resident through his description of Shaft's angry state of mind. Every element of the black ghetto experience of the 1970s is mentioned: the first brawl, the first confrontation with the police officer chasing him, but whom he successfully escapes, the concrete walls which constitute his everyday universe, the bullets that missed him and the Vietnam trauma.[3] Despite this anger, the literary character does not support black radical organizations. On the contrary, he harshly criticizes Ben

Buford, the leader of a black revolutionary group which he simply associates with mercenaries.[4]

This stiff criticism had disappeared from the movie's 1971 version. In the same scene involving Shaft, Buford and Bumpy Jonas (Knocks Persons in the novel), it is Ben Buford who preaches to Jonas, and not Shaft scolding Buford. The latter insists that he does not lead a group of mercenaries but a revolutionary organization defending a sound cause. He eventually agrees to involve his men in the liberation of Jonas's daughter only in exchange for the money necessary to free the "brothers" and "sisters of combat" imprisoned by the "honky government." The last phrase is then emphasized with a close-up on the character's face. Absent from the novel's plot, the reason for the financial deal between Jonas and Buford gives credit to the revolutionary and to his cause. Shaft is mute during Buford's entire monologue. He is more garrulous, though, in another scene with police officer Vic Androzzi during which he defends the revolutionaries the police tries to capture. By the end of the movie, it is thanks to the radical group's involvement in the liberation of the hostage that Jonas's daughter is safely taken out of the mafia's hands.

Thus, in this first adaptation of the novel, Shaft undoubtedly supports the black radical organization more than the literary character did. In the novel, Shaft's ability to progress in a white environment or in a black one was the reason why Persons relied on him to find his daughter. Similarly, that capacity was the reason why Buford suspected and dreaded him. For that matter, the novel's conclusion details Shaft's decision to leave the country and his community and his desire to become a race-less character.[5] Conversely, the blaxploitation movie emphasized the extent to which Shaft belongs to his racial community and pointed out a vivid racial opposition. In the scene in Androzzi's office where Shaft answers the police's questions, he puts forward both his blackness and his community: "Warms my black heart to see you so concerned about us minority folks." Androzzi attempts to respond, while debunking the racial perspective Shaft is purposely giving to the police's involvement in the affair: "Oh come on Shaft, what is it with this black shit, huh?" Taking a black pen and putting it next to Shaft's face, he adds: "You ain't so black." Shaft's daring and witty response copies the white policeman's gesture. Grabbing a white coffee cup and laying it on the officer's face, he concludes: "And you ain't so white either, baby."

Considering the period when the movie was made, the scene was crucial as it symbolically meant that the black man, who had just thrown another black man out of his office window (though accidentally), could still get the final word with a white officer, in the police station.

In 2002, Isaac Julien, who authored *Baadasssss Cinema*, a documentary on the genre, explained that the blaxploitation movies revealed the every-day life of the black urban population and a political and historical reality that had never been tackled in American popular culture before.[6] Other authors would rather highlight that these elements — Shaft's closeness with the black separatist discourse and his distrust of the police — were deliberately intensified by the movie's producers to attract the ghetto residents the film originally targeted. Black cinema specialist Donald Bogle argues that *Shaft* is merely a white private's ordinary story, but with a "black sensitivity."[7] Fred Williamson, a symbolic figure of the genre, explains that, at its beginning, Hollywood producers cared little about the contentious and displeasing content of the films which brought in considerable profits and attracted both black and white viewers, eager to discover an emerging black hip hop culture.[8] As opposed to the literary character, in the movie, Shaft's particularities were indeed heightened and connected to black cultural traits: the "afro," the walking attitude, the assertiveness of "baby" ending every line, or the character's behavior towards the institutions and most particularly towards the police.[9] Certain elements that were added in the adaptation of the novel do thus emphasize the mercantile exploitation of black culture.

If Shaft daringly mocks the police, he does not criticize the system or the police's violence against black ghetto residents, as did Melvin Van Peebles's *Sweet Sweetback's Baadasssss Song.*[10] The movie's real bad guys are the mafia's mob. Thus, Régis Dubois states that *Shaft* is a "fake" black film which illustrated Hollywood's strategy to profit from the period's black protestation movement.[11] Similarly to what Bogle argued, Dubois suggests that the movie lacks any political engagement and that in producing *Shaft*, MGM simply re-created a black action hero who is not much different from a white one.[12] Thus, one is likely to think that the producers' decisions to use two black directors were not randomly made. When given the direction of the 1971 version, Gordon Parks was the first African American director of a major studio's film (*The Learning Tree*, 1969). John Singleton, who directed *Shaft 2000*, is the only black director to have been nominated for an Oscar in the best director category. According to Anne Crémieux, both Parks and Singleton had the ability to value black culture while seducing all the other racial groups.[13]

Yet *Shaft 2000* does not give as much screen time to the ghetto as Tidyman did in the novel. The racist hate crime which starts the movie takes place in a trendy club patronized by both the victim and the murderer. In addition, the last shots of the movie depict the entire city rather than the ghetto, contrary to the 1971 version, whose action is limited to the ghetto's boundaries. The racial separatist discourse has disappeared from the 2000 version. On the contrary, Shaft, played by Samuel L. Jackson, often criticizes his racial group's bitterness towards the police. The radical organization that contributed to the movie's conclusion in 1971 does not appear in John Singleton's film. The new Shaft can solve the crime thanks to his partners, although he quits the police in the middle of the story.

The uni-racial cast of the plot's main action is no longer possible in contemporary America. The new Shaft lives in a multiethnic society, at a time when multiculturalism and other similar concepts have been phrased to apparently solve racial tensions and handle the multiplicity of cultures. As Jackson/Shaft says, "It's Giuliani's time." Thus, the movie's producers transformed Tidyman's novel so that it would speak to all racial and ethnic groups likely to identify with an African American hero.[14] While the first adaptation was aimed at a black spectatorship, the 2000 adaptation targeted a much more modern and multiracial audience. Such multiculturalism is shown through the police officers with whom Shaft works.

In the scene when the whole team is introduced, Shaft and his colleagues are on the verge of apprehending drug dealers. He poses with his partner, Vasquez, who, as her name suggests, is Hispanic. They are joined by two new partners, Jack Rosetti, who is obviously Italian-American, and Jimmy Grooves, just as evidently African American. While they quietly plan to enter the dealers' hideout, another detective is opening its door. He is Caucasian and is named Lugger.[15]

In this scene, and throughout the movie, the characters who contribute to justice are brought closer to American values. Sometimes, an American flag flutters next to them or to their houses. Inversely, those who defy American justice are estranged from the nation and its symbols, similarly to the youngsters who shout Spanish insults to Shaft and throw things at him as he runs after a drug dealer. The multiculturalism of the detectives is opposed to the racial uniformity of the drug dealers. The scene reaches its climax when the multicultural team faces the drug baron and his men. With a high-angle shot, the director intensifies the confrontation between a team of multiracial policemen and a group of Dominican drug dealers, in other words, a group of integrated minorities who respect and defend the laws of the system, opposed to one single minority who does not. The rules of integration and those of justice are thus paralleled.

Out of the race-less literary character, Shaft was transformed into a hero that defends and acclaims multiculturalism. Yet, this racial mixing is limited inside and outside the film narrative. Indeed, Detective Vasquez is not played by a Hispanic actress but an African American one, Vanessa Williams. Interestingly, at no point in the movie is her hair uncovered or left loose. It is constantly tied back so that her haircut, for which the actress is already famous among viewers, may not remind them of her true origins. Only at Shaft's surprise birthday party can the viewers see her briefly with her curled hair. Similarly, the Dominican drug dealer that Shaft will track until the movie's end is played by a black actor, Jeffrey Wright. Obviously, the desire to have Hispanic characters, whether "good" or "bad," depicted the producers' will to represent and attract diverse racial groups, and to avoid the racial dichotomy that pervades Parks' first version. Yet, this desire is blurred by the use of African American characters to play Hispanic parts. Likewise, if police detectives belong to diverse ethnic and racial groups, only African American policemen are heard congratulating Shaft for his arrests. As Anne Crémieux mentioned, Singleton found the means to satisfy a multiethnic audience generally and a black spectatorship specifically. Yet, racial mixing does not seem to be compromised when it comes to intimate relationships.

Shaft's Sexuality and the Limits of Multiculturalism

Ernest Tidyman purposely depicted Shaft as a sensual and sexual character. In the first adaptation, Gordon Parks wanted Richard Roundtree to keep his mustache, as he thought it had as much importance in the character's sexual appeal and virility as his "afro" and his brown leather jacket.[16] In the new version, Samuel L. Jackson gave up the "afro" for a bald head and a perfectly-trimmed goatee. A man's bald head is the primary element that the spectator views of Shaft's character. The movie titles mix bluish images of an African American couple making love, scored by Isaac Hayes' musical theme. If spectators can neatly distinguish the woman's face, they can only guess Jackson's bald head. Then, the director combines those images with those of the man putting his clothes back on, while the woman is still enjoying the moment. One understands that the man is Jackson, since his bald head is at the center of the frame in the next shot, while the camera is following him through a crowd of bystanders up to the crime scene. Therefore, in the movie's single love scene, the main character has not yet been introduced to the viewers, and only pieces of bodies are clearly visible.

This contrasts with the original *Shaft*, where bodies of the leading character and of his female partners are fully seen, whether they are white or black. Two love scenes are portrayed in the 1971 version: one in which Shaft waits for his girl friend, naked on her couch; the other one with a white woman he met in a bar and who furtively joins him while he is having a shower, in keeping with Tidyman's original literary writing. Filters are used to attenuate the impact of the scenes: in the first one, the camera is put vertically and the intercourse is seen through the colorful decorations put on the ceiling; in the second one, the interracial couple making love is observed from behind the shower door.

However, although Tidyman detailed the love scenes of his character with white women, Jackson/Shaft does not have such overt contacts with female characters, especially white ones. In addition, in seduction scenes with black female characters, Shaft is frequently in different shots from the women he is supposed to ravish later on, instead of traditional close shots.

Of course, the new Shaft is not an entirely sexless character. At one moment in the movie, he stares at a woman who passes by and that he thinks "hot." Yet, the woman goes almost unseen, as the episode is put within the transition between two sequences. In the following scene, Richard Roundtree, the original Shaft who guest-stars as Shaft/Jackson's uncle in this version, mentions his nephew's reputed sexual power. To a bartender who glamorously kisses Shaft, he says: "Alice, Alice, ease up on my nephew. Or that boy's gonna poke a hole in something." Thus, the new Shaft assuredly has desires and sexual potentiality, but it is not displayed for the viewers' appreciation or judgment.

The relationship between Shaft and the white witness he is to protect are depicted with more timidity. At the beginning of the movie, he first calls her by her first name when they are alone, but resorts to a solemn "Madam" when he mentions her to a policeman who has joined them. All contact is made through clothing and no skin contact is clearly established in front of the camera, even in rhythmic action scenes involving the two characters. In the introduction scene, once Shaft has arrested the main suspect, he heads towards the nervous white bartender. He brings her to a mirror which stands behind her so that she can see the blood marks on her face. Their hands are hidden or off-screen. Only the movement of the characters suggest to the viewers that he touches her.

Throughout the movie, the contacts between the interracial pair are forced, awkward or thwarted. Only once do the viewers see skin contact, though the characters' faces are again hidden (the witness) and off-screen (Shaft).

At the end of the movie, when the witness' life is no longer in danger, Shaft touches and comforts her inelegantly. She is lying, face down, on the ground and he puts his hand under her shoulder. The characters thus cannot establish a reassuring and logical eye-contact.

Again, in the following scene, on the steps of the courthouse, he embraces her to reassure her. Yet, the face of one or the other character is alternately put at the center of the shots. All these efforts to display interracial contact while not making them suggestive to the viewers contrast with the original adaptation, where Richard Roundtree overtly touched the white woman he met in the bar. Close-ups deliberately focused on the two characters' hands with an angle that displayed the woman's décolleté. The interracial pair was thus seen openly kissing several times during those scenes.

In this new adaptation, the lack of interracial contact is not limited to Shaft's character. No physical contact intervenes between the black victim and his white fiancée, in the flashback scene. To warm her up, he does touch her when they enter the bar, but his hands only rub her black coat. Similarly, once he has endured a racial insult from his future murderer, he tries to comfort her, but his hand suddenly escapes hers. As she is trying to take her coat off, it is the clothing that he brushes and not her hand. In the new adaptation, the only character who *seems* to have a prolific sexuality is none other than Richard Roundtree, the original Shaft. At the end of the birthday party, he is depicted leaving the bar with two young women, probably Hispanic and Caucasian, who rush to his side when he waves his finger in their direction. Only the original Shaft has thus kept his social, financial and sexual powers.

Régis Dubois argues that, since the 1990s, the new black cinema heroes have been more reserved than their 1970s counterparts.[17] Political correctness has obviously erased the sexual liberation of black characters that the blaxploitation had momentarily allowed. Dubois adds that behind this modern attitude lies the desire of producers and directors to confer a reassuring image of these powerful black male protagonists. This explains why they have become vigorous defenders of American laws and justice.[18] Their new hyper-heroism is inextricably connected to their asexuality. The two police detectives in *Bad Boys* (Michael Bay, 1995) illustrate Dubois's point. They arrest the drug dealer and protect the white female witness, without whom the condemnation is impossible. Yet, contrary to elementary Hollywood narrative codes,[19] neither of the two policemen has a love story with the witness, even Will Smith, who is depicted as an irresistible womanizer throughout the movie.

The 1990s black heroes dwell in a white and "de-racialised universe"[20] which sometimes, but only rarely, involves other black female characters that stand for the heroes' girlfriends, wives and fiancées. The only two seduction scenes in which Jackson is allowed a possible sexual encounter take place in the bar he regularly frequents. At first, he flirts with a former mistress who now is dating one of his friends. Nothing happens between the two, since that friend interrupts Shaft's courting. The situation was all prepared in advance as it was a trick to lead him to the room where all his friends are waiting to throw him a surprise birthday party. Then, by the end of the party, he exchanges some evocative words with Alice, the non-white bartender, who the viewer is given to understand is an irregular mistress. After this brief conversation, the scene ends, and Shaft's sexual appeal is left to the viewers' imagination.

In this new version, the absence of love scenes is problematic in comparison to the novel and the first adaptation. The novel provides a plethora of the leading character's sexual performances. As for the first adaptation, it respects this major component of the hero's traits. In the 2000 version, apart from the suggestions hinted at in the movie titles and during the brief seduction scenes with his former mistress, the new Shaft does not have a sexual life, much like the new black Hollywood characters starring in mixed casting movies. However, this sexual potentiality was central to the blaxploitation characters as it echoed their new social, political and cultural powers. Thus, nowadays, contemporary African American heroes are closer to the sexless ones played by actors such as Sydney Poitier and Harry Belafonte in the 1950s and 1960s. The difference now resides in the motive for their intervention in the story: they no longer fight for racial equality but for American justice.

Ernest Tidyman imagined Shaft as a virile, vigorous and aggressive literary hero. By the end of the first chapter of the novel, Shaft had already gotten rid of two thugs who were ordered to bring him down to Knocks Persons, throwing one out of the window and pressing his gun to the other's head for information. In the blaxploitation version, the black thug accidentally fell out of the office window as he was about to pounce on Shaft. In *Shaft 2000*, a black man is indeed thrown out of a window, not by Shaft who is not even in the scene, but by the Dominican drug baron. If this last version is more violent than the previous one, Shaft's character does not perpetrate much of the movie's brutality. If he does, it is justified by the villain's atrocity which undeniably deserves punishment.

Shaft's violence and aggressiveness are less visible, though, when he confronts the white murderer, Walter Wade, Jr. (Christian Bale). From the beginning of the movie, Wade is made despicable when he smiles at what he calls his black victim's "homeboy's [...] rhythm," when the victim is actually having a lethal convulsive seizure on the ambulance's stretcher. Shaft's response to Wade after the racial comment — two punches — are thus justified to the viewers. However, the blows are swift and almost concealed compared to the numerous close-ups on the blood-drenched face of a drug dealer Shaft beats later on in the movie. Shaft's violent gestures against the white murderer are made as unnoticeable as any physical contact he may have with white female characters. For instance, when Shaft arrests Wade, the close shots do not allow the viewers to clearly see the arrest. They can only imagine it from the sight, then from the sound of the handcuffs. Similarly, when Shaft apprehends Wade a second time and walks him to his cell, the two men face each other in front of the cell's door. The position of the camera allows the viewers to see the characters' faces. Then, the camera's angle shifts, hides Wade's face, and exposes Shaft's. The latter pushes the suspect in the cell. Yet, the viewer cannot see Shaft's hand push Wade inside the cell. Again, it can only be imagined.

Paradoxically, Shaft's contacts with Peoples Hernandez, the Dominican character played by an African American actor, are made more obvious and direct. In the first version, the hero resorted to violence as a means to defend himself. In the 2000 movie, since Shaft only brutalizes the characters who are morally depicted as evil, he uses violence as a punishment. Indeed, to obtain information from a black mother living in the ghetto, Shaft stuns the neighborhood's drug dealer who was trying to recruit the woman's son in his gang. While he uses his gun to hit the young man, a white patrol officer driving through the ghetto passes by him. Both nod at each other, the officer drives off and Shaft continues his beating, though he is a former police detective at that moment of the movie. That scene would have raised the indignation of blaxploitation viewers. Yet, the close-ups on the black villain's bloody face are made acceptable, because the drug dealer is morally reprehensible and Shaft is a black character.

The character's race and his new profession allow him gestures and actions that a white protagonist would not have. In the 1971 version, Androzzi was threatening to take Shaft's private detective's license should he refuse to collaborate with the police. Shaft is thus compelled to give accounts about the man's plunge from his window. However, this element was not present in the novel, where there is little confrontation between the police officer and the private detective, and where the latter is even called by the police to have access to the impenetrable gangster world of Harlem. In *Shaft 2000*, it is the lead character that carries on this confrontation between his race and his occupation.

Shaft's new position is the most distinctive element from Ernest Tidyman's novel. The author had imagined his hero as a rootless character and as one who would neither collaborate with the police nor run away from them. However, the new Shaft is first a homicide detective, before he is transferred to Narcotics, and eventually quits the job. Isaac Hayes's musical theme had even underlined that Shaft was "the cat that [wouldn't] cop out." John Singleton has kept Hayes' score, so well-known in the audience's imagination, though it has little relevance in the new adaptation. Through the movie's setting, the director sometimes makes every effort to have the viewers consider Jackson as a credible Shaft, in spite of his new occupation. Indeed, in the bar where his birthday party is celebrated, a sign reading "The cop is your friend" hangs on the wall behind the bartender. In the movie's titles, the original score plays on images that repeatedly announce the character's position: bluish images appear on the screen, alternating with images of Shaft's police badge. The latter appears whenever the singers pronounce Shaft's name or Singleton's name appears on screen, as if to stress that this important detail brought to the main character is the director's decision. The police siren accompanies the music and eventually starts the movie.

The viewers can thus quickly grasp that the plot is in New York City and that it is as representative of Shaft's universe as the police is. The references to the latter are omnipresent in the first images. John Shaft walks through the crowd of bystanders with his police badge on his chest. In the next scene, the close shot which pictures a conversation between Shaft and another policeman clearly focuses on the letters of the NYPD which decorate the policeman's uniform collar. Similar letters appear on the jackets of the forensic scientists. Likewise, Shaft's first lines are an assessment of his new position. Questioning the policeman on the procedure taken around the victim, Shaft vexes the man who understands that he is taken for a beginner. To the man's frustration, Shaft answers that he too knows his job.

Such affirmation of his new position at the very beginning of the movie makes his resignation surprising and problematic to the image it gives of the system. Nonetheless, similarly to the blaxploitation heroes who appeared some years after the beginning of the genre, the new Shaft is not opposed to the police but to the mob. The system is thereby not questioned as it was in *Sweet Sweetback's Baadasssss Song*. Only a few faulty elements of the system must be taken out by the hero so that justice functions correctly. Thus, at the beginning of the movie, Wade commits a racial hate crime and thus stands as the story's villain. Progressively, he becomes the victim of the Dominican drug baron, who takes over the villain's role. By the end of the film, the frightened witness finally agrees to testify against Wade who is arrested and ready to be tried. However, though American justice is about to be dutifully applied, Wade is shot down by his victim's mother. Since Shaft kills the Dominican drug dealer in a final confrontation, the two villains die. Whatever the racial community to which they belong, both are punished by moral laws as they would have by men's.

In the novel's conclusion, the hero was leaving his community as much as he was rejecting the police. At the end of the first adaptation, Shaft was laughing away, exhilarated by the last trick he played on the city's police. His victorious guffaw implicitly pointed out the police's incapacity to handle and solve the problems that might affect Harlem's black community. In the new adaptation, aimed at a multicultural audience, a politically correct message is delivered: racial or ethnic groups can coexist and claim their specific identity as long as they still remember to abide by the American laws. Thus the villains' multi-ethnicity (Dominican-American; Caucasian-American; Italian-American; African American) is not made as problematic as it is for Shaft to be an African American detective. In 1971, Maurice Peterson, a journalist for *Essence* magazine argued that Shaft was a man free of racial doubts. He was proud to be black but that did not come as an obsession to him.[21] This pride was central to the first adaptation of the novel and, as it opposed the white police, it inevitably opposed American institutions. In 1971, when the novel was published and the first movie released, the double identity of the black population was not yet resolved. In thirty years, the term "African American" has enabled the group to expose the doubleness and simultaneity of being black and American, as is the case for other ethnic groups. However, racial identity is more central to *Shaft 2000* than it was in the 1971 version, and is frequently related to the lead character's position as a police detective.

The debate has shifted from being black and/or American to being black and/or a policeman. The first mention of the issue is made by Lugger, a white detective who pushes Shaft to "pick a color, black or blue." Shaft himself expresses the ambiguity of his position to his uncle: "I remember when I took that job thinking I could fight from inside, and you telling me about all the problems. That color thing — Too black for the uniform, too blue for the brothers." It is symbolic that he should raise the issue in a conversation with his uncle, the original Shaft, the one who would not "cop out." It seems that, all along the investigation, his double identity as a black policeman is not feasible. Nonetheless, it is by fighting to prevent American justice from being "bought off by the green" that he manages to find his true position within the film's society. By the end of the movie, he proves that he is worthy of being a policeman as he killed the (Dominican) villain, eased the desire for justice of a (black) mother, found the (white) murderer, and protected the (white Italian) witness, as well as the city and the entire American justice system.

Nonetheless, when he performs all those actions successfully, he is no longer a policeman, since he has quit the police in the middle of the movie. To John Singleton, who readapted Ernest Tidyman's novel and authored the scenario of the last version, this detail tends to suggest that Shaft cannot combine his racial ethnicity and his occupation as a police detective. Similarly, if we pay a close attention to the actors that are on screen in the closing sequence, we remark that multi-ethnicity has also disappeared. All the actors who remain in this last scene are African Americans: Shaft, Shaft's uncle, Vasquez (played by black actress Vanessa Williams), a black police detective who is frequently seen but who has little dialogue in the movie, and a black woman who comes to complain about her violent lover. Shaft and his uncle walk out of the police station as two private detectives, and are joined by rap singer Busta Rhymes whose character intends to enter Shaft's new family business. As a black director, John Singleton seems to have more difficulties in handling an African American character in a politically-correct period and with the task to satisfy a multicultural audience, than Ernest Tidyman, as a white author, to accurately write his black character in the 1970s. The two contemporary concepts, political correctness and multiculturalism, allow two readings of the movie, an explicit one which favors the cohabitation of different groups and the success of American justice, and another implicit one which seems to put forward a single group isolated from the rest of society.

Conclusion

Ernest Tidyman's novel underlined a racial binary opposition between black and white people, with Shaft standing in the middle of the divide. In the two filmic versions, some elements of the story were put forward in each version, depending on the racial discourse of the period, so as to satisfy the audience the movie targeted. In the blaxploitation adaptation in the 1970s, the racial gap was intensified and white characters were immediately depicted as evil. Inversely, black characters were all good, whether they were respectable or not. Nevertheless, the 1971 version delivered a message of equality for black viewers who could see a black character put in a position traditionally held by a white one. To Edward Mapp, this was representative of a growing equality in the 1960s and 1970s.[22] The new version of the movie, marked by political correctness, cannot adopt such a vision of racial groups. Indeed, equality being guaranteed and protected by the laws, mentioning any challenge to it would amount to questioning American justice. The system of justice is placed at the heart of the new adaptation and is protected by the nation's multicultural individuals. However, the last images of the movie suggest that multiculturalism and political correctness do not prevent periodic racial separatism. On the contrary, it promotes it, especially when dealing with interracial intimacy.

NOTES

1. *Shaft 2000* was produced with a $46 million budget and brought in $70 million.
2. James Robert Parish, *Black Action Films: Plots, Critiques, Casts and Credits for 235 Theatrical and Made-for-Television Releases*, Jefferson, NC: McFarland, 1989, 252.
3. Ernest Tidyman, *Les nuits rouges de Harlem*, Paris: Gallimard, 1971, 50–51.
4. *Ibid.*, 218–219.

5. *Ibid.*, 249.
6. Terry Lawson, "Blaxploitation Demanding New Respect," *Milwaukee Journal Sentinel*, July 25, 2002. FindArticles.com. 16 Apr. 2007. http://www.findarticles.com/p/articles/mi_qn4196/is_20020725/ai_n10808366.
7. Donald Bogle, *Toms, Coons, Mulattoes, Mammies and Bucks: An Interpretive History of Blacks in American Films*, New York: Continuum, 1989, 239.
8. Lawson, "Blaxploitation Demanding New Respect." However, Ernest Tidyman's literary character was not representative of Harlem, since he lived in Greenwich Village where he worked as a professional.
9. Régis Dubois, *Le Cinéma des noirs américains: entre intégration et contestation*, Paris: Editions du Cerf, 2005, 140.
10. Anne Crémieux, *Les Cinéastes noirs américains et le rêve hollywoodien*, Paris: L'Harmattan, 2004, 37.
11. Dubois, *Le Cinéma des noirs américains entre intégration et contestation*, 139–141.
12. *Ibid.*, 143.
13. Crémieux, *Les Cinéastes noirs américains et le rêve hollywoodien*, 37.
14. *Ibid.*, 159.
15. In Tidyman's novel, all the police detectives were white. However, the author did not insist upon it, as they were primarily policemen.
16. Donald Bogle, *Blacks in American Films and Television: An Encyclopaedia*, New York: Simon & Schuster, 1989, 460.
17. Régis Dubois, *Images du noir dans le cinéma américain blanc (1980–1995)*, Paris: L'Harmattan, 1997, 68.
18. *Ibid.*, 69.
19. *Ibid.*
20. *Ibid.*, 70.
21. Parish, *Black Action Films*, 254.
22. Edward Mapp, *Blacks in American Film: Today and Yesterday*, Metuchen, NJ: Scarecrow, 1992, 251.

BIBLIOGRAPHY

Bogle, Donald. *Blacks in American Films and Television: An Encyclopaedia*. New York: Simon & Schuster, 1989.
_____. *Toms, Coons, Mulattoes, Mammies and Bucks: An Interpretive History of Blacks in American Films*. New York: Continuum, 1989.
Crémieux, Anne. *Les Cinéastes noirs américains et le rêve hollywoodien*. Paris: L'Harmattan, 2004.
Dubois, Régis. *Le Cinéma des noirs américains: entre intégration et contestation*. Paris: Editions du Cerf, 2005.
_____. *Images du noir dans le cinéma américain blanc (1980–1995)*. Paris: L'Harmattan, 1997.
Lawson, Terry. "Blaxploitation Demanding New Respect." *Milwaukee Journal Sentinel*, July 25, 2002, FindArticles.com. 16 Apr. 2007. http://www.findarticles.com/p/articles/mi_qn4196/is_20020725/ai_n10808366.
Mapp, Edward. *Blacks in American Film: Today and Yesterday*. Metuchen, NJ: Scarecrow, 1992.
Parish, James Robert. *Black Action Films: Plots, Critiques, Casts and Credits for 235 Theatrical and Made-for Television Releases*. Jefferson, NC: McFarland, 1989.
Shaft. Gordon Parks, dir., Ernest Tidyman, scr. Metro-Goldwyn-Meyer, 1971.
Shaft. John Singleton, dir., Richard Price, Shane Salerno, John Singleton, scr. Paramount Pictures, 2000.
Tidyman, Ernest. *Shaft*. New York: Macmillan, 1970. Trans. *Les Nuits rouges de Harlem*, Florian Robinet, trans. Paris: Gallimard, 1971.

Sexual Politics: *The Last September*, Novel and Film

Shannon Wells-Lassagne

The film adaptation of *The Last September* was much anticipated: both
its director, Deborah Warner, and its screenwriter, John Banville, were widely
acclaimed in their own domains (theater and fiction, respectively), before
making their first foray into the cinema, and their source material, Elizabeth
Bowen's second novel, was considered by many to be the masterpiece of an
underappreciated modernist writer. Given its star cast (Maggie Smith, Michael
Gabon, Jane Birkin, Fiona Shaw) and its apparition in 1999, in the wake of
the period drama frenzy launched by *Chariots of Fire* (1981) and continued
notably with films like *Howard's End* (1992), its future must have seemed
assured. When it came out, however, it was subject to puzzlement rather than
praise: the radical changes to the source material displeased Bowen fans, while
the uneven tone displeased those expecting fare typical of period dramas. My
argument is that both of these failings are in fact due to its dual affiliation:
the film *The Last September* is not just an adaptation to the screen, it is an
adaptation of the original novel to political and social critical stances. Warner's
changes to Bowen's text tell us much about what modern readers appreciate
or find disturbing in Bowen's texts, while she holds a James Joyce-style looking-glass to both Ireland and modern society more generally.

Bowen's *The Last September* is set in Ireland during the Troubles of 1919–
1921 leading up to Irish independence. This armed conflict, however, is very
much in the background of the novel: any violence is absent from the novel,
and the English soldiers come to defend the interests of the Protestant Ascendancy who rule on their behalf are seen almost exclusively as prospective dance
and tennis partners in a manner very similar to Jane Austen's gallant soldiers
during the Napoleonic Wars. The story centers on Danielstown, an Anglo-

Irish Big House, and its inhabitants, Sir Richard and Lady Naylor, their house-guests Marda Norton and Hugo and Francie Montmorency, and their Oxford-educated nephew Laurence and niece Lois. Lois's relationship with Gerald, a young British soldier (or rather, their inability to have a relationship, despite the young man's ardor) becomes an allegory for the fraught relationship between the Anglo-Irish and the English. A more promising relationship is the one that links Lois to Marda Norton, an older woman for whom Lois displays a certain fascination. However the end of the novel suggests that neither of these relationships are feasible, and that the only hope is for the Anglo-Irish protagonist to escape her culture altogether: Gerald is shot, Marda gets married, and Lois goes off to Tours to improve her French, while the Big House, symbol of Anglo-Irish oppression (of the tenantry and of themselves) is burnt by rebels.

In many ways, choosing Elizabeth Bowen's fiction as a source for a film seems an inspired choice because of the very nature of her prose. As Deborah Warner comments in an interview,

> [...] I came to it knowing [...] Elizabeth Bowen [...] was somewhere a filmmaker. There was no question that if she had [sic] another career choice, she would have made films, because her delight in the minutiae of detail, how she describes [...] light [...] are all facets of filmmaking. She's a very good designer, she's a very good cinematographer, she's a very good [...] scriptwriter. So it was absolutely right that this become a film, and I was happy to be the conduit for that to happen.[1]

The insistence on the very cinematic nature of Bowen's texts (and of *The Last September* in particular) suggests that *The Last September* is almost already a film in and of itself, where decisions as to costumes, lighting, montage and camera angles are already present in the prose; of course, one might ask what role the director reserves for herself if the novel imposes such a strong vision of the finished product. However, what Warner goes on to discuss in her comments on the novel, and what appears most clearly in her interpretation of the source material, is not the very visual nature of the original text, but its political content:

> It's also a very sobering reminder to us all that things change, that we may feel very sure of where we are [...] America feels very sure of where it is, England feels pretty sure of where it is, so too the Anglo-Irish felt very sure of where they were. And yet, by the end of that year of which this last September is a part, they were to be eclipsed and never seen again, because Ireland needed to move towards its democracy, towards its future, and I think it becomes a very meaningful and very very contemporary tale in that respect.[2]

Actress Fiona Shaw (who plays Marda) goes even further, suggesting that "*The Last September* is more pertinent now than it was when it was written."[3]

In both cases, the cinema adaptation is a means to bring to the fore the political undertones of Bowen's fiction, and to apply them to the present political situation (both women mention the Balkan War, for example).

In this case, then, the simple decision to focus on politics (sexual or otherwise), becomes a desire not just to adapt but to interpret, to give new emphasis to these aspects of the novel. I believe that while many aspects of the novel are very cunningly transposed to the screen, and other changes stem from the necessity of streamlining the original story, there are a certain number which reflect the beliefs of screenwriter John Banville and director Deborah Warner which differ markedly from those of Elizabeth Bowen. Thus, the director and screenwriter are not "the conduit" for Bowen to become the filmmaker she was always meant to be; rather, they are using *The Last September* as a jumping-off point for their own vision of politics and art. Therefore, I'll be examining the textual and cinematic versions of *The Last September* first by focusing on the political ramifications of the different stories before going on to investigate the way novel and film deal with the question of genre, whether it be through cinematic prose or literary cinema.

Isolation and Rapprochement

The allegorical nature of *The Last September* is implicit in its very title: while it is the last September to be experienced in the symbolic structure of the Anglo-Irish Big House Danielstown before its imminent destruction by rebels, it is also the last September of innocence for the protagonist before going out into the world. The loss of innocence is thus the central theme of this fiction (as it is in most, if not all, of Bowen's work). Lois's experiences become representative of the Anglo-Irish as a whole, where their willful ignorance parallels the protagonist's inexperience. As such, my antithetical title, "Isolation and *Rapprochement*," expresses not only the double nature of the plot, hovering between individual actions and their representativity, but also what I believe to be one of the fundamental differences between *The Last September* as written by Elizabeth Bowen and as filmed by Deborah Warner.

Both English and Irish, neither English nor Irish, the Protestant Ascendancy in Bowen is essentially defined only by its isolation, its marginality, even when faced with a war that threatens their way of life. Lois's comments on the topic show her exasperation: "'How is it that in this country that ought to be full of such violent realness, there seems nothing for me but clothes and what people say? I might just as well be in some kind of cocoon.'"[4]

The fact that Lois makes this comment to her English suitor Gerard, of course, suggests that this Anglo-Irish isolation is not absolute: indeed, much of the novel deals with their fraught relationship with the English, in whose name they rule and whose soldiers are currently present to defend them. However, the interaction between the two groups is far from simple. The fact that Lois's English suitor Gerald's last name is Lesworth is not unintentional: class warfare is alive and well in Bowen's novel, however muted and comically treated it may be, and the English are decidedly worth less in the Anglo-Irish mentality than those they are protecting. While the Anglo-Irish are distanced from the English by a feeling of superiority and snobbery, their separation from the Irish tenantry is total in the novel: Irish characters are mentioned but rarely appear, and all interaction between gentry and tenantry is limited to polite conversation. The rebels themselves are not so much a group of individuals as a sort of supernatural force, omnipresent, omniscient, and all-powerful. Thus when Lois encounters a rebel running through the forest at night, she first takes him for a ghost:

> First, she did not hear footsteps coming, and as she began to notice the displaced darkness thought what she dreaded was coming [...]— she was indeed clairvoyant, exposed to horror and going to see a ghost. [...] It must be because of Ireland he was in such a hurry [...] His intentions burnt on the dark an almost visible trail; he might well have been a murderer, he seemed so inspired.[5]

Indeed, the Irish of Bowen's novel are "part of the landscape," and while this dehumanizes them utterly, it also makes the country itself seem to be rising up against them: "The house seemed to be pressing low in apprehension, hiding its face [...]. It seemed to gather its trees close in fright and amazement at the wide, light, lovely unloving country, the unwilling bosom whereon it was set."[6]

Lois and her family find themselves isolated from the English and the Irish in both personal and political terms; indeed, it becomes clear that in this novel, the two are indissociable. In fact, the only emotional attachment Lois does seem able to form is to Marda, a visitor to Danielstown whose sophistication fascinates her. The ambiguity of this relationship has led many to speculate on the homosexual overtones of Bowen's work, but given the overall dynamic of the novel, it seems that it primarily implies an Anglo-Irish character and society that are turned in on themselves, who prefer the looking-glass that an older, more sophisticated version of oneself offers.

Meanwhile, Deborah Warner and John Banville's version of *The Last September* shows an Anglo-Irish society that is very much a part of the Irish community. Indeed, the first words of the film are not spoken by any of the Anglo-Irish main characters, but by the Irish servants, wanting to replace the requested sorrel soup with its County Cork equivalent, nettle soup, thus suggesting that the primacy of the English influence of the novel has been replaced with the frequently abrasive ingredients in Ireland's own melting pot. Indeed, throughout this adaptation of *The Last September*, an accent is placed on the presence of Irish servants within this supposed stronghold of the Protestant Ascendancy. The film version of *The Last September* has the Anglo-Irish characters repeatedly insisting that they, too, are Irish (to the confusion of the English characters with whom they interact), thus clearly implying that though the Anglo-Irish may maintain relations with the English for practical reasons (they are the means by which the Anglo-Irish maintain their power), their inclination is to side with the Irish.

The Irishness of the Anglo-Irish characters is in fact incarnated by the screenwriter's decision to transform formerly Anglo-Irish characters into Irish ones, cementing the closer relationship between the gentry and their tenantry: for example Lois's closest friend in the novel, Livvy Thompson, is transformed into Livvy Connelly, an Irishwoman whose brother, Peter (unrelated to her in the novel) is a known rebel. In so doing, Banville and Warner increase the proximity of both rebels and colonizers to the Anglo-Irish; thus the gap between the different communities that seems unbreachable in the novel becomes surmountable. Warner makes this desire to cross over from one community to the other obvious in her persistent use of doorways and thresholds to frame her shots, causing the viewer to "close the gap" between inside and out through the gaze.

The marginal nature of the Anglo-Irish is also decreased by the presence of war and of violence on the screen: because the reader of Bowen's novel is only told of attacks, the same way the Anglo-Irish characters themselves are, the characters' distance from the conflict is shared by the reader. In Warner's version of *The Last September* the subjective view of the war from a purely Anglo-Irish standpoint is replaced by a more objective view, where the audience sees episodes of both army brutality and IRA assassinations, and indeed where the protagonist is the cause and the witness to one of these assassinations. This is of course partly a projection of the camera's objective perspective as contrasted with the subjectivity of prose; however, it also transforms the Anglo-Irish from willfully ignorant bystanders to helpless observers, making the Anglo-Irish protagonist the heart of the battle for predominance in Ireland between the Irish and the British. Likewise, the conflict itself is transformed from a simple subject of conversation among others to a crucial element in Lois's love relationships — indeed, in the film, Lois's love relationship no longer symbolizes Anglo-Irish inability to engage, but rather the very nature of Ireland, caught between the English and the Irish.

Here, Gerald's suit fails because Lois prefers Peter Connelly, a rebel who in this version of the story is Livvy's brother, avidly pursued by the Black and Tans. (In the novel there is a minor character named Peter Connor, but he is married, relatively unknown, and quickly captured). The film's Peter Connelly is a childhood friend and lifelong love of Lois's, once again bringing the Anglo-Irish and the Irish closer together.

The mill scene, which is singular in the novel and multiple in the film, allows us to more closely examine the ramifications of the differences between the two *The Last September*s: when Lois, Marda and Hugo see the mill in Bowen's text, it is described in explicitly Gothic tones, as "the ghost of the Palace Hotel," and one of many that have "never quite stripped and whitened to skeletons' decency."[7] Fear is the immediate reaction, and Lois refuses to go inside until Marda pulls her in. The mill is given both political and sexual significance: Hugo bitterly remarks that it is the result of English law strangling commerce (a comment that goes unheard), and the mill contains an anonymous rebel, who holds the two women at gunpoint. The gun accidentally goes off, and Marda's hand is injured: when she puts it to her mouth the blood on her lips suggests perhaps the most famous of the Protestant Gothic inventions, Stoker's vampire, implying that it is in fact the guilty recognition of the Anglo-Irish having sucked their own country dry.[8] The sexual significance of the mill is perhaps equally obvious, since Lois's fear at entering is associated with the pleasure of Marda's arm around her waist. Once inside, the rebel's gun becomes a specifically phallic image, though it differs radically from the macho image usually given to guns: "Neither of them had seen a pistol at this angle; it was short-looking, scarcely more than a button."[9]

The Gothic aspect of the mill disappears in the film version of *The Last September*, as does the fear that accompanies it: not only is Lois not afraid of the mill, she used to play there as a child, and she enters alone to discover her childhood friend Peter. The haunting image of the corpse of Irish trade, the manifestation of Anglo-Irish sins, becomes the symbol of "simpler times" where Anglo-Irish and Irish played together in innocence (though this may not be as simple a relationship as it appears, since in Banville's script even as children, the Anglo-Irish Lois was the miller, and the Irish children were her helpers). The idea of the Irish countryside falling victim to English and Anglo-Irish misdoings is absent, and a power struggle between the Irish and the Anglo-Irish takes its place: in her relationship with Peter, Lois struggles to maintain power that Peter now wants for himself (memorably uttering the phrase, "I'll be the miller this time..."), and sex borders on rape. What is implied, however, is that harm only comes to the couple because of British interference: when Gerald learns that Peter is in the mill, he fears Lois has been taken hostage, and she begs Peter to shoot her to save her reputation (thus she has the bloodied hand, though the vampire image is absent). If their relationship must end, it is because the English are hot on his trail.

Thus the sexual politics of the novel, which are both ambiguous and divergent from more normative heterosexual desire, are simultaneously exacerbated and normalized in the film version of the story: Bowen's work, which is traditionally characterized as depicting "life with the lid on,"[10] becomes a literally bodice-ripping tale of star-crossed lovers (what one critic called "an Irish West Side Story")[11] where outsider Gerald interferes with the course of true (if difficult, or even violent) love. This normalization of the traditional male and female roles of the tale is all the more surprising in a film by Deborah Warner, as it is at odds with her custom of gender-bending: Warner has made a habit of casting Fiona Shaw in male roles in works like *Richard II* and Beckett's *Footfalls*: given that Shaw plays the role of Marda Norton, anyone familiar her work would have undoubtedly expected her to maintain or even heighten the ambiguous relationship between Lois and Marda. Likewise, incestuous relations are recurrent in Banville novels like *Birchwood*, his take on the genre of the Anglo-Irish Big House, something that is implicit in the original Lois/Marda relationship, and which is absent in the film. Ironically then, both screenwriter and director are much more conservative than they are in their other works.

These changes, in my view, diminish both the political and sexual implications of the original text: while at the end of Bowen's novel Lois leaves on her own, bypassing Marda and going on to her own endeavors, the film's Lois leaves with Marda on her honeymoon, fleeing from the failure of her two relationships with Gerald and Peter, but finding comfort in someone else's (loveless) marriage. Likewise, by making Gerald's rejection, and indeed his death, a simple matter of male rivalry, the larger political implications of his role are swept aside. As a characterization of the English, Gerald is no longer menacing in his very "niceness," his adherence to social norms; he is simply ineffectual. Thus Lois's love relations become the personification of the changing characterizations of the novel's different factions, and the widening of the subject matter from Anglo-Ireland to Ireland as a whole; the implications, however, are radically different from Bowen's own. Ironically enough, the absence of Gothic repression and the minimizing of Anglo-Irish guilt in general suggest a much more positive view of an Irish future, something perhaps most clearly symbolized by the change in the ending of the film. The novel ends with the "execution" of the Big House by rebels, and Lady Naylor and Sir Richard refusing to exchange glances, "for in the light from the sky they saw too distinctly,"[12] implying that though Lois has escaped, Anglo-Ireland will continue to refuse the truth of its situation. In the film, however, the house does not burn, and the final shot is of Lois's departure with Marda and her swing sitting empty, suggesting that what has been lost is essentially innocence, but that Anglo-Ireland itself (as symbolized by the house) will continue as long as its interaction with the outside world does: only the English influence has been banished.

Although some of these changes could be rationalized as simplifications in accordance with the more restrictive time and narrative frame allotted to feature-length films, I would argue that it also reflects the changing vision of Irish history where revisionist theories have become increasingly important. Revisionists seek to replace the "nationalist myths" of Ireland's independence with a more balanced vision of the fight for independence. In a sense, the movement from the marginality of the novel's action to the larger picture of war, and to the more balanced vision of both Anglo-Irish and Irish is not just a means of adapting the subjectivity typical of a modernist novel to the objectivity of film; it is also the transposition of a more radical view of history to a newer and more balanced approach. As an observer of the war and a member of the Protestant Ascendancy, Elizabeth Bowen could allow herself the biting criticism of the Anglo-Irish, whereas Banville and Warner's version of the story manifests a desire to attenuate this criticism (and therefore this isolation), emphasizing the shared Irishness of the Anglo-Irish with their tenantry. In so doing, I would argue that the changes made serve an explicitly modern political purpose, where "The Troubles" the film recounts refer indirectly to the more recent Troubles of Northern Ireland, and where this attenuated gap between two communities may be an effort to foster reconciliation.

A Question of Genre: Vision and Text in The Last September

Of course, the changes made to the plot of Bowen's novel encompass only part of the process entailed by film adaptation — the purely visual imagery is also crucial in any analysis of *The Last September*'s text and film forms. As was mentioned above, Bowen's texts are particularly rich in visual imagery, be it the long descriptive passages or the references to actual paintings:

> In the dining-room, the little party sat down under the crowd of portraits. Under that constant interchange from the high-up faces staring across [... the party] had a thin, over-bright look, seemed on the air of the room unconvincingly painted, startled, transitory. [...] each so enisled and distant that a remark made at random, falling short of a neighbour, seemed a cry of appeal, the six, in spite of an emphasis of speech and gesture they unconsciously heightened, dwin-

dled personally. While above, the immutable figures [...] made of the lower cheerfulness, dining and talking, the faintest exterior fiction.[13]

As is obvious from the above passage, visual references serve both a mimetic and an artistic purpose: though the family portraits serve to set the scene quite effectively, they are also a clear manifestation of the weight of tradition that keeps the Anglo-Irish from being "more convincingly painted," or rather causes them to "dwindle personally." However, this reference to the visual also calls into question the *textual* nature of the novel: in relation to the paintings, the characters become "the faintest exterior fiction"—a clear reference to their literary nature. Thus, by emphasizing the visual in her novels, Bowen is in fact calling attention to the aesthetics of her work, its very artistry, breaking down the suspension of disbelief and obliging the reader to engage with the novel as text.

Likewise, the reference to genre that I mentioned earlier, whether it be the Gothic, the Big House novel, or quite simply the love story, all seem to be deliberately evoked so as to be exploited and then subverted: thus the marginality of the Anglo-Irish characters serves a second, artistic function, showing the author skirting several more traditional narratives in order to both emphasize the limitations of these (and indeed all) narratives, and to demand that the reader (and her protagonist) create their own outside the framework of the novel. Therefore, given the implications of the visuality of Bowen's texts, Warner's own references to vision and film become particularly interesting.

Though the dinner scene from which the above passage is taken is filmed in an atrium, thus ridding us of the family portraits (though by filming the group from outside the atrium, the viewers gets some diminished sense of the Anglo-Irish characters as being "enisled"), other juxtapositions of painting and action make this idea of the weight of past traditions clear: thus the arrival of the Montmorencys during the opening credits is proceeded by a shot of a painting of a figure hunting on horseback (and significantly, it is here that Warner chose to place the reference to Bowen's book), while what was originally a carriage ride between Lois and Hugo is transformed into a similar scene on horseback, with the same colors, the same clothes, and the same action. Once again, the mimetic function is accompanied by a more artistic function, as the painting/action parallel, the idea of the characters mimicking fashions and actions of a past suggest a *mise en abyme* of the genre of period or costume drama within which the film itself is functioning. By volunteering this parallel between the painting of an earlier time and the film in which it appears, Warner too seeks to renew and subvert the genre.

The repeated use of a double exposure effect, showing both the painting and the reflection of the person looking at it, again suggests the power of tradition to influence behavior (it is because Lois is looking at her own reflection in a family portrait and playing her character of proper Anglo-Irish lady that she gives Gerald encouragement, calling him darling). Lois's departure from Danielstown with Marda is unattended by the other members of the household, but a parting shot of a family portrait seen from the window gives the impression that it is registering this escape, and suggests that Lois might be escaping from the heritage industry as well as her family traditions.

However, though Warner may be seeking to escape from the weight of tradition implicit in the period drama by making the artifice and artistry of the film manifest, she does not escape from another very traditional narrative: the romance. In an interview about the film, Warner herself confirmed this: *The Last September* is "a love story" (bringing us back to our *West Side Story* reference), something that Bowen's novel toys with only to ultimately reject. Given the very different nature of the two media and the very different economic circumstances in which they are situated, it is perhaps inevitable that a film should be obliged to conform to a marketable genre in a way that Bowen was able to avoid with her novel.

Though Banville and Warner are far from faithful to Bowen's novel, their choices are thought-provoking, and in many ways allow the viewer to better understand the political implications of the author's original plot. More importantly, like the use of double exposure discussed above, the film *The Last September* shows us a reflection of its filmmakers and of ourselves: in the desire for reconciliation that it manifests, in the desire to innovate the genre of period drama while maintaining a certain marketability. Warner's *The Last September* is a reflection of our times in the same way that Bowen's was a reflection of her own.

NOTES

1. *The Last September*, Deborah Warner, dir., John Banville, scr., Matrix Films, 1999. DVD bonus.

2. *Ibid.*

3. *Ibid.*

4. Elizabeth Bowen, *The Last September* (1929), London: Penguin, 1952, 49.

5. *Ibid.*, 33–34.

6. *Ibid.*, 66.

7. *Ibid.*, 122–123.

8. Julian Moynahan, *Anglo-Irish: The Literary Imagination in a Hyphenated Culture*, Princeton: Princeton University Press, 1995, 244.

9. Bowen, *The Last September*, 124.

10. Elizabeth Bowen, *English Novelists* (1942), London: Collins, 1947, 25.

11. "*The Last September*," *Scope* online journal, http://www.nottingham.ac.uk/film/scopearchive/filmrev/last-september.htm.

12. Bowen, *The Last September*, 206.
13. *Ibid.*, 24.

BIBLIOGRAPHY

Banville, John, *Birchwood* (1973). London: Picador, 1998.
Bowen, Elizabeth. *English Novelists* (1942). London: Collins, 1947.
_____. *The Last September* (1929). London: Penguin, 1952.
_____. *The Last September.* Deborah Warner, dir., John Banville, scr. Matrix Films, 1999.
_____. "*The Last September.*" *Scope* online journal, http://www.nottingham.ac.uk/film/scopearchive/filmrev/last-september.htm.
_____. *The Mulberry Tree: Writings of Elizabeth Bowen.* Hermione Lee, ed. San Diego: Harcourt Brace Jovanovich, 1986.
_____. *Seven Winters and Afterthought* (1950). New York, Alfred A. Knopf, 1962.
Moynahan, Julian. *Anglo-Irish: The Literary Imagination in a Hyphenated Culture.* Princeton, Princeton: University Press, 1995.

Jane Austen Goes to Bollywood ... with a Pinch of Salt

Florence Cabaret

This essay addresses the question of the moment when a novel is adapted to the screen and studies some of the ideological and aesthetic options such a transfer reveals. Jane Austen's *Pride and Prejudice* (1813) stands as a particularly relevant choice since it is a novel which already has a fairly long history of adaptations, starting with a first MGM version in 1940 by Robert Z. Leonard and ending (so far) with the latest 2005 adaptation by Joe Wright. What is more, over the past ten years, the theoretical and academic fervor triggered by the transposition of plays and novels on the silver screen has also consecrated "Jane Austen on screen" as a respectable niche for thorough researchers. As such, even the most "unfaithful" adaptations of Jane Austen appear as legitimate and fruitful objects of studies — which prompted me to choose Gurinder Chadha's *Bride and Prejudice* (2004), as it could firstly be characterized as a far from respectful adaptation of *Pride and Prejudice* or, as the postmodernist approach would have it, as an adaptation which is clearly on the side of appropriation and intervention. Therefore, bearing in mind that Gurinder Chadha shot this film after *Bend It Like Beckham* (2002), in which she reclaimed another icon of British culture, I would like to sustain the idea that *Bride and Prejudice* can be envisaged as a postcolonial "writing back"[1] to one of the most famous embodiments of the British cultural canon. Indeed, in her film, the British Indian-born director has kept the basic story line of the novel, which centers on the two elder Bennett sisters falling in love or in contempt, coping with social and personal obstacles before eventually getting married. But this story line has been inserted in a film which is also a musical and only lasts about one hour and a half, so that obviously Gurinder Chadha does not have much time for the transposition of Jane Austen's in-

140

depth psychological portrayal of her characters. This first departure from the novel is quite representative of the general displacement of a film which does not comply with the rules of the "period film" and transposes Austen's world into the beginning of the twenty-first century while setting the plot in three different countries and continents (India, Great Britain and the U.S.A.). Such a geographical de-territorialization deliberately twists Jane Austen's attachment for the local and may first appear to favor an unsettling global perspective for the unwinding of the characters' relations. I would like to explore this tension between the local and the global as we shift from novel to film thanks to three vantage points: 1) the implications of this change of location and scale as far as the political and historical agenda of the film is concerned, 2) the consequences for the treatment of the issue of marriage and of the relationships between men and women, 3) the film as a means not only to write back to Jane Austen's novel but also to other adaptations of *Pride and Prejudice*, to Indian cinema (and the contemporary Bollywood craze) as well as American cinema.

Deterritorializing Pride and Prejudice: *Some Ideological Implications*

The first obvious repercussion of the geographical and historical transfer of Austen's plot materializes in characterization. In the film, the characters' social status is constantly associated with national and ethnic belonging: by doing so, Chadha recycles one of Austen's central concerns (the importance of social positions) and adapts it to a group of contemporary upper-class protagonists straddling several continents and cultural codes. Mr. Darcy is now William Darcy, an American citizen and rich hotel owner; he is the best friend of Balraj Bingley, an Indian-born British citizen and lawyer. The two of them are invited to a wedding ceremony in India, where they meet the two Bakshi sisters, Jaya and Lalita, who are the daughters of a small landowner and respectively stand for Jane Bennett and Elizabeth Bennett. The Non-Resident Indian soon falls in love with Jaya while the American Darcy and the Indian Lalita launch into the well-known game orchestrated by their respective pride and prejudice about Indian backwardness and American contempt for others. Before acknowledging their love for each other, they get rid of two obstacles: Lalita rejects the proposal of the Indian accountant M. Kholi living in Los Angeles (who replaces the clergyman Mr. Collins) and Darcy literally knocks out his rival John Wickham, who is a British globe-trotter living in London's Little Venice. This reshuffling of social status combined with the characters' national origins stages the change of hands of wealth and world power since the turn of the eighteenth century. From novel to film, we shift from the implicit emerging of the British Empire in Austen's universe to the loss of such world supremacy. In Chadha's film, we see that world power has been transferred from Great Britain to the U.S.A., which has two major consequences for the grounding of the plot. The former Indian "jewel of the crown" has turned into an independent democracy and emerging country which has seductive and antagonistic relationships with both Great Britain and the U.S.A., like the characters in the film. Indian emigration has given birth to a varied Indian diaspora which is acquiring a significant position in the west — with upper-class groups progressively merging with their Western counterparts and having ambivalent relationships with their own native land. This set of data is also relevant when we come to reflect on the choice of the actress Aishwarya Ray to embody the equivalent of Elizabeth Bennett. She is an Indian actress whose very fair skin and very clear eyes fit beauty criteria that are particularly valued in India, but which may also hint at the possibility of inter racial unions. What is more, she has been renowned as the most beautiful woman not only in India but in the whole world since she won the Miss India and Miss World beauty pageants in 1994 and 1995 respectively. Since then, she has also become a global top-model who has been hired by L'Oréal, Coca Cola and De Beers as one of their representatives in advertisement campaigns. Thus the body of the actress and what she symbolizes ethnically and economically participate in this encounter between the global and the local that is at stake in the film. However, this constant play between the local and the global ironically echoes Jane Austen's attachment for the local and sometimes reproduces her opposition of countryside to town, as well as her characters' conversations about the advantages and drawbacks of geographical proximity or distance.[2] As such not only do the changes in the characters' identities testify to the ideological shift from novel to film, but the way places, distances and closeness are discussed and shown on the screen contributes to the reappraisal of this Austenian issue.

In spite of the seemingly global mobility of the film protagonists, some of them assert their strong attachment for the place where they were born and point to their own desire for roots in a world of constant migrancy. Unlike his wife, Lalita's father expresses his wish to see his daughters married with an Indian resident so that they will not be living too far from him. As for the non-resident Indian Mr. Kholi, he bluntly admits that he comes back home to find himself a local wife, by which he means a good and devoted Indian woman and not a woman obsessed with her job or a woman turned lesbian such as he may come across in the U.S.A. Darcy himself declares that he

would like to live in the same house as his wife and not in two separate countries like his parents. But more centrally, the choice of Amritsar — a rural town
in the upper north of India — for the location of the Bakshi house also epit-
omizes this tension between the local and global. From the outset of the film,
Amritsar is introduced through an alternation of synecdochic views framing
either a local or a more global approach of space. The first shot reveals the
Golden Temple, which is a symbol of Amritsar for its inhabitants, but also
for Indian people and tourists; then we are alternately shown scenes of the
lush fields of the rural surrounding area, where Mr. Bakshi and Lalita supervise
the work of their employees, and scenes of Amritsar's international airport,
where Balraj Bingley, his sister Kiran and Darcy are seen as they leave the
plane. Then we follow them as they reach the streets of Amritsar (through a
series of high angles shots of the populous streets and close ups on the face
of Darcy to expose the reaction of the westerner discovering this Indian town)
and, as the title of the film appears on the screen, the façade of the Bakshi
family's nineteenth-century western-style house is revealed to us. In terms of
history, Amritsar is also strongly evocative of key moments in the national
and international history of India. It calls to mind India's connections with
the British Empire (with the notorious 1919 Amritsar massacre), India's independence and the simultaneous partition of India and Pakistan (as in 1947
many communal riots took place in Amritasr given the town's proximity with
the new border), as well as the history of independent India (with Indira
Gandhi's Operation Bluestar in 1984 and the massacre of Sikh separatists who
had taken refuge in the Golden Temple). The last massacre is often regarded
as the embodiment of a national state policy of defense of national unity and
territorial integrity so as to fight what the Indian government calls religious
fundamentalism, a policy which is itself reminiscent of another "war on ter-
rorism" launched in 2001 from the U.S.A. Thus, even though the Temple
appears untouched in the film, such a choice hints at a less glossed-over version
of the place, but also at common interests shared by local and global politics.
The fact that the region of Punjab, where Amritsar is located, is frequently
used by Indian filmmakers as the setting of their films also reinforces the idea
that this film puts the question of Indian people's attachment to their moth-
erland. As Jigna Desai explains, the choice of Punjab may be linked to the
significance and wealth of the Punjabi diaspora, but it also shows that "Punjab
functions in the Indian imaginary as the site where cultural values have been
maintained, where Indianness has been preserved unsullied."[3] So Punjab, like
the Southern English country side of Jane Austen may also be described as a
receptacle and preserver of age-old traditions in a time of change.[4] And in
Jane Austen's novel, as well as in Gurinder Chadha's film, marriage stands as

a choice symbol of traditions and human connections. As such, when Chadha sets all Jane Austen's ball scenes within the context of several wedding ceremonies, she underscores our perception of marriage as an anthropological motif which itself reveals a cross-cultural "anthropological desire for knowledge and intimacy with the other."[5]

The Universally Acknowledged Truth of Arranged Marriages

As an "elementary structure of kinship," marriage serves as a bridge between Jane Austen's world and Gurinder Chadha's world, between the eighteenth and nineteenth centuries, between Great Britain, India and the U.S.A. In the film, the frequent recurrence of marriage as a linguistic and iconic topic operates on two levels. It satisfies a certain Western "nostalgia for family and kinship intimacy" supposedly shrined in Jane Austen's universe by "seeing the possibilities contained in other cultures."[6] Simultaneously, the motif of the wedding also functions as a form of reassurance for diasporic groups thanks to the fictionalized "'maintaining' of traditional familial structures and practices in spite of displacement."[7] Thus, in several scenes, the film playfully associates the national and cultural variations of such a fundamental pattern of connections: with the indoors ceremonies of a Sikh marriage in Amritsar at the beginning, with the dream sequence of Lalita's European wedding in a Swiss landscape, with an Indian marriage in the U.S., with the closing of the film on the outdoor festivities celebrating the two sisters' marriages in Amritsar, one of them being an inter-racial marriage. What is more, all these wedding ceremonies entail an impressive display of wealth and consumption, offering us a visual feast of a thriving India and prosperous America — from the accumulation of flowers, food, silk saris and colorful costumes animated by group songs and dances to the luxury of Mr. Kholi's recently-built new American house as well as of the Beverly Hills hotel where his marriage is to take place. So if both in the novel and the film marriage is used as a way to epitomize family ties and cultural stability, it also stages bourgeois-turning-liberal conceptions of marriage, and shares the same strategy of capital transmission.[8]

That is the reason why we can say that in Chadha's film, arranged marriages are not exactly depicted as an old-fashioned Indian specificity but rather as a "universally acknowledged truth," i.e., as a practice which is quite suited to contemporary busy South Asian migrants looking for a "traditional Indian wife" like the first groom or like Mr. Kholi, but also quite suited to workoholic rich westerners like Darcy. By ironically rewriting Jane Austen's own ironically phrased universal truth in the opening sentence of the novel, Chadha contests the cliché representation of India's backwardness by providing common spaces of identification for the dominant "modern" culture.[9] Visually speaking, the arranged marriage is no longer a locus of difference between Amritsar, London and Los Angeles, as illustrated by the similar tourist-like approach of each town and the smooth blending of one wedding into another. From India to the U.S.A. people appear to be sharing similar behavior. For instance, Lalita's Indian mother is shown as being as manipulative as Darcy's American mother when it comes to trapping or warding off somebody for their children. And if the brides' and grooms' social backgrounds are part of the issue of the acceptability of this or that union, the film never refers to other prevailing obstacles in India such as the caste system or the necessity of dowries, which are regarded as signs of India's backwardness when compared to what is depicted as the liberal turn of contemporary unions in the Western world.

Still, if the question of arranged marriages provides a bridge between novel and film, Chadha clearly states that it is no longer a means of material survival for the woman and her family, or a way of conforming to the moral rules of a certain kind of society. The arranged marriage has turned into a means of social promotion for the Indian bride and family in the sense that it is a means of living abroad and getting more opportunities in the West. If the film does not make a big show of working women, from the first shots we are given to understand that Lalita works on the farm of her father as she is seen supervising field work and checking her father's book accounts. Such a shift in perspective overlooks the more repressive environment of the novel and the depiction of women's positions in a patriarchal society. However, the predicament of many women in contemporary India as regards baby boy preference and marriage is alluded to by the father in an apparently off-hand remark, when he replies to his wife that if it is so difficult to get four daughters married, they should have drowned two of them when they were born. By having Mr. Bakshi poke fun at his wife, in a manner which is reminiscent of Mr. Bennett's teasing mind when he comments on his wife's quest for suitable matches for their daughters, the film and the novel point to the evolution of the status of women in some countries and social classes, though not in the same proportions. Like other South Asian diasporic women film directors, Chadha can be said to be "writing against narratives of victimhood" with a film staging "a narrative of [female] agency to multiple audiences simultaneously."[10] Somehow the film also echoes contemporary readings (and filings) of Jane Austen as a proto-feminist, with Elizabeth Bennett as the arch heroine starting to rebel against the fate imposed on women at the end of the eighteenth century. Indeed, the film may well reproduce the idea that marriage is a necessary condition for the upper middle-class Indian girl to leave her family and live abroad, but several hints indicate the possibility of further changes: first when Lalita chaperones her sister Jaya but is obviously not shocked to see her swimming in Balraj's arms, and also when a lascivious song and dance by R&B singer Ashanti obviously paves the way for the lovers' night. The character of Kiran, Balraj Bingley's sister, is also quite representative of the contemporary possibility for Indian diasporic women to live abroad and remain single without her parents pressing her to marry and have children (whereas her brother appears to be the object of such demands). Finally, one of the first conversations between Lalita and her best friend Chambra Lamba[11] provides the opportunity of a telling joke about the prospect of Lalita getting married to Darcy and then getting a divorce so that Lalita and Chandra can share the money between the two of them. The humorous tone and concluding laughter lightly discards the possibility of unscrupulous women manipulating men for financial purposes before legally getting rid of them; it also discards the possibility of a homosexual relationship between the two friends.

This daring and plotting potential of women is also exemplified in the conversations between Darcy and Lalita, which are much shorter and blunter than in the novel, and reveal a new treatment of the character of Darcy. Indeed, Chadha's film appears to desecrate the role of a protagonist who has long been perceived as the embodiment of the English male hero, of the English upper-class and imperial pride. Even though recent adaptations reflect in their own ways a more sensitive conception of the character, Chadha goes much farther in her undermining of Darcy, especially when she frames him between two bawdy allusions during the first wedding scene. Indeed, one of his first cues reveals his fear of being sick if he eats Indian food. And a few moments later, when he first tries to dance with Lalita, he is seen constantly losing the Indian trousers he did not manage to tie properly, so that he is forced to leave Lalita abruptly and without a word of explanation while he is laughed at by Balraj, Kiran and another Indian guest. Actually, as soon as he disembarks at the airport, he is shown as disoriented, absolutely clueless and regularly torn between opposite impulses. He is in constant need of explanations, either from Balraj (who explains to him the dance and game opposing the group of young men to that of the young women during the wedding festivities) or from Kiran (who translates the words of their songs for him). One of the final scenes completes the debunking process when he appears in the middle of a group of Indian drummers, caricaturally and ridiculously reconciled with the Indian dances and songs that he found so grotesque when he first discussed them with Lalita. The choice of Martin Henderson to play the role has also been the butt of many criticisms as he was reproached with being nothing more than a pretty face and unsubstantial actor who, contrary to Colin Firth in the 1995 BBC version, did not emerge as a revelation in this film. But quite interestingly, the "revelation" of the film may be that Darcy is no longer the male figure characters and viewers should be attracted to. As Mrs. Bakshi and Mrs. Lamba remark on first seeing him and discussing his fortune: "Too bad he is not an Indian!" The character of Balraj, though less present on the screen, may stand as a serious foil in this adaptation as he is depicted as more subtle and daring when, for instance, he launches into a dance in which he leads the group of dancers to seduce Jaya, or when he unmasks Darcy's ambivalent attitude towards Lalita — so that he appears less subdued and submitted to his friend than in the novel. What is more, the role is played by British Indian actor Naveen Andrews, who is famous for several other parts he played in the adaptation of Michael Ondatjee's *English Patient* (by Anthony Minghella, 1996),[12] but also in *Kama Sutra* (by Mira Nair, 1996),[13] and who may have benefited from the reputation of sensuality and eroticism associated with these two films. As for the character of Mr. Kholi played by Nitin Chandra Ganatra, however comical and ridiculous he may appear, he is obviously made to steal the show from Darcy with, among other examples, his motto "No life without wife" which is turned into a mock musical number performed by the four Bakshi sisters. Even though Chadha's portrayal is fairly biting, the actor's performance propels Mr. Kholi to the fore by associating him with the most hilarious and memorable moments of the film (from his arrival at the Bakshi house, to the dinner where he espouses his philosophy, to his dancing at the wedding, not to mention his proposal to Lalita). This implicit favoring of roles which were originally conceived as secondary roles by Jane Austen may be a way for Gurinder Chadha to ironically promote Indian actors[14] by conjuring up associations with other renowned films or by having them walk on western grounds. The social greediness of the Indian-born accountant is thus metaphorized in the vision of a Mr. Kholi roaring like an MGM lion in Kholywood, hinting at Chadha's own playful absorption of other film codes and symbols, whether they originate in Hollywood or Bollywood.

"Writing Back" to Other Jane Austen Adaptations and Film Traditions

Film intertextuality and celebration of other film traditions could also account for Chadha's choice of marriage as the focal point of her film. Indeed, if marriage is one of the backbones of Jane Austen's novel, it is also a *motif* which is quite typical of Indian popular movies as recently illustrated by the craze of the so-called "Bollywood" films. The pun on the title, *Bride and Prejudice*, is an invitation both to a humorous rewriting of *Pride and Prejudice*, as well as to a de-centering of the focus on marriage as seen from the female/bride perspective, from the B of Bollywood[15] and maybe as well from B series films. So that Gurinder Chadha not only writes back to Jane Austen but also to Jane Austen as interpreted by other film directors before her and also to Indian and American cinema. For instance, the emphasis laid by Chadha on arranged marriages may function as an echo of the adaptation of *Emma* by Douglas MacGrath (1996), in which the protagonist is essentially presented as an unfelicitous matchmaker. One may also think of the adaptation of *Mansfield Park* by Patricia Rozema (1999), whose postcolonial approach explicitly re-inscribes Jane Austen's characters within the context of the rise of the British Empire. As for adaptations choosing to locate Jane Austen in a contemporary context, the trail has already been blazed by Amy Heckerling when she transposed Emma in twentieth-century U.S.A. with her *Clueless* (1995). But more pointedly, one may think of the way the male and female gaze have been shot and staged in the 1995 BBC adaptation of *Pride and Prejudice*, especially during the ball scenes. Many scenes in Andrew Davies's version show Darcy oscillating from controlling gazer to fascinated onlooker while in Chadha's version, Darcy is characterized by a puzzled and dominated, mesmerized gaze (cf. the scenes where Lalita, Jaya and Chandra are in the upper galleries, relishing the view downstairs while Darcy is shown looking up and averting his glances), which is another way of weakening his position from the start. In Chadha's film, Darcy is also compelled to witness the first encounter between Lalita and Wickham on the Goa beach, which is an obvious departure from Jane Austen's novel and the 1995 BBC adaptation, so that he is turned into a powerless and moody *voyeur* as Wickham walks out of the sea. And it is tempting to interpret this scene as a cheeky variation of Darcy's dive into the small lake nearby Pemberley, which brought many spectators of the BBC adaptation to surmise about more intimate scenes between the hero and heroine.

Surprisingly enough, Chadha's use of the codes of Indian cinema provides a relevant staging of Austenian chastity and modesty, which is partly faithfully transposed here, following Indian film conventions ruled by Indian censorship which imposes that no kiss and no sex scene should be seen on the screen. Yet, bodies are obviously set into relief during the lively dance scenes which are choreographed either as a form of challenge (first wedding dance), or as a sensual mode of seduction (Goa beach scene), or as a clumsy/harmonious physical cooperation between men and women (second wedding dance). Similarly, the film plays with the ways Indian filmmakers bypass censorship with explicit wet-sari scenes when in the final film credits, Gurinder Chadha is seen re-enacting Darcy and Lalita's fountain scene as she dances with her screenplay writer, Paul Mayeda Berges, who "savagely" kisses her at the end of this humorous sequence.[16] I may also refer to another fantasized scene unveiling Lalita's dream of her European wedding, when the heroine sees herself powerless in the arms of Darcy about to kiss her behind a curtain of pouring rain. What is more, this scene which is situated in the Swiss Alps is a clear reference to this choice of location by Indian film makers as a substitute for the Himalaya or Kashmir landscapes which would blow up their budget or which would be too dangerous because of political unrest in Kashmir. Lastly, an Indian film is literally used as backdrop for the final confontation between Darcy and Wickam as it takes place in a London cinema showing a Bollywood film and a fight between a villain about to rape a screaming woman just before the good guy arrives and knocks him off—a scene which is reduplicated by Darcy as he hits his rival/the seducer of Lakhi (Lalita's young sister). But once again, the game of references combine two sets of cultural codes as this kind of *mise en abyme* device is also quite typical of famous fight scenes in American and English movies.[17] Thus, several associations come to mind: western films with the views of the Grand Canyon where Darcy takes Lalita for a helicopter ride, musicals (with the song of the four sisters, the restaurant scene with the Mexicans, the dancing scene between fountains, the beach scene with the gospel choir), but also American serials such as *Bay Watch* with the two Californian surfers used in ludicrous backing vocals, not to mention music videos with the Goa beach scene.

However far we seem to have moved from Jane Austen's text, Gurinder Chadha's *Bride and Prejudice* is a good example of what a contemporary film adaptation of a literary work of art may be about. It does not necessarily stand in a position of reverence to the original text and therefore may result in the playful blending of the canonical source with unexpected references to an apparently alien geographical and historical context, with expected references to the world of films and with the more or less conscious interferences of the way the novel has been variously interpreted by recent literary trends (feminist studies, new historicist studies, postcolonial studies in the case of Jane Austen). The result testifies to a number of evolutions, from the general to the specific: the growing importance and attraction embodied by the world of film when compared to the world of literature; the cohabitation of so-called low culture and high culture (so that Elizabeth Bennett no longer plays the piano in a British mansion and has become Lalita playing the guitar on the Goa beach); the geopolitical shift from Great Britain to the U.S.A. with India reshuffling the cards of the world power game, which is necessarily reproduced in the cinematographic area where financial interests are more and more significant; the evolution of the way some Indian diasporic artists relate to the British canon as they reshape it less in a polemic way (writing/striking back) than in a more celebrating appropriation, which may nonetheless be interpreted as a strong political and artistic statement. But in the end, Chadha's film inevitably leads us back to the novel and to the spotting of both famous and apparently more marginal passages, three of which may be read back as ironical commentaries on Chada's film:

> It is a truth universally acknowledged, that a single man in possession of a good fortune, must be in want of a wife.[18]

> "It must be very agreeable to her to be settled within so easy a distance of her own family and friends."
> "An easy distance you call it? It is nearly fifty miles."
> "And what is fifty miles of good road? Little more than half a day's journey. Yes, I call it a very easy distance."[19]

> "What a charming amusement for young people this is, Mr. Darcy!—There is nothing like dancing after all.—I consider it as one of the first refinements of polished societies."
> "Certainly, Sir;—and it has the advantage also of being in vogue amongst the less polished societies of the world.—Every savage can dance."[20]

NOTES

1. A phrase coined by Salman Rushdie after the title of the famous Star Wars saga, *The Empire Strikes Back*.

2. One may think of the conversation between Mr. Darcy and Elizabeth Bennett.

3. Jigna Desai, *Beyond Bollywood: The Cultural Politics of South Asian Diasporic Films*, London: Routledge, 2004, 221.

4. Netherfield, the place leased by the Bingleys as their country residence in Austen's novel, is replaced by a location in Goa (a place which is famous for Europeans' encounter with Indian exoticism since the 1970s in particular) and, more precisely, by a gated luxury hotel which Darcy would like to buy. This transposition raises the issue of land owning, with the consequence that some places are lost to their local inhabitants. By connecting it with the issue of tourism, the film rejuvenate Austen's study of financial domination through property and land acquisitions.

5. Desai, *Beyond Bollywood*, 222.

6. *Ibid.*, 229.

7. *Ibid.*, 221.

8. *Ibid.*, 229.

9. *Ibid.*, 222.

10. *Ibid.*, 212.

11. She plays the equivalent of Charlotte Lucas, Elizabeth's confidante who will marry Mr. Collins, just as Chambra accepts Mr. Kholi's proposal.

12. Also starring Juliette Binoche, Ralph Fiennes, Kristin Scott Thomas ... and Colin Firth.

13. Along with Indira Varma, who played his lover in Mira Nair's film and who is his sister in *Bride and Prejudice*.

14. It might also be a way for her to indirectly comment upon the position of the U.S.A. in "the East"—trying to have the lead role but in constant need of go-betweens and sometimes ending up superseded by them.

15. A word which is itself coined after the two great film industries in the world today, i.e., those of Bombay/Mumbay and Hollywood.

16. I would like to thank Ariane Hudelet for drawing my attention to this interesting detail.

17. One may think of Terry Gilliam's *Twelve Monkeys* (1995) or of Wes Craven's *Scream 2* (1997).

18. Jane Austen, *The Annotated Pride and Prejudice* (1813), David M. Shapard, ed., New York: Anchor, 2004, 2.

19. *Ibid.*, 328.

20. *Ibid.*, 44.

BIBLIOGRAPHY

Austen, Jane. *The Annotated Pride and Prejudice*. David M. Shapard, ed. New York: Anchor, 2004.

Bride and Prejudice. Gurinder Chadha, dir., Paul Mayeda Berges, Gurinder Chadha, scrs. Pathé Pictures International, 2004.

Clark, Robert, ed. *New Casebooks:* Sense and Sensibility *and* Pride and Prejudice. *Contemporary Critical Essays*. London: St. Martin's Press, 1994.

Clueless. Amy Heckerling, dir., scr. Paramount Pictures, 1995.

Desai, Jigna. *Beyond Bollywood: The Cultural Politics of South Asian Diasporic Films*. London: Routledge, 2004.

The English Patient. Anthony Minghella, dir., scr. Miramax Films, 1996.

Gard, Roger. *Jane Austen's Novels: The Art of Clarity*. New Haven: Yale University Press, 1992.

Kama Sutra. Mira Nair, dir., Helena Kriel, and Mira Nair, scrs. Channel Four Films, 1996.

Macdonald, Gina, and Andrew F. Macdonald, eds. *Jane Austen on Screen*. Cambridge: Cambridge University Press, 2003.

Mansfield Park. Patricia Rozema, dir., scr. Arts Council of England, 1999.

Monaghan, David, ed. *New Casebooks:* Emma, *Contemporary Critical Essays*. Basingstoke: Macmillan, 1992.

Monaghan, David, Ariane Hudelet, and John Wiltshire. *The Cinematic Jane Austen: Essays on the Film Sensibilities of the Novels*. Jefferson, NC: McFarland, 2009.

Parrill, Sue. *Jane Austen on Film and Television: A Critical Study of the Adaptations*. Jefferson, NC: McFarland, 2002.

Pendakur, Manhunath. *Indian Popular Cinema: Industry, Ideology and Consciousness*. Cresskill, NJ: Hampton Press, 2003.

Pride and Prejudice. Simon Langton, dir., Andrew Davies, scr. British Broadcasting Corporation, 1995.

Pride and Prejudice. Robert Z. Leonard, dir., Aldous Huxley, Jane Murfin, scr. Metro-Goldwyn-Mayer, 1940.

Pride and Prejudice. Joe Wright, dir., Deborah Moggach, scr. Focus Features, 2005.

Sutherland, Kathryn. *Jane Austen's Textual Lives: From Aeschylus to Bollywood*. Oxford: Oxford University Press, 2005.

Troost, Linda, and Sayre Greenfield, eds. *Jane Austen in Hollywood*. Lexington: University Press of Kentucky, 2001.

Vasuvedan, Ravi S., ed. *Making Meaning in Indian Cinema*, 5th ed. New Delhi: Oxford University Press, 2005.

Surface and Depth in *Korea*

Nicole Cloarec

As Brian McFarlane recalls in the introduction of his study,[1] cinema has always turned to literature as an endless source of storylines.[2] As the vast majority of filmic adaptations consists of adaptations of novels, it comes as no surprise that a great number of criticisms towards adaptations focus on their necessary selections of narrative events and elements. In this context, adaptations of short texts are often praised for being particularly "faithful" to the original,[3] notwithstanding the problematic nature of this critical judgment. John Huston's *The Dead* is but one example: rather than the various alterations — however slight they may be — what we keep in mind is the successful rendering of the atmosphere created by the text. More recently Ang Lee's adaptation of Annie Proulx's *Brokeback Mountain*[4] is surprisingly long (more than 2 hours) for about 50 pages of large-fonted text, adding to the storyline a number of *Americana* scenes. As far as alterations are concerned, it seems that additions are more easily accepted than subtractions, as if omissions were more visible than additions which are more likely to blend into the whole.

However, Brian McFarlane makes an interesting distinction between different types of short texts: "Perhaps the novella, too short to demand of the film-maker the drastic excisions invariably required by the film version of a full-length novel and too long to need the invention of new episodes which the transposition of a short story into a full-length film is likely to require, is the most congenial fictional form for the 'faithful' adaptor."[5]

I will not discuss here the moot point of where a short story ends and where a novella begins,[6] nor where the latter ends and becomes a novel. In the case I have chosen to study, there is no possible doubt: John McGahern's short story *Korea*[7] is remarkably short (5 pages in the 1992 collection). Its filmic adaptation is also quite short as regards commercial standards; nonetheless it was produced and distributed as a feature film.

McGahern's short story offers an exemplary case of narrative economy, combining minute descriptions of the surface of things and events[8] with an oblique rendering of the characters' inner drama. In one review of the film, published in *The Scotsman,* the journalist wittily states that the film is "so beautifully adapted that every comma breathes"[9] — I'm not sure I know how to recognize breathing commas but what is certainly true is that the silences of the short story have been invested by the film. Black's *Korea* presents the rather unusual case of a filmic adaptation where the entire process of adaptation consists in expanding the original highly-condensed narrative, in unfolding its every sentence as it were. This development reveals, to the utmost degree, that the essence of filmic adaptation is not based on texts which are to be transposed on screen but on specific readings of these texts. This is all the more true as McGahern's story not only ends with an absence of closure but, more importantly, with an ambiguous simile which forces the reader to make his own personal interpretation.

In this article I would like to show in what ways McGahern's short story remains present in the film *Korea* and is not reduced to a mere "storyline." It seems to me that the answer can be developed into three main lines of arguments. First, the film takes up the challenge to convey the specific dichotomy between the smooth surface of the narrative — as smooth as the surface of the lake in the film — and the depth of inner dramas that come back obliquely to the characters' conscience, be it the past of a family drama or of the nation's traumatic history. Moreover, if it is true that a short story is written from its ending,[10] then the film manages to convey this specificity by choosing to offer a visual interpretation of the ambiguous simile ending the short story while preserving the full force of its impact. Third and last, I will investigate the choice of McGahern's short story from an intertextual perspective. As Christopher Orr remarks about the notion of intertextuality: "Within this critical context, the issue is not whether the adapted film is faithful to its source but rather how the choice of a specific source and how the approach to that source serve the film's ideology."[11]

As its title does not clearly indicate, the short story *Korea* is set in Ireland in the early 1950s. Its main protagonist — and narrator — is a young man who, while fishing with his father for a living, asks him about his past experience during the War of Independence. The narrative, which is set in the past, starts *in medias res* with the son's question. His father's story is then told in two moments: first in an indirect mode, focusing on the traumatic memory of the execution of a young boy he witnessed when he was a prisoner in 1919, then in the direct narration of a second memory which comes both as a contrast and an echo to the first: some years later, as he was on his honeymoon at the seaside, the image of furze pods bursting into the air conjured up the image of the execution of the young boy when he tore open his tunic and made its buttons fly into the air. The second part of the story deals with the son's sudden awareness as he unwittingly overhears a conversation between his father and a neighbor about the reputedly substantial amount of compensation a man called Moran received from the U.S. army after his son has been killed in action in the Korean war. He then understands why his father has been suggesting to him to go to America "the land of opportunity" where there is room for ambition unlike "in this poky place" where "all there's room for is to make holes in pints of porter."

Because McGahern's characterization remains sketchy (there are no names, no physical descriptions), the film does not run the risk of betraying the characters' physiques. What prevails is the son's inner thoughts about his father whose past he tries to understand as much as to escape. As far as emotions are concerned, McGahern uses great stylistic restraint, thus creating the impression that much is left unsaid. Cathal Black explained in an interview that the only direction he gave to the actors was to play "down," to be more suggestive than expressive, to keep a lid on emotions.[12] In the film, the main focus is still on the relationship between father and son, and although the film, like many adaptations, shows the propensity to expand and add dialogues, the whole *mise en scène* stresses what remains implicit in this relationship. Unsurprisingly, the tension-fraught dialogues are classically filmed in shots-counter shots, but the camera often links the two characters in silence by panning from one to the other. Very often, when one is seen in the foreground, the other appears in the background in an over-the-shoulder shot and the repeated changes of focus from father to son show they constantly feel each other's presence even when they do not talk or refuse to talk. When the characters do not resort to small talk and ready-made sentences, they are often shown talking while turning their backs or avoiding each other's eyes. This is the case when the father relates his traumatic past to Eamon, looking out sideways through the window (:35) or when he first suggests that Eamon should go to America (:43). This posture is not restricted to the father-son relationship but characterizes almost all important relationships in the film, like the first meeting between Eamon and Una or the first dialogue between John Doyle and his long-standing enemy Ben Moran. Filming the characters' backs not only stresses their difficulty to communicate but it also highlights their reluctance to express or to show their feelings. Last but not least, it creates an off-screen space inside the frame, leaving much suggestion for the viewer.

The film resorts to the traditional device of the voice over to convey the first person narrative. Even though there is no point in looking for any strict equivalent between narrative and filmic enunciation, what is striking in the film is that the son is nearly always in a position of observation. Hence the importance of looks in shot-counter-shot scenes and suggesting point-of-view shots. Eamon is repeatedly shown looking at his father's photograph, or watching his father through the pub window; he is filmed standing in the background witnessing his father's departure after he has received the letter announcing that his fishing license will be taken away (:33); and when he overhears his father's conversation with a neighbor about the much–discussed financial compensation for Luke Moran's death, his vision is filtered through the lavatory door that is slightly ajar. What is more, Eamon has a female double in the character of Una who stands witness to the two fathers' fraught relationship, and most importantly, to the relationship between father and son, up to its climactic dénouement.

If the recourse to a voice over is a classical device in films to make up for what cinema cannot show, namely a character's inner voice and thoughts, it has the advantage from a narrative point of view of establishing a double temporality, superimposing the present of past events and the present from which the events are recollected and reconsidered. Eamon's voice over intervenes four times in *Korea*. The first two are additions that develop background information about the father's past during the Irish civil war, where the son acts as a spokesman for the past generation. The other two are quotes from the text focusing on the son's ambivalent feelings towards his father. What is interesting to note is that these passages form a circular pattern, opening and closing the film, which is quite conventional, but most specifically, framing the father's narration of his traumatic past that constitutes the core of the story and occurs right in the middle of the film. The past is literally embedded in the present and in the son's consciousness. The film highlights the pervasive presence of the past that lies underneath the smooth surface of everyday life, contrasting the peacefulness of the lake and the struggle of the trapped eels filmed underwater. Contrary to the short story, the traumatic memory itself, of the execution of the young boy that the father witnessed in prison, is presented in three incomplete segments scattered throughout the film, as if the memory was too painful to be grasped as a whole. The first flashback occurs while the father is nodding off, after a close-up on his picture in uniform followed by a tilt-up on the gun hanging on the wall nearby (:14). The scene stresses the involuntary memory process through the superimposition of two conflicting memories that contrast each other and yet echo each other. Brief shots of a prison corridor and a prison yard alternate with longer shots of yellow furze by the sea, and the two series of shots are linked further by the same musical leitmotiv, played softly on a violin for one, with additional drums and distortions for the other. However, the flashback ends before the execution and the shooting sound overlaps into the present of the father awakening. The execution proper will be visualized only at the near end of the film in a second flashback (:58) while the father is sleeping on the jetty. In between (:35), the whole story is told by the father who is filmed in a middle shot looking sideways out through the window, except for a very brief shot of the prison bars and another of the blooming yellow furze, ensuring a visual connection with the first flashback.

As in most of McGahern's writings, History weighs on the present through an enclosing frame of recurrences, people being entrapped in the thralls of a repetitive temporality like the recurring shots of the eels contorted in the wire cage. The whole film is indeed structured through circular patterns, with the closing scene echoing the opening scene, both set in the same place, showing the same people performing the same activity. What is more, a number of sequences are also structured in a circular pattern, the neat symmetrical organization of shots creating a sort of independent entity detached from the overall temporality of the film.[13] As in the short story, temporal landmarks are unobtrusive in the film. And although the short story's diegetic time lasts less than 24 hours, the narrative is dotted with minute descriptions of daily activities related to fishing and gardening which the film expands into repetitive activities over a number of days without providing any specific temporal landmarks. Significantly enough, the main part of the film is shot in the cold blue light of early morning and late evening; day-time scenes are filmed in a much changing weather, creating discontinuity from one scene to the next or even within the same scene, which makes it difficult for the viewer to tell whether the events occur on the same day or not.

This is all the more true as the film is punctuated with ellipses through the use of black screens, of bright flashes that are associated with memories, dreams and mental images,[14] and surprising cuts. After the father's narration of the scene which has been haunting him, the son inquires further into the execution "It's a wonder their hands weren't tied" (:40) but although the dialogue appears in continuity, the characters who were at home are now on the lake. Similarly, after the radio has announced the death of an Irish soldier in Korea, the official announcement of Luke Moran's demise occurs off screen while we are shown a brief shot of the exterior of the Morans' house followed by a short shot of the eels underwater. A last example (:15) is offered when Eamon, helping his father gardening, is filmed in a close up looking off screen as we can hear the sounds of a cortege of mourners, but there is no countershot. The next shot is taken from the coffin's perspective inside the hearse.[15]

In both the story and the film, the present is somehow engulfed by both the repetitive time of daily work and the recurring past of traumatic events.[16] In addition to inserts of photographs which punctuate the film, the radio plays a prominent part in conveying the intrusive presence of an absence, be it in time or space. The radio is indeed strongly associated to Eamon's late mother who received it as a wedding present and spent most of her free time listening to it. The radio coalesces the mother's past dream of going to America and the contemporary news about the ongoing war in Korea, as well as the father's attachment to the past (the radio set works on batteries) in opposition to the advancing modernity represented by the electrification of the village.

While in the short story the name of the country Korea is mentioned only once apart from the title, the ongoing war is much more present in the film. The story of Luke Moran is thus integrated in the diegetic present and his funeral is developed into a whole scene, with a striking procession on the lake rowing to the graveyard located on an island. Cathal Black explained in an interview that "the burial on the lake was the main image that attracted me to the story. It contained the most powerful symbol that the society cherished, emigration and the attraction of foreign places and the wealth supposedly available there. Essentially, I suppose it was a story about a society that is feeding on itself, slowly eating itself up."[17] As Luke Moran's death is indirectly announced on the radio, the overlapping sound of the news links the two families in a crosscutting, contrasting their social status (a bright interior with middleclass ornaments at the Morans' versus a bare interior in the dark at the Doyles') while uniting them (both are having dinner and will be affected by the news).

The Moran family is thus the source of major additions in the film which develop the mere name *Moran* into a full-fledged family. Luke's sister Una provides the romantic subplot, totally absent from the short story. Eamon and Una are Romeo-and-Juliet-like lovers (except it doesn't end tragically), son and daughter of long-standing enemies. The enduring animus between the fathers Doyle and Moran is itself related to the period of the civil war, highlighting the father's bitterness about his fight for "a country he had fought for but was stolen from him." Ben Moran's affluent life is also associated with the changes brought about by "progress" (tourism and most specifically electricity), which John Doyle keeps disparaging. Whenever the subject of electricity is raised, the father keeps repeating that "some things never change," contrasting the superficial change of modernity with the deep enduring scars of the past. Most of all, the introduction of Una turns the father-son relationship into a triangle and complexifies the father's motivation for his decision to send his son to America, which is made explicit after he catches a glimpse of Eamon walking with Una in the woods (:43). Whereas in the short story the father's motivation remains difficult to grasp because of the conciseness of the narrative, the film multiplies the possible explanations. At first dead set against America (repeating sentences like: "We didn't fight for our country to have our sons sent to Korea to die," "there's far too much talk about America" [:29]), John Doyle is subject to a number of pressures before making up his mind. The loss of his fishing license, which is just mentioned in the story as likely to happen, the continuous talk of neighbors trying to know the exact amount of the financial compensation, the "treason" of his son in love with his arch-enemy's daughter, the bitter disillusionment he feels towards a country that let him down and condemns a third of its youth to emigrate,[18] are as many possible reasons.

Interestingly enough, the film emphasizes the idea that the father's words are not his own as he merely repeats the old cliché about America "the land of opportunity" after we see him hearing the same speech delivered by a worker in the railway station (:29). The film here brings the full impact of a scene to translate the narrator's comment: "I was wary of the big words. They were not in his own voice." In a similar way, the film opts to interpret the ambiguous passage in the conditional "He'd scrape the fare, I'd be conscripted there, each month he'd get so many dollars while I served, and he'd get ten thousand if I was killed." Whereas the story's ending would suggest all conditionals refer to mere conjecture on the part of the narrator, the film dissociates the first conditional from the others, transforming it into the actuality of a future in the past.

Ambiguity is indeed what makes the short story's interpretation problematic, forcing each reader to make his own. In this respect, its very ending is emblematic. Not only is it inconclusive but it ends with a highly ambivalent simile: "I'd never felt so close to him before, not even when he'd carried me on his shoulders above the laughing crowd to the Final. Each move he made I watched as closely *as if* I too had to prepare myself to murder."[19] The actuality of the film medium makes it necessary to offer a visual interpretation of this "as if." In so doing, the film gives an equivalent of the readership contract specific to short stories: a final twist, whose surprise was nonetheless prepared from the beginning (mainly through the recurrent close shots of the gun). Far from making the last words of the story superfluous as they are pronounced in voice over, it gives them a new depth of meaning.

However the film does not stop there and its additional ending may be the true interpretation implicit in the son's will to break the vicious circle of repetitions. Hope is embodied in Una waiting on the jetty when she gives her hand to help Eamon's father. John Doyle accepts it after a moment's hesitation. He then draws her attention to the call of a kingfisher, echoing Eamon's remark to Una then to his father in a sort of communion. The kingfisher motif operates here as a bond that unites the triangle formed by Eamon, his father and Una. In the last shot, the father goes off screen leaving the young couple face to face at a distance. The film's ending remains inconclusive but the last image suggests that the new generation may be able to bring about reconciliation with the nation's past and within the nation itself.

Cathal Black's first short film *Wheels*, shot in 1976, was based on another short story by John McGahern[20] and relates the visit in the countryside of a young man to his taciturn father who bears him a grudge after his son refused to let him live with him in Dublin. The son is divided between feelings of guilt and relief to be free from his father's sterile life. The film-maker explains: "At the time I thought that McGahern's *The Dark* was a revealing and original work. I thought that there was a dark heart to the country that wasn't being expressed but McGahern seemed to bring this out."[21] Far from being just a provider of stories, McGahern appears to be a model as for the status of art and artists in Ireland. Cathal Black makes his own the writer's double agenda which combines an uncompromising investigation into the "darker" side of Ireland and of the nation's history[22] with an unflinching aesthetic approach to his medium. The fate of his second film *Our Boys,* shot in 1981, is strikingly similar to McGahern's second novel *The Dark* (1965). Black's fiction drama about a Christian Brothers school in Dublin in the early 1960s denounces its brutality, the physical abuse and the life-long effects it had had on its pupils.[23] It was banned from the screen by the RTÉ[24] for 10 years even though the public broadcaster had helped produce the film.

In a context of harsh competition from Hollywood, Cathal Black, along with filmmakers such as Joe Comerford, Bob Quinn or Thaddeus O'Sullivan,[25] refuses to abide by the Irish producers' concern with producing uncritical material, conform to Hollywood's standards and palatable to audiences abroad.[26] *Korea* offers a remarkable balance between expansions and adjunctions of narrative elements (especially the romantic subplot) and the aesthetic restraint of the *mise en scène*. If the recurrent long shots showing the two characters in their boat in the middle of the lake may stress the beauty of the scenery, they also convey the distancing perspective of the camera, highlighting their isolation and powerlessness faced with Nature and History. In the first scene introducing the two main characters or in the scene of Eamon's despair near the lake, the camera slowly tracks forward but never goes as far as framing the characters in a medium shot, as if it didn't want to intrude too much into their inner lives. This unobtrusiveness is also present in the recurrent filming of the characters' backs as I have mentioned before, and the use of screens, as when the father is filmed through a misty window or when after a tilt down from outside through the window of the Doyles' house, a change of lighting draws focus on the curtain (1:10). Most dramatic action happens off screen in surprising cuts. And once the visual immediacy of the setting has ensured a reality effect, the photography becomes highly stylized. The lake appears almost in black and white (:7) with its silvery water. Characters are filmed like black shadows thanks to backlighting, as when Eamon rows Una to her brother's tomb. Some shots are like refined geometry, like the white orb of the full moon at night or the spherical halo of the radio lamp in a black screen.

Thanks to highly stylized photography and the use of elliptical montage, *Korea* combines a vivid realistic account of everyday life with a preoccupation to delve underneath, to go beneath the surface of things. As Cathal Black himself remarks: "It is the easiest thing in the world to be superficially controversial. It is far harder to get under the skin of people's lives and neither condemn nor applaud, just quietly observe."[27] To come back full circle and quote Brian McFarlane again, I think Cathal Black's *Korea* fully demonstrates that "fidelity to the text is not measured merely by what is retained and how that is presented but also by the extent and nature of inventions and departures from the original."[28]

NOTES

1. Brian McFarlane, *Novel to Film: An Introduction to the Theory of Adaptation*, Oxford: Clarendon Press, 1996.

2. "The film-makers themselves have been drawing on literary sources, and especially novels of varying degrees of cultural prestige, since film first established itself as pre-eminently a narrative medium." *Ibid.*, 3.

3. "Unlike most translations of literary works to the screen [...] this screenplay remains almost completely faithful to *The Dead*, adopting the characters, plot, dialogue and structure of the novella ad following it almost line by line, at times even words for words...," Producer's Notes, quoted in Lea Baechler, *James Joyce Quarterly,* Fall 1988, 521–522.

4. New York: Scribner, 2005, first published in *The New Yorker* in 1997.

5. McFarlane about Peter Bogdanovich's 1974 film based on Henry James's *Daisy Miller*, 145.

6. In publishing terms, a novella is long enough to be published on its own.

7. John McGahern, *Collected Stories*, London: Vintage 1994 (New York: Alfred A. Knopf, 1993), 54–58, first published in *Nightlines*, 1970.

8. What was said of *The Dead* is as relevant to McGahern's short story: "most of the novella consists of meticulous descriptions of the surface of events — precisely what is required of a good screenplay." Producer's Notes to the first screenplay, quoted in Baechler, 521–522.

9. Quoted in the press review.

10. According to Georges Poulet, short stories are written from the end: "Elle se bâtit

à partir de la fin. Très fréquemment cette fin est surprenante, et c'est pour amener cette surprise finale que se trouve organisé ce qui précède" ("It is constructed from its ending. Very often the end is surprising, and what precedes it is organized to lead us to this final surprise," editor's translation). Quoted in Jean-Pierre de Beaumarchais, Daniel Couty, and Alain Rey, *Dictionnaire des littératures de langue française*, Paris: Bordas, 1662.

11. "The Discourse on Adaptation," *Wide Angle* 6/2 1984, 72, quoted in McFarlane, 9.

12. Interview with Cathal Black by Vincent Brown, published in *Film West* n°24, also available at http://www.iol.ie/~galfilm/filmwest/24cathal.htm.

13. To give but one example (:12):
   1- shot of the full moon at night
   2- medium shot of the exterior of the house with focus on Eamon's face in the foreground
   3- father indoors opens the door in the background → change of focus
   4=2- father closes the door without going out → focus back on Eamon at the same place
   5=1- full moon

14. Bright flashes are used for the evocation of the furze, with the voice over "his past in my dreams" (:31), during Eamon's hallucinations of Luke in front of fire (:52).

15. This unusual viewpoint will be echoed near the end of the film when Eamon, in a feverish nightmare, will return the dead boy's look as it were and see Luke in front of a fire, highlighting the haunting identification of the living boy to the dead one.

16. This intermingling of time is made explicit by the father near the end of film when father and son go fishing for the last time (1:05): "That's the case she had with her when she went to the hospital to die. I spent all the time I could with her. It's time. The last time."

17. Interview by Vincent Browne.

18. In the newspaper John Doyle reads at the pub (:48.20), the headline reads, "Emigration Figures Increasing" and the article begins, "A third of Ireland's 14-year-olds will have emigrated before they reach 50 if present trends continue."

19. My emphasis.

20. Published in *Nightlines* (1970) which also contains "Korea."

21. Interview by Vincent Browne.

22. Contrary to the younger generation which is more prone to adopt "post-modern" Hollywood aesthetics, many of the filmmakers from the first wave (Quinn, Comerford, Black, Murphy, Thaddeus O'Sullivan) have returned again and again to themes that attempt to explore the meaning of the past for contemporary Ireland.

23. Interwoven into the fiction are interviews of former pupils and archive sequences (footage of a St. Patrick's Day parade in Dublin and a sequence from the Eucharistic Congress held in Dublin in 1932). See Martin McLoone, *Irish Film: The Emergence of a Contemporary Cinema*, London: British Film Institute, 2000, 138–140.

24. RTÉ is Raidió Teilifís Éireann, Ireland's public service broadcaster.

25. A group of filmmakers who collaborate on one another's films.

26. Cathal Black has his own production company. However the main problem remains distribution.

27. Interview by Vincent Browne.

28. McFarlane, 163.

BIBLIOGRAPHY

Baechler, Lea. "Producer's Notes: Korea." *James Joyce Quarterly,* Fall 1988, 521–22.

Browne, Vincent. "Interview with Cathal Black." *Film West* n°24, www.iol.ie/~galfilm/ filmwest/24cathal.htm.

Couty, Daniel, Jean-Pierre de Beaumarchais, and Alain Rey. *Dictionnaire des littératures de langue française.* Paris: Bordas, 1992.

McGahern, John. *Collected Stories.* London: Vintage, 1994.

McLoone Martin. *Irish Film: The Emergence of a Contemporary Cinema.* London: British Film Institute, 2000.

Proulx, Annie. *Brokeback Mountain.* New York: Scribner, 2005.

The Visible in *Howards End*
and *The Remains of the Day*

Karim Chabani

Much of the academic debate on "heritage films," central to film studies in Great Britain in the 1990s, discussed Merchant-Ivory films (such as *Howards End* and, to a lesser extent, *The Remains of the Day*), viewing them as archetypal of this genre. The kinds of questions posed within such scholarship tend to focus on ideology and national representation. Without questioning the validity of such discourse, I believe it would be a mistake to obfuscate other aspects of these works by neglecting a comparison with the novels that inspired them, thus probing the aesthetic transformation at stake.

In such a comparative analysis, we could proceed to enumerate the differences, variations and similarities between them with some relevance. The problem, however, for us is more acute and requires precise attention be paid to the specificity of the media concerned. With such an agenda in mind, I hope to show in what follows that an attentive reading of *Howards End* and *The Remains of the Day* brings the notion of invisibility to the fore. Such a notion becomes obviously problematic when it comes to be transferred to a visual medium. Therefore I also plan to argue that *fidelity*, a concept that has been dismissed in recent academic discussions pertaining to literature on screen but which is deeply rooted in the actual narrative content of the works under scrutiny here, takes on a more dialectical dimension and thus offers a useful if provisional critical paradigm.

From the Unsaid to the Unseen (and Back)

To return to invisibility in *Howards End* and *The Remains of the Day*, and before arguing on whether it can be shown, the question emerges: how can it be *told*? For both novels, this very notion operates within the narrative and constructs the main characters.

By way of an illustration, Stevens dwells at length upon his own invisibility when he is on duty.[1] What he presents as a professional asset becomes an idiosyncratic feature, defining his very character so that visibility (or the lack thereof) entails an ontological dimension. The butler attempted to "minimise [his] presence"[2] to the extent that he is ignored by others, all behaving as if he were not there — or not at all.[3] Without allowing the reader to decide between a personal trait or a professional attribute, an always-already ghostly Stevens appears to belong to the shadows, ontologically flickering between presence and absence.

When *reflecting* on the "greatness of the English landscape," he finds its outstanding quality to be its inconspicuousness. His endeavor to remain out of view eventually compromises his own vision. As a protagonist, he does not see the landscape and as a narrator, he hardly ever resorts to description (i.e., the locus of visibility in a literary text). Interestingly, he is fully aware of such an "omission":

> But I see I am becoming preoccupied with these memories and this is perhaps a little foolish. This present journey represents, after all, a rare opportunity for me to savour to the full the many splendours of the English countryside, and I know I shall regret it later if I allow myself to become unduly diverted. In fact, I notice I have yet to record anything of my journey to this city — aside from mentioning briefly that halt on the hillside road at the very start of it. This is an omission indeed, given how much I enjoyed yesterday's motoring.[4]

Literally he sees but his own blindness, not only to his surroundings but to the reasons for such a "preoccupation" with the past. His memories indeed "pre-occupy" the textual space and, if nothing ever "takes place" in *The Remains of the Day*, it is because there is no *place*, only space. Memories condense into a reflective screen that blocks out the landscape, thus transmuted into a soulscape. Haunted not by the genius of the place but by the soul of the traveler, does the scenery become a mere setting?

A reversed cinematic metaphor aptly translates this rare phenomenon. Set in mechanical motion ("motoring"), Stevens posits himself as a camera, "recording" his journey. Unfortunately, Stevens-as-a-narrator is no less insistent in his delusional attitude than Stevens-as-a-character and ends up acting as a projector. The pictorial materiality of the verdant English landscape (so dear to Ivory's aesthetic) is whitewashed — as it were — and fades into a blank canvas, a screen of sorts. His evanescent memories are like light-rays he projects onto it. At the heart of *The Remains of the Day* is therefore not the invisible *per se* but the visible that the butler failed to see. The reader must therefore see what was *unseen* by an unreliable narrator—a common strategy in literature of which Stevens is emblematic and here commented upon by David Lodge:

> The point of using an unreliable narrator is indeed to reveal in an interesting way the gap between appearance and reality, and to show how human beings distort or conceal the latter. This need not be a conscious, or mischievous, intention on their part. The narrator of Kazuo Ishiguro's novel is not an evil man, but his life has been based on the suppression and evasion of truth, about himself and others.[5]

The *unseen* in *Howards End* is of an altogether different nature precisely because it does not partake of the same narratorial discourse. John Hillis Miller remarks on the omnipresence of the very word which he situates on the same spectrum as a list of other terms:

> A just reading of *Howards End* depends on how you take the word *unseen* and its synonyms, the "invisible" [95], "the unknown" [110], "infinity" [91], "the submerged" [83], "a more inward light" [108], "the inconceivable" [204], "the glow" [327], the "idea of Death" [236], and so on. [...] Among other such repetitions, the word *unseen* echoes discreetly and unostentatiously through the novel like a musical motif.[6]

In visual terms, instead of a blank space as in *The Remains of the Day*, the unseen is more of a blur, a repeated encounter with the unnameable. I would however not agree that these words and phrases are strictly synonymous; the dissemination of the "unseen" within the text does not play the music of chance. All occurrences consistently connect this undefined notion to Margaret[7] (unlike the other terms selected by Hillis Miller), and I shall attempt to delineate briefly its semantic trajectory—following the main character's own evolution throughout the novel.

On the first two occasions the term is mentioned its meaning remains hazy. The reader, like Margaret herself, acquires a form of *familiarity* with the term whereas an unveiling of the concept it conveys is perpetually deferred. It is *via* her encounter with Ruth Wilcox that Margaret will apprehend the unseen; only at this juncture can she realize that it is in private—as opposed to social gatherings—that the unseen can be properly approached: "But in public, who shall express the unseen adequately? It is private life that holds out the mirror to infinity; personal intercourse, and that alone, that ever hints at a personality beyond our daily vision."[8]

After this pivotal realization (and Mrs. Wilcox's *unwritten* death), Margaret refuses to *discuss* the term. She intuitively perceives what it refers to—something of which other characters[9] are incapable—and its ill-defined nature appears to repel constructed discourse. Margaret grows to *comprehend* it by taking (or inheriting) the *place* of Ruth Wilcox. It entails the same paradox as the German *unheimlich*: at home (*heim*)[10] with such a notion, she knows its content remains elusive, a secret (*heimlich*). In what follows, this Freudian notion shall function as the fundamental nexus between the unseen and vision in the films adapted from these novels.

An Uncanny Fidelity

Both the film adaptation of *The Remains of the Day* and that of *Howards End* attempt to "transpose" (an aptly musical term) "the impact of the unseen on the seen"[11] or, more pragmatically put, the rendering of the unseen in film. A much-criticized notion, fidelity questions the conditions of possibility of cinematic adaptation in this instance as it is at the very core of their respective plots.

After Mrs. Wilcox "gave up the ghost," the story of *Howards End* (the film, the novel, but also the house) takes a decisive turn with a symmetrical betrayal.[12] The Wilcoxes' unfaithfulness betrays a lack of respect for the spectre[13]; they fail to see how the unseen, the rules of the *familiarity* and *propriety* that developed between Margaret and Ruth transcend the laws of *family* and *property*. Furthermore the reflection on matrimony also hinges on fidelity: the wedding of Margaret and Henry is perceived as a betrayal by both sides. In an improbable illustration of the epigraph, adultery *connects* characters: hence the nodal position of the Basts, whose extramarital ties links Helen and Henry, otherwise opposed in all but their initials.

Ivory plays variations on the same theme in the film adaptation of *The Remains of the Day*. Indeed, the film intertwines (dis)respect toward a deceased mother and infidelity in matrimony. Whereas the maternal figure was scrupulously avoided in the novel, Stevens's father confesses that his wife was unfaithful to him, saying "The love went out of me when I found her carrying on." The unseen ("love"), absence ("went out") mingle in betrayal ("carrying on") in a phrase that however suggests persistence. The viewer in this instance can hear and see what Stevens-as-a-narrator would never say. Significantly, Stevens-as-portrayed-by-Hopkins looks away at this point, literally refusing to face the truth. Here lies the core of our analysis: how can an adaptation be faithful, not to the letter of literature, but to its spirit, its *ghost* as it were? How can film *show* (as opposed to *tell*) the unseen?

The butler's blind faith in his father(s) is the main thematic thread (threat) and is figuratively illustrated by gestures of concealment. After the butler had respectfully drawn the curtain on the meeting between Ribbentrop and Chamberlain, Lord Darlington's own god-son tried to convince Stevens that his master was used as a pawn by the Nazis and said repeatedly "Can't you see?" When Miss Kenton attempted to show Stevens the evidence of his father's physical decay, he simply closed a door on her.[14] Stevens obviously tries to (b)lock out all elements that could betray the weaknesses of his "fathers": they are "ob-scene" and therefore ought to remain unseen.

Conversely, the spectators see what the butler turns a blind eye to and it looks "uncanny." The return of the repressed is perceptible, i.e., not visible but legible. For instance, the Chinaman that was misplaced by Stevens senior is shown with a curiously wagging head in an uncanny shot, singled out by a mock–Chinese theme. Stevens immediately turned away from that almost ironic statue, as if terrified by an object he should be *familiar* with.

Likewise, a process of defamiliarization manifests the unseen in *Howards End*, but in that instance, Margaret welcomes it. When the two sisters finally met at Howards End where their furniture had been moved, they both noticed that the carpet fit perfectly and that their father's sword also matched the room. Margaret even says: "Isn't it surprising that the sword looks right too?" Another paternal symbol, it indicates that they found a new home (*Heim*): the unseen that returned in this particular case is not a repressed disturbance as with Stevens but rather the unseen as Meg incrementally perceived. These familiar objects "look right," they show a new (and undefined) familiarity.

Waves of Haunting

Such a faith in the unseen is accompanied by a disbelief in vision. To separate visibility from presence facilitates the distinction between film and other visual arts. On the other hand, it also shows that the ontological question of film relies first and foremost on phenomenology. In the first few shots of the film version of *The Remains of the Day*, Ivory draws our attention to the illusory nature of the cinematic form. Caught up in his daily routine, Stevens walked through Darlington Hall surrounded by the vanishing images of his past. Even Miss Kenton appeared and disappeared in this ghostly fashion in a shot when she was seen through a rounded window, mimetically suggesting a camera-lens. The viewer cannot then decide if such shots are to be interpreted either as subjective or reflexive. This introductory sequence therefore functions as an encoding moment and the viewer can rightly feel suspicious. Reformulating the analogy between Stevens-as-a-narrator and a film projector, the sequence depicts, not the narrator, but the very *medium* as unreliable.

Such a principle of uncertainty governs the interpretation of the entire film. Indeed the film works through alternating sections representing Stevens's journey and his earlier days at Darlington Hall. Are the latter to be understood as analepses (flash-backs) or anamneses (subjective — and therefore potentially reconstructed — memories)? One can hardly venture a positive answer in this regard. However, all of these four narrative shifts are triggered by an element of the dialogue or a situation, so that the effect is closer to that of involuntary reminiscence than of a fragmentary narratological technique. In addition, some scenes are highly unlikely, such as Lord Darlington making fast amends for the dismissing of the Jewish servants, or the repetition of the exact same words in the father's death-scene and when he parts with Miss Kenton. On the other hand, the aforementioned sequences that accounted for elements "visibly" suppressed by the butler seem to run counter to this interpretation.

As a consequence, in order to give a faithful interpretation of these works, it seems important to maintain this ontological undecidability. One then feels justified in borrowing Derrida's coin-word "hauntology," a phrase that may aptly define the oscillation between data and traces of such images, gliding through the partitions between film and novel, in a cinematic genre foregrounding its reconstruction of the past. Derrida in his reflection on haunting calls upon a "visor effect,"[15] by which he means that ghosts have a distinctive capacity for seeing without being seen. The analogy with film spectators is obvious enough, but Derrida takes it one step further and defines the cinema as "magnificent mourning" and every film as "a magnified work of mourning."[16] As such, the cinema shares with Stevens (and Ruth Wilcox, as we shall see in the next section) his most idiosyncratic — and ghostly — features.

The fragmented chronological axis allows therefore for a manifestation of haunting *via montage* in the both versions of *The Remains of the Day*. The linear narrative of Forster's *Howards End* does not allow for such displacements; so how is Ruth Wilcox's haunting presence to be suggested? As Hillis Miller points out, a film cannot use verbal repetition as a possible locus for haunting:

> The absence of the narrator makes the film of *Howards End, faithful* as it is to the novel and admirable as it is as a film, fundamentally different. [...] The film, which has its own strong visual resources not available to the novel, [...] leaves out many of the verbal repetitions (for example, of the word *unseen*) that generate so much of the meaning of the novel.[17]

Here, the critic seems oblivious to his own suggestion: the word "unseen" functions as a "musical motif." The unseen is expressed in music: the opening sequence when Mrs. Wilcox walked through her garden and cast a benevolent glance at her own family through a window shares the same theme as Margaret's encounter with Howards End. A neighbor tells her then, "I took you for Ruth Wilcox. You have her way of walking around the house." The viewer's sentiment is thus confirmed: he hears her walk too. Margaret and Mrs. Wilcox share the pace, the same tempo, the same theme.

Music becomes the gates to the underworld, through which the dead return to the living[18] — only more so for a character whose death is expressed without a word, only through a melancholy melody... The soundtrack can therefore maintain an intimation of the unseen, an invisible omnipresence *matching* the dimension of this character: "I feel that you and Henry and I are only fragments of that woman's mind. She knows everything. She is everything." Two pages after Margaret makes this statement, the narrator asks as a conclusion to chapter 40: "Was [Leonard Bast] part of her mind too?"[19] Music in film is the answer to this question since the piece played to say the unnameable, i.e., the unseen and unspoken death of Mrs. Wilcox is entitled "The Basts."[20] As the soundtrack establishes another winding path between the characters, her melodious epitaph enacts the notorious epigraph "Only Connect."

Figuring Absence

By way of a conclusion, I intend to borrow two figures of cinematic rhetoric singled out by the French film scholar Marc Vernet in his work *Figures de l'absence*.[21] In this work, Vernet focuses on the representation, or rather the figuration, of the invisible in films. His first remarks centre on what he calls "*l'en-deçà*" (the beneath), a distant shot where some element blocks or interferes with the spectator's vision. According to Vernet, these characteristics combine to create the effect of a gaze-bearing presence. The camera's point of view materializes then — partly or in totality — the geographical or psychic presence of a character.[22]

In the film *Howards End*, the opening sequence functions as an encoding key-scene where the bearer of the gaze is identified with Ruth Wilcox. Her presence in the afore-mentioned scene where Margaret discovered Howards End, was signaled by peculiar-angle shots. Whereas Ruth Wilcox was looking at a familiar scene through the window from *without*, when Margaret duplicated her gesture, she was shot through that same window from within the house. Once Margaret had entered the house, she was seen from a distance in a low-angle shot. The use of the depth of field corresponds to no other demand of the narrative than the suggestion of a denaturalized, defamiliarized, and as such personalized point of view. The locus of that gaze, justifying the angle, remains *unseen* and nonetheless perceptible, i.e., *comprehensible*.

In the film *The Remains of the Day*, similar examples seem less relevant but another figure remarked on by Vernet recurs interestingly. The critic coins the phrase *regard-à-la-caméra* (looking-at-the-camera) to refer to frontal close-ups focused on a character's face, seemingly looking at the spectator, or at least to be directed to something on that side of the screen.[23] The repartition of the occurrences of such shots seems to indicate that they are an effect of Stevens's journey: after the first half of the film (from which they are completely absent) the shot thus defined recurs no less than eight times. Half of these occurrences are connected to past events: in this case, they signal the wrongs that Stevens intends to right.

Vernet notes that this type of shot is commonly used to denote an "encounter with death"[24] and, strikingly, the first occurrence of such looking-at-the-camera is situated immediately after the death of the father. Stevens's face is blown up to such an extent that the dead body is off-screen. As he refused to see his father's shortcomings, he obliterates his father's death. The repressed object is under erasure, as it were, only dialectically perceptible through the assumed object of such an intent gaze. This scene is duplicated when Stevens lets Miss Kenton go to her trysts. His blank stare indicates passivity: he will not stop her, no more than he would express his feelings. He has to be a spectator of his own tragedy. Then again, the cinematic metaphor becomes self-evident here: like the camera, he records the action. Looking *at* the camera gives him the look *of* the camera.

The second series of this type of shot functions as a coda, recalling and gathering the previous occurrences. The scene in the restaurant where Miss Kenton (now Mrs. Benn) announced to him that she had no intention of returning to her former occupations reflects her departure to meet Mr. Benn. But this time, the butler is not protected by the cold reticular window-panes: whereas he had refused to face her departure, he needed to accept her refusal to come back. After mixing memory and desire, the butler needs to face rejection and old age. In the next sequence, on the pier, his long and melancholy blank stare echoes his face when his father had died. Unlike Oedipus, when Stevens realizes his irretrievable mistakes, he does not blind himself but opens his eyes to the waste of his life. His face is an answer to Mrs. Benn's question "What are you looking forward to?" There is nothing to look forward to: the entire screen is occupied by a non-seeing gaze. The viewer sees nothing but that there is nothing to see. At this stage, the cinematic illusion falters and yields to photography. Roland Barthes noted that only in photography, as opposed to film, can the character look straight at the viewer.[25] The butler is represented as a photograph (or a still, one is even tempted to say a still-life), i.e., without a future (because, Barthes contends, it is motionless) and therefore pathetic and melancholy.[26]

Both film adaptations are haunted by literature, by the novels that inspired them of course but also by a larger intertext primarily constituted by the literary network of Merchant-Ivory adaptations.[27] Conversely, they become spectral themselves. Indeed they ignore the barriers between the arts and glide adrift towards the immaterial mobility of music or the still and sepulchral photographic imprint. The spectral nature of the cinematic medium (foregrounded by Derrida among others) seemed perfectly *adapted* for the ghostly characters of the novels *The Remains of the Day* and *Howards End* so that they have found in their filmic counterparts faithful "ghost images."

NOTES

1. Kazuo Ishiguro, *The Remains of the Day*, London: Faber and Faber, 1996, 73.
2. *Ibid.*, 72.
3. *Ibid.*, 74, 80.
4. *Ibid.*, 67.
5. David Lodge, *The Art of Fiction*, Harmondsworth: Penguin, 1992, 155.
6. John Hillis Miller, "E.M. Forster: Just reading *Howards End*," in E.M. Forster, *Howards End*, New York, Bedford Books, 1997, 467. The pages mentioned have been modified to match the edition used in this article.
7. E.M. Forster, *Howards End*, Harmondsworth: Penguin, 1989, 44, 87, 90, 108, 112, 203.
8. *Ibid.*, 90. See the definition of "intercourse" (third sense) in the *Oxford English Dictionary*, 2d ed. on CD-ROM: "Communion between man and that which is spiritual or unseen."
9. Be it her sister Helen or her daughter-in-law Dolly. *Ibid.*, 112, 203.
10. A term that points to Howards End, the very house that materializes what brings the two women together.
11. *Ibid.*, 90, 108.
12. Compare "They neglected a personal appeal. The woman who had died had told them 'do this,' and they answered 'we will not'" (*Ibid.*, 107) and "Mrs. Wilcox had been treacherous to the family, to the laws of property, to her own written word" (*Ibid.*, 108).
13. For an elaboration on this anagram, see Jacques Derrida, *Echographies de la Télévision*, Paris: Galilée, 1997, 139.
14. Illustrating the very image for repression given in Sigmund Freud, *Five Lectures on Psychoanalysis* (1909), New York: W.W. Norton, 1989, 23.
15. Jacques Derrida, *Spectres de Marx*, Paris: Galilée, 1993, 26.
16. Thierry Jousse, interview with Jacques Derrida, *Cahiers du Cinéma*, n°556, April 2001, 77–78.
17. Miller, 467. (Emphasis mine).
18. See Françoise Proust, *L'Histoire à contretemps*, Paris: Cerf, 1994, 68.
19. Respectively, E.M. Forster, *Howards End*, 305, 307.
20. See the soundtrack CD: Richard Robbins, *Howards End*, Nimbus, 1992.
21. Marc Vernet, *Figures de l'absence*, Paris: l'Etoile, 1988.
22. *Ibid.*, 33–35.
23. *Ibid.*, 11.
24. *Ibid.*, 23.
25. Roland Barthes, "Droit dans les yeux," *L'Obvie et l'obtus*, Paris: Seuil, 1982, 282.
26. Roland Barthes, *La Chambre claire*, Paris: Seuil, 1980, 140.

27. This effect in enhanced by similarities in terms of casting and crew (stage designer, director of photography, soundtrack composer, editor, costume designers).

BIBLIOGRAPHY

Barthes, Roland. *La Chambre claire.* Paris, Seuil, 1980.
_____. "Droit dans les yeux." *L'Obvie et l'obtus.* Paris: Seuil, 1982, 279–283.
Derrida, Jacques. *Echographies de la Télévision.* Paris: Galilée, 1997.
_____. *Spectres de Marx: L'état de la dette, le travail du deuil et la nouvelle Internationale.* Paris: Galilée, 1993.
Forster, E.M. *Howards End.* Harmondsworth: Penguin, 1989.
Freud, Sigmund. *Five Lectures on Psychoanalysis* (1909). New York: W.W. Norton, 1989.
Howards End. James Ivory, dir., Ruth Prawer Jhabvala, scr. Merchant Ivory Productions, 1992.
Ishiguro, Kazuo. *The Remains of the Day.* London: Faber and Faber, 1996.
Jousse, Thierry. "Interview with Jacques Derrida." *Cahiers du Cinéma,* n°556, April 2001, 77–78.
Lodge, David. *The Art of Fiction.* Harmondsworth: Penguin, 1992.
Miller, John Hillis. "E.M. Forster: Just Reading *Howards End.*" *Others.* Princeton, NJ: Princeton University Press, 2001, 182–205.
Proust, Françoise. *L'Histoire à contretemps.* Paris: Éditions du Cerf, 1994.
Remains of the Day. James Ivory, dir., Ruth Prawer Jhabvala, scr. Merchant Ivory Productions, 1993.
Robbins, Richard. *Howards End* Soundtrack. Nimbus, 1992.
Vernet, Marc. *Figures de l'absence.* Paris: Éditions de l'Etoile, 1988.

Adapting E.M. Forster's Subversive Aesthetics

Laurent Mellet

Forster spoke or wrote very little on cinema and when he occasionally did, this was what he would say: "I won't have any of my own stuff filmed — one of my few remaining principles."[1] The Edwardian novelist was very dubious about the ability of a film to convey any emotion at all, and he was even more doubtful whether a film adaptation could lead to anything but the impoverishment of the original novel.[2] Yet five out of Forster's six novels were adapted for the screen, including three by James Ivory (*A Room with a View*, *Maurice* and *Howards End*, between 1986 and 1992) and one by David Lean (*A Passage to India*, in 1984).[3] The critics and the few researchers have always stressed the way these films merely draw a nostalgic embellished image of England's past, oversimplifying what was at stake in the novels. At the same time the films are seen today as perfect adaptations, seemingly faithful to the original work and displaying a classic and now benchmark aesthetic. Bearing in mind Forster's mistrust of cinema and refusal to have his own work adapted, we have to reassess the films and show how this paradoxical critical view may betray as well as reveal the gist of Forster's writing. Beyond the many unifying elements of Ivory's pictures and the label of "heritage movies," aiming first and foremost to a smooth reconstruction of the past, what the films also reflect is the process of film adaptation itself in its manifold relations to *space* and *time*, and to the issue of *modernity*. The translation of a work into a new medium can either stifle, disclose or push on with its modernity, and this question can only be asked within the framework of space and time as specific devices of each genre. For Forster: "In space things touch, in time things part."[4] This aesthetic motto and its many possible subversions lay the groundwork for this paper about adaptation and modernity.

174

Showing and Overshowing the Text

Virginia Woolf was really the first reviewer of Forster, who was to prove quite difficult to classify — now an Edwardian, now a Georgian novelist. The essays of Woolf on Forster hinge around the idea of a writer unbalanced between too many realistic and material details, and his liberal speech on and faith in human relationships.[5] The films seem to agree with Woolf on this point, with an obsessive desire to recreate the material space of bygone days. They teem with accurate details and put forward a visual and historical profusion which indicates a deliberate gap between then and now. Significantly, this is what is often condemned by the critics, who view the films as mere historical or cultural documents. The opening of Lean's *Passage to India*, for instance, looks like a celebration of imperialist England *and* the wonders of India, Lean adding a sumptuous voyage and arrival of the English with the viceroy.[6] More generally, these adaptations largely *show* the scenic backgrounds of the novels, whether it be Florence in *A Room with a View*, Cambridge in *Maurice* or London in *Howards End*. Again this is something that the critics have often deplored, claiming that such visual explicitness was totally at odds with Forster's more subtle style.

We are faced here with one of the inevitable, and not always very productive, sore spots of film adaptation. What is relevant is that this *showing* quality of the films may turn into some kind of *overshowing*, since indeed it not only makes the text explicit, but also displays what the writing tried to conceal. In his book *English Heritage, English Cinema*, as in many essays, Andrew Higson argues that James Ivory shot here the epitome of what he calls "heritage films," with an "aesthetic of display." He writes: "Visual effect, the complete spectacle of the past, becomes an autonomous attraction in itself [...] [allowing] the image to come to the fore precisely as image, as spectacle, as the unfettered display of heritage properties."[7] What Higson criticizes in Ivory's adaptations is the way the director films Florence or London rather than Forster's novels and characters. To him many "splendid shots" are "narratively unmotivated"[8] inasmuch as they do not correspond to any character's look within the frame or to any narrator's outside. His definition is interesting though perhaps a bit naïve — why should a cinema picture be motivated to be a good shot? But its main interest is indeed to point back to Forster. In a first extract from *Howards End*, visual splendor, "narratively unmotivated" shots and elegance could sum up Ivory's work, and evoke Forster's distrust of cinema.[9] The scene is exactly what Higson would condemn, since the slow camera movement on the hospital does not film what Charles and Evie Wilcox are looking at and is thus gratuitous for Higson, who writes that such an image works as a mere enjoyable view for the audience. However the sequence, the whole of which was added to the text by Ivory, is very significant and heralds much of what is to come in the story, emphasizing the legacy between the two Mrs. Wilcoxes and the future union between Margaret and Henry. But indeed these shots on the magnificent façade, then on the beautiful flowers and countryside of Howards End, utterly run counter to Forster's approach to place and character in his novel. Generally speaking, Forster does not describe his locations and rather follows an aesthetic of the invisible: there is hardly anything to be visualized from Forster's writing. This really is one of its basic traits, which again sheds light on the fundamental ambiguity in adapting the novels.

Revealing Forster's Modernity

What Higson did not see is that the films also manage to express this writing of the invisible, and do not merely betray the text with sumptuous shots of sumptuous locations. In *Maurice*, for instance, the classic fade to black is always used to point to the necessity of hiding oneself and hushing things up: when the servant Simcox mentions the scandal around Lord Risley's trial to Clive, thus hinting at Clive's own shameful homosexuality, the latter snarls: "You will never mention that subject again, Simcox, while you remain in employment here."—a concluding sentence that also leads to a prudish fade to black.[10] The first establishing shot of Cambridge also seems to be "motivated" enough, not only aiming at displaying the buildings' splendor.[11] Here the panoramic shot goes past the hero without noticing him, without really shooting him — the invisibility of Maurice, on which the first chapters of the novel are based, is thus fittingly preserved in the film. The camera sweeps around the room and turns Maurice into nothing more than part of the furniture, a mere prop. His first appearance as a grown-up reveals his commonness, which, along with his invisibility and blindness, is determinant in Forster's characterization. For most of Forster's heroes, this progressive move from invisibility to visibility, and from blindness to vision, constitutes a coherent metaphor for their evolution and the basic challenge of the plots. Ivory's overshowing strategy can therefore become pregnant with meaning inasmuch as it provides a proper illustration of this move and opening to the visual. His many framed and even overframed shots, with their pictorial dimension leading the eye and revealing the visible, may work as visual equivalents to the narrative voice of the novels, which now and then tries to remind the characters of this requirement to see and be seen. So if Ivory's excess of illustration may first be construed as a misrepresentation of Forster's writing, the evolution in that writing itself can also argue that this pictorial, and sometimes theatrical, dimension of the films is quite relevant. One passage from *A Room with a View* makes this explicit. Contrary to Forster, Ivory chooses to show the encounter between Cecil and the Emersons in the National Gallery.[12] This encounter is very dramatic and even ironically dramatic, since Cecil is the one who will bring Lucy's former lover closer to her, and here Ivory seems to play around this very idea of showing and meaning. The scene is banal though quite astonishing, between a painting and a theatre stage, and of course the set has been carefully selected. The three characters appear against Paolo Uccello's *Battle of San Romano*, which replaces the novel's perhaps wiser works by Luca Signorelli. There is no depth of field except that from the painting, as if Lucy's two suitors, facing each other, were already part of the battlefield fighting for her love. And beyond this visual meaning, this excerpt works as an original vindication of the process of adaptation. Paradoxically enough, the scene stands between the painting and the stage, with people passing by in the foreground watching the actors. Yet it might justify the films' emphasis on the visible by loading it with meaning and echoing this watershed in the novels. Lucy indeed will then have to watch and see who she really loves.

Forster's writing sometimes endeavored to experiment with this primacy of the visual, and what the critics condemn in the films may appear rather appropriate in a Forster adaptation. That is why these film versions can eventually be said to reveal Forster's *modernity*. By that we mean first the way Forster would now and then reverse his way of writing, no longer concealing things, but moving from the voice to the eye, from telling to showing. And such a move can be seen as modern if we refer to what lies at the core of any research on film adaptation — the problem of aesthetic genre categories. In his *Laocoon* (1766), G.E. Lessing argues against the *ut pictura poesis* for a specificity of each genre in its relation to space and time. Painting is for him the art of the *Nebeneinander*, juxtaposing bodies in space, and poetry that of the *Nacheinander*, presenting actions one after the other in a temporal linearity.[13] Lessing then admits that this pattern can be worked on and that actions may sometimes be painted and bodies appear in poetry. But basically the image is the space of the body and its description, while the text is the time of the event and its narration. Inverting this pattern is a step towards modernity, and Forster's writing eventually belies Lessing's categories, claiming that words do not necessarily tell an action in time, but can also depict a scene in space. What is worth noticing is that Ivory always said he was interested in Forster's characters more than plots: "Forster's plots are not very important to our enjoyment, perhaps — less important than the characters' lives that he develops, the atmosphere he creates that surrounds those lives."[14] Being convinced by the character more than the event, Ivory implies that despite what the critics always say, it was Forster's modernity that motivated and conducted his adaptations, and not any precious recreation of an embellished past. When he writes that Forster's characters are more real than his events, Ivory brings to the fore the subversive and modern quality of the novelist, whose work is much closer to Lessing's painting of a body than continuous word narrative. Ivory thus points back to Forster's subversion of Lessing's categories, with a character in space prevailing on a plot in time.

From Lessing to Deleuze: Choosing Silence

However, if this emphasis on Forster's aesthetic modernity stems from the films' *mise en abyme* of his work on the visual, their own recourse to space and time fails to parallel the novels' modernity. On the issue of time again there is a gap between how the critics read the films and Ivory's intentions. The films are often criticized for the way they idealize the Edwardian period and people. For Higson: "Some audiences certainly saw [*Howards End*] as nostalgic — and some delighted in it for that very reason, while others were horrified by the way it seemed to recreate an ideal, prelapsarian England as seen through rose-tinted spectacles."[15]

Yet Ivory claimed he was after the contemporary, or eternal, relevance of the novels. He never wished to give the audience such a restricted vision of England nor of Forster's message. Indeed he considered that in the films the "liberal-humanist" dimension of this message should not be seen in the context of that "prelapsarian England," but rather transferred in the society of the 1980s and 1990s. There is therefore no nostalgia on his part, but a constant wish to focus on Forster's characters' enduring significance.[16] *Maurice* and the context of AIDS in the late 80s, or the narrow-mindedness of a cleft society, whether it be the one of Forster in *Howards End* or of that living under Mrs. Thatcher's reign, are examples of this modern echo of Forster that Ivory wished to make us hear.[17] In this regard the way Gilles Deleuze picks up on Lessing's theories of space and time is quite relevant. In *L'Image-temps* Deleuze writes that for the cinema modernity means the capacity to free oneself from the narrative, to inject time into space, and voice into the image[18]: a moving picture is modern when it includes external time and voice. And this is where the films by Ivory seem to reach their limits, since they do not correspond to the definition given by Deleuze. Even regarding the message of Forster's plots, the films utterly lack the tone of the novels, often ironical and sarcastic. They may reveal Forster's modernity and transition from chronological telling to dilated showing, but they fail to apply this form of modernity to their own aesthetics of space and time, for there is no voice in them inasmuch as they remain silent about Forster's ambiguous views on his own England, and therefore even their topical relevance is somewhat diluted and lost. Action never really comes to a halt, however interested the director may have been in characters and moods, and the films have no breathing space outside the framework of their illustration process. The theory of Deleuze is quite intricate and refers to a more ambitious and reflexive type of cinema than Ivory's. Yet it drives us back to this issue of space and time, image and voice, and underlines why the films convincingly display Forster's modernity within the bounds of their own classicism.

Ironically enough, the only moments when they manage to *say* something more or something other than the plots, are when they choose silence.[19] In the first embrace between the two platonic lovers of *Maurice*, silence is what enables us to hear the emotion of touch and caress[20]: after a few words, the *Miserere* by Allegri stops, while the camera prudishly moves back. The two men do not dare look at each other, and silence emerges from the singing of birds, rustle of clothes, crackling of the rattan chair and short breathing. The very noisy arrival of Maurice's friends into the room is all the more brutal and meaningful. The passage is based on a type of sensuality created by this fake silence — fake since there are many things to be heard and deciphered besides birds and clothes, and it may be in such a silent shot that Ivory meets Deleuze's definition of external voice and discourse. Only silence could echo the novel's slow and cautious orchestration of desire, and here the essentials of Forster's writing can be heard outside what the image shows. The way the heroes fail to understand what is happening to them, their physical awkwardness, the intensity of the moment — what the narrative voice often underlines in the novel, or simply the tone of the book and its implications, convincingly ooze from the mute discourse of the film. A "mute discourse" indeed, a discourse rising from silence, and such is the last ironical space-and-time feature of Ivory's adaptations. Here maybe the modernity proposed by Deleuze could characterize the films, as the one implied by Lessing Forster's novels. These progressively opened on the visual, and the films sometimes can move from the visual to the vocal, however silent it may be, and break off for a moment so as to let something else enter the visual space, just as Deleuze put forward.

"In Space Things Touch, in Time Things Part": Three Different Voices

Ivory's movies therefore turn out to be less academic and shallow than they seem to be. All the more so if we now consider David Lean's adaptation of *A Passage to India*, still around the issue of space and time, since the aesthetics of this film will actually shed light on Ivory's modernity. In the novel Adela Quested is haunted by this strange aphorism: "In space things touch, in time things part."[21] This sentence may sound like a continuation of Lessing: things are juxtaposed in space, therefore in contact, while temporal elements succeed one another and cannot be simultaneous. The episode of the Marabar Caves, and of the alleged rape of Adela by Aziz, will shatter and once again reverse this aesthetic order: while Forster does not *show* anything of the scene, which happens in the blank between two chapters, the narrator then *writes in the chronology of the text*, writes in time, the possibility of the rape, thus of contact between bodies. His writing in that last novel invalidates the primacy of space and loads time with the prime meaning of the scene. Here space separates the bodies, whether it be the Caves themselves, where for instance, "The two flames approach and strive to unite, but cannot,"[22] or the space of the text that seems to deny and erase the rape. But the narrative then gives many clues that could argue in favor of contact. The invisibility of the event is compensated for by the writing of another text within the text, which Forster endows with another voice that seems to say the rape did happen: "the orifices were always the same size [... Miss Quested's field-glasses] were lying at the verge of a cave, halfway down an entrance tunnel. [...] the leather strap had broken."[23] The phallic symbol of the glasses, even more obvious in the manuscripts of the novel, when Forster actually wrote if not the rape, the assault,[24] and the breaking of hymen lying behind that of the strap, work as textual evidence of the rape in the chronology of the narrative. So if for Adela, "In space things touch, in time things part," on the contrary Forster's coherent writing claims that "in space things part, and in time things touch." The text chronologically writes the possibility of contact and touch, while showing the opposite. The original motto confirmed Lessing's categories. With this last inversion Forster goes still further. He first challenged Lessing with the opening of the text on the visual. Now he implies that this visual is not the proper opening for literature, that only in its chronological dimension can it succeed in making things touch and get in contact — as if already, or again, questioning the need for adaptation.

Lean's film does not push on with this thematic and aesthetic inversion around space and time. It is of course highly different from Ivory's adaptations, and could be said to fail where Ivory's did according to the critics, when they did that much. The film is often very far from Forster's novel and writing still based on the invisible and what defies the representational power of fiction. In his last novel Forster brings to the fore this dimension of his style, questioning it and equating it with the impossibility of writing India as of giving any coherent literary image of man. Most of the time the film ignores the complex and aporetic human relationships tackled by Forster, preferring to *display*, as Higson writes of Ivory, India and the British Empire. More specifically, the scene of the Marabar Caves is famous for its negation of Forster's meaningful mystery and ellipsis.[25] Of course the film here does not *show* nor *say* that the rape actually happens. We do not know whether Aziz does enter the cave or not. Yet the emphasis on Adela's erotic malaise, here and before, when she seeks sexual comfort from Ronny or goes through another sensual crisis when admiring erotic statues, clearly goes further than the novel. The close-up on their touching hands, Adela's embarrassment when she asks Aziz about his wife, and then his growing discomfort—"in space things touch," indeed, and Lean films the two characters as stepping towards each other. The rape is here visibly potential, more than potential with this final cut from Adela's tears and look at her own body, to water flowing and gurgling.

So Lean's *Passage to India* meets Lessing's categories indeed: "in space things touch," and later during the trial, "in time things will part," since in the film it is *voice* which drives Adela to understand her mistake in accusing Aziz. In the end the actual reality of the rape is not what matters, and the film may not be as explicit as what is often said. What is relevant is the way David Lean follows a classic aesthetic, further away than Ivory's from the modernity proposed by Deleuze — no external voice at all here to comment on this moment in the caves, but a mere visual clarification of what is at stake with Forster.

Forster's subversion of aesthetic categories is thus smoothed over in Lean's adaptation. Subversion, and even *subversions*: we mentioned how his writing first challenged Lessing's *Nebeneinander* and *Nacheinander* by proving, sparingly and less successfully perhaps than with the modernist writers, that a text can turn into an image, suspend time and write space. After this first move towards modernity, Forster steps back and confirms Lessing in spite of himself since it is not in this textual space that things can touch, and his writing cannot make us *see* people connect, to refer to the famous epigraph of *Howards End*, "Only connect..." Eventually Forster suggests a third movement: in *A Passage to India*, things and bodies do touch but in time chronology, in this art of the *Nacheinander*, and such is the last subversion by Forster, who weaves a complex but coherent aesthetic around the notions of space and time in his novels. Such are also the limits of his modernity, and indeed modernism: Forster accepts and works within the bounds of fiction, trying to make people connect in the writing and in time, before giving up and turning his back on fiction.

As for Ivory's films, at the end of the day they too can prove rather close to Forster's approach to genre modernity. The embrace in *Maurice* may point back to image as a mere surface of touch. But silence and mute discourse remind one of Deleuze. Of course Ivory does not go as far as Forster and does not imply that "in time things touch," except through his wish to underline the contemporary echoes of Forster's world and plots — but that really is not the most convincing aspect of the films. Yet this external discourse is a trace of modernity, all the more so if we now conclude on the way the space created by the frame of the picture disproves the idea that "in space things touch." The different images of a sequence from *Howards End* seem to show that contact is impossible, while a certain tone of voice in the same sequence may be saying the opposite.[26] The disharmony in the couple at that time is visible, and the two characters fail to get closer in space. Only time, then, can do this, and the black dissolves can be construed as external spaces with an external voice trying to reconcile Margaret and Henry. The first dissolve closes on Henry hiding behind his hand and opens on a new shot with the two characters now together. Then Margaret vainly follows him and Ivory cuts on Henry leaving off-camera, then filmed with his back to the camera and in reverse shot with Margaret, who holds out her hand to him, partly out of shot and Henry's moves into it just before another dissolve. At last the couple gets together in a more academic shot. Out of the frame, out of space, those black gaps can be seen as some external source or voice aiming at contradicting what is visible, building some tension between what the film shows and what it says, between space and time.[27]

According to Gaston Bachelard: "In its thousand crevices, space is much like compressed time. That's the purpose of space."[28] Here cinematographic space disappears in these dissolves and allows time to emerge and take control of the narrative. Editing is of course one way to answer the demands of Deleuze. Space and time are not only the basic coordinates of human life — they lie at the origin of creation, on the blank page as on the silver screen, and of reception, but may also turn out to be the inevitable axes along which film adaptation must be approached so as to assess its modernity. Along the necessary genre transpositions, a film can be as subversive as a novel according to the way each medium relies on and resorts to its various expressive potentialities — spatial and temporal above all.

NOTES

1. Interview of E.M. Forster by J.W. Lambert, "Mr. Forster at the Play," *Sunday Times*, 4 August 1963, 21.

2. It is a well-known fact that during his lifetime Forster systematically refused to have his work adapted, however insistent and persuasive Satyajit Ray, for instance, may have tried to sound when meeting Forster about *A Passage to India*.

3. *Where Angels Fear to Tread* was shot by Charles Sturridge in 1991. *The Longest Journey* is the only novel by Forster never made into a film.

4. E.M. Forster, *A Passage to India* (1924), London: Penguin, 2000, 199.

5. See for instance Virginia Woolf, "The Novels of E.M. Forster" (1927), in *The Death of the Moth and Other Essays* (1942), San Diego: Harcourt Brace Jovanovich, 1970, 162–175.

6. So much so that the film is often said to be more imperialist than the novel, where British pomp is less visible.

7. Andrew Higson, *English Heritage, English Cinema: Costume Drama since 1980*, Oxford: Oxford University Press, 2003, 84 and 172.

8. *Ibid.*, 173.

9. First extract: *Howards End*, :38.50 to :41.

10. *Maurice*, :53.

11. Second extract: *Maurice*, :06 to :06.30.

12. Third extract: *A Room with a View*, :56.30 to :58.

13. Gotthold Ephraim Lessing, *Laocoon* (1766), E.A. McCormick, trans., Baltimore: Johns Hopkins University Press, 1984, XVI, 78.

14. James Ivory, "Introduction," in *Howards End*, E.M. Forster, New York: Modern Library, 1999, xii.

15. Higson, *English Heritage, English Cinema: Costume Drama since 1980*, 147.

16. "The problem of living honestly with one's emotions will be with us, I guess, as long as people make films, write plays, or write novels. [...] Maurice contemplated suicide in the novel because of his 'unspeakable' lusts. Or look at Blanche DuBois; she's never dated as a figure, any more than Lucy Honeychurch in *A Room with a View*, with all her muddled ideas" (James Ivory in R.E. Long, *James Ivory in Conversation*, Berkeley: University of California Press, 2005, 214).

17. "Like *A Room with a View* and *Howards End*, [*Maurice*] was fun to make, and was another illustration of Forster's ability to speak to modern audiences. It came out at exactly the right time: in 1987, after the first big AIDS hysteria had passed, when people were feeling concerned, guilty, and more open-hearted towards homosexuals" (James Ivory in an unpublished letter to the Modern Archive Centre of King's College Library, Cambridge, 1992). More generally there would be a lot to add about these common points between Edwardian and "Thatcherian" Englands. See Claire Monk, *Sex, Politics and the Past: Merchant Ivory, the Heritage Film, and its Critics in 1980s and 1990s Britain*, unpublished MA dissertation, British Film Institute, 1994, and Cairns Craig, "Rooms Without a View," in *Sight and Sound*, June 1991, 10.

18. Gilles Deleuze, *L'Image-temps*, Paris: Les Éditions de Minuit, 1985, 298 and 303.

19. Robert Bresson claims: "LE CINÉMA SONORE A INVENTÉ LE SILENCE" (Robert Bresson, *Notes sur le cinématographe* [1975], Paris: Gallimard, 1995, 50).

20. Fourth extract: *Maurice*, :20 to :22.

21. Forster, *A Passage to India*, 199.

22. *Ibid.*, 138.

23. *Ibid.*, 165 and 166.

24. "[Adela] got hold of the glasses and pushed them at her assailant's mouth. She could

not push hard, but it was enough to hurt him" (*The Manuscripts of* A Passage to India, corr. Oliver Stallybrass, London: Edward Arnold, 1978, 242).

25. Fifth extract: *A Passage to India*, 1:17.20 to 1:23.

26. Sixth extract: *Howards End*, 1:31.50 to 1:33.50 (the quarrel between Margaret and Henry after she has discovered he had a mistress when first married).

27. This tension is also present in the sequence in which Margaret and Henry have lunch at Simpson's, based on the same dichotomy between what is shown and what is said (*Howards End*, :59.20 to 1:02.20).

28. "Dans ses mille alvéoles, l'espace tient du temps comprimé. L'espace sert à ça" (author's translation). Gaston Bachelard, *La Poétique de l'espace* (1957), Paris: Presses Universitaires de France, 2001, 27.

BIBLIOGRAPHY

Bachelard, Gaston. *La Poétique de l'espace* (1957). Paris: Presses Universitaires de France, 2001.

Bresson, Robert. *Notes sur le cinématographe* (1975). Paris: Gallimard, 1995.

Cairns, Craig. "Rooms Without a View." *Sight and Sound*, June 1991, 10.

Forster, E.M. *The Manuscripts of* A Passage to India. Oliver Stallybrass, ed. London: Edward Arnold, 1978.

_____. *A Passage to India* (1924). London: Penguin, 2000.

Ivory, James. "Introduction." *Howards End*, E.M. Forster. New York: Modern Library, 1999, xi–xx.

Lambert, J.W. "Mr. Forster at the Play." *Sunday Times*, 4 August 1963, 21.

Lessing, Gotthold Ephraim. *Laocoon* (1766). Trans. E.A. McCormick. Baltimore: Johns Hopkins University Press, 1984.

Long, Robert Emmet. *James Ivory in Conversation*. Berkeley: University of California Press, 2005.

Maurice. James Ivory, dir., Kit Hesketh-Harvey, James Ivory, scrs. Merchant Ivory Productions, 1987.

Monk, Claire. *Sex, Politics and the Past: Merchant Ivory, the Heritage Film, and its Critics in 1980s and 1990s Britain*. Unpublished MA dissertation, British Film Institute, 1994.

Passage to India. David Lean, dir., scr. EMI films, 1984.

Room with a View. James Ivory, dir., Ruth Prawer Jhabvala, scr. Goldcrest Films International, 1984.

Where Angels Fear to Tread. Charles Sturridge, dir., Tim Sullivan, Derek Granger, Charles Sturridge, scr., Compact Films, 1991.

Woolf, Virginia. "The Novels of E.M. Forster" (1927). *The Death of the Moth and Other Essays* (1942). San Diego: Harcourt Brace Jovanovich, 1970, 162–175.

Re-Adaptation as Part of the Myth: Orson Welles and *Don Quixote*'s "Outings"

Sébastien Lefait

When we tackle the subject of a figure of mythical dimension such as Don Quixote, the question of re-adaptation always crops up at some point, as if it was implied by the mythical dimension itself. Indeed, a literary character may be called a myth *because* it recurs in many different works of art, sometimes under various shapes, while remaining instantly identifiable. To take but one example, Dorian Gray is undoubtedly related to Doctor Faustus, which makes the work by Oscar Wilde yet another adaptation of the original, which is itself a version of the Promethean myth.[1] A myth, by essence, is constantly readapted.

The case is different for *Don Quixote*. The book comes first, and there seems to be no original story to be found. The story was not mythical to start with, it became a myth by itself. But there is another major difference between Faustus and Quixote. For the latter, the universal quality of the story is not what prompts artists to tell it again and again. As a matter of fact, *Don Quixote*, because of its structure and contents, calls for many re-adaptations, while the Faustian story somehow merely happens to have been repeated. According to Marthe Robert, *Don Quixote* is a book that is bound to remain undone or even unstarted, a work that needs to be constantly rewritten.[2] Her view seems to suggest that the re-adaptation process is part of the quixotic myth. Besides, each time the story is retold, its meaning is renewed, as Borges shows through one of his characters, Pierre Ménard, who rewrites *Don Quixote* word for word centuries after the original was published, yet does not write the same book.

This need for new adaptations of the story mainly comes from the second part of Cervantes's work, which may be considered to be an adaptation of the first. The main character decides to "go out" and seek adventure again, but he has not changed, even if his condition seemed to have healed at the end of the first part. The situations narrated in book 2 are of course new, but they are not totally different from the ones to be found in book 1: whether he is confronted with windmills or a puppet show, Quixote always misinterprets events according to his readings, and makes giants or villains out of inanimate objects. As Marthe Robert shows, the book can be read unchronologically, since the narrated events do not follow from one another and do not become gradually more complex, but just accumulate like a series of unrelated short stories.[3]

The second part, then, is at the same time a *sequel* and a *repetition*. Indeed, in chapter 3 of book 2, the bachelor Samson Carrasco gives the reader a brief summary of what happened in book 1, taken from what he has read in a recently published work. In other words, book 1 appears as a book at the beginning of book 2, and is mentioned several times throughout. This makes book 2 even more similar to an adaptation, since the characters mentioned here are literally taken from a book (part 1), and given doubles in another (part 2).

Another dimension of the process should be taken into account. Just like the film adaptation of a novel, the second part of *Don Quixote*, makes the characters seem more *real*. If the Knight of the Sad Countenance lives in a fictional world because his imagination distorts everything (in part 2, he is, both literally and figuratively, *in a book*), it has to mean that the world outside, the one to which his body belongs, is real. The supposed author of book 1, Cid Hamet Benengeli, is mentioned again in book 2, as the author of both the first volume and the second, which makes him at the same time a character in the book and, as the author, a person out of the book, even if he is just another of Cervantes's creations. Don Quixote and Sancho Panza are in the same situation, and therefore as "real" as Cid Hamet Benengeli is. Chapter 59 goes even further in trying to endow the characters with "reality," since it mentions a fake sequel of *Don Quixote*, written by an author named Avellaneda. Indeed, there actually *is* a fake sequel of *Don Quixote*, and Avellaneda really existed. Reality thus intrudes into the novel, and allows Cervantes to criticize the forger, and his characters to prove they are *real* because their counterparts in Avellaneda's work are impostors. The fake sequel exists, which tends to prove the other sequel, i.e., book 2, to be real too, even if it is in fact as fictional as its author Cid Hamet. As the one and only Don Quixote, Cervantes's character then decides not to go to Saragoza just because the impostor went there, i.e., to expose him as fake and to prove he is the *true* Don Quixote.[4]

Re-adaptation, then, is part and parcel of *Don Quixote*, and contributes to making the character mythical. But it also contributes to making *Don Quixote* a reflexive work, through the *mise en abyme* process. In *Les Mots et les choses*, Michel Foucault shows that its specular dimension allows the book to investigate the relationship between language and truth. For him, *Don Quixote* is "the hero of the same."[5] The romances he has been reading tell him his duty, since he draws from them what he ought to say and to do, and his feats tend to prove that what happens in the romances is true.[6] In other words, he makes the world outside look like what it is in the books.[7] Of course, the fact that he fails to do so tends to prove that he is wrong, that fiction is bound to remain untrue.

But Cervantes's reflection does not end there, as the general opinion about *Don Quixote* goes. For Michel Foucault, book 2 is essential to the understanding of the work, in that it demonstrates that language has not become totally powerless. Book 1 plays in book 2 the part that romances used to play in book 1. Don Quixote must now be faithful not to his dreams, but to what he has become in the previous volume, he has to prove *himself* real.[8] He therefore owes his existence to language only, and his truth is *inside* the words of the book, it is self-sufficient and does not have to be related to the 'real' world.[9] Authors do not have to search the world for truths to express anymore, since they are able to create their own truth.[10]

The most interesting aspect of the reflection is not only that it is created by a new form, the novel, but that it also justifies the use of this new form. Indeed, as Georg Lukács indicates, *Don Quixote* shows that authors should not write epic romances any more because the epic genre is no longer related to Truth.[11] Hence the rise of the novel, which allows for another form of perfect relationship between word and Truth. For Lukács, Cervantes had the visionary intuition that things had changed, and took the change into account to create a new literary genre in order to make it possible again to express a truth.[12] To put it simply, *Don Quixote* deals with the death of the epic and the necessary birth of the novel.[13]

Consequently, when it comes to adapting the book, most directors realize it would be difficult to make a film about the rise of the novel, which is probably why they choose to take no heed of book 2 and of the reflexive dimension it introduces, and merely use film narrative technique to tell the story of book 1 *again*.

Orson Welles, however, does not. Just like book 2, his *Don Quixote*, the film of a lifetime that was released years after his death, presents one of the knight's new 'outings.' The original story is transformed, Don Quixote and Sancho are transposed into our world, where they hear they are about to be the heroes of a movie by ... Orson Welles himself. The re-adaptation process, then, is at the heart of both the novel and the film, in which two *versions* of the main characters meet. The re-adaptation required by the original text leads Welles to change the plot. Apparently, his aim is to preserve the reflexive quality of the book. In this, he is encouraged by the object of the reflection, the relationship between fact and fiction which, according to Youssef Ishaghpour is the whole point of Welles's work.[14] Analyzing the film in further detail is now necessary to determine how Welles manages to keep this essential dimension of the myth, and to elicit the conclusions he draws from the reflexive dimension of *Don Quixote*.

When watching one of the sequences that make up the film of *Don Quixote* as it was edited in the early 90s, for example the purple patch sequence of the hero's fight against the windmills, one might get the feeling that the finished film would have been a traditional, linear adaptation of the book. But that impression is proven wrong when one takes the whole reconstructed film into account. Indeed, it includes "real life" sequences, quasi documentary scenes in which Quixote and Sancho, or Welles himself, appear in contemporary Spain, for example in the context of a bullfight. As a matter of fact, as Youssef Ishaghpour indicates, Welles did not want to shoot the kind of adaptation he had shot in *The Trial* or in his Shakespearian films, because the book is made of references to past literature and to itself.[15] His film, then, includes passages of traditional adaptation, along with passages of contemporary transposition, which allow for a reflection on traditional adaptation itself. Welles seems to have been aware that, as André Helbo shows, an adaptor cannot be faithful to the original text without changing its meaning,[16] which is exactly what Borges proves in *Pierre Ménard*. Consequently, a traditional theatrical or filmic adaptation of the book is virtually impossible, as Marthe Robert explicitly notes,[17] but an adaptation that is not totally faithful to the text may be successful. Hence Welles's choice of a new way to adapt, a way that was supposed to take account of the book's inadaptability in its very title. Indeed, at some point, Welles chose *When are you going to finish Don Quixote* as the title for his movie,[18] not just because he never had enough money or time to finish it but probably also because he was aware of the *necessarily* unfinished character of the work, in a much more intuitive way than critics such as Marthe Robert.[19] Strangely enough, Welles's film is not the only film *about* the difficulty to adapt in the usual way: Keith Fulton and Louis Pepe's *Lost in La Mancha* is another instance, and it is very close to Welles's film in the way it works and deals with the *problem* of adapting *Don Quixote*.

The opening sequence of the film gives a good notion of Welles's conception of adaptation. The last shot shows a statue of Don Quixote with a book in his hand. Then, after a dissolve which almost amounts to *morphing*, the statue takes life in the next shot, which shows the character, played by Francisco Reiguera reading a book aloud. This last statue is one of the many included in the opening sequence, as if to illustrate Welles's desire to adapt the myth of Don Quixote, what it means today, rather than the original story. The dissolve, a blatant intervention of the film director, seems to mean here that Welles's aim is to give life to the (contemporary) statue, i.e., to the monument of European literature, rather than to the character in the book. Hence his voice-over comments about telling the spectator the truth about Don Quixote.[20] But the sequence that follows might perfectly be an excerpt from a traditional adaptation, at least until the shot freezes, since no contemporary elements appear in it, so that the mixture of traditional adaptation and transposition into the modern world is preserved. Indeed, the film also includes sequences taken from Cervantes's book, but told in the context of Welles's time. One of them is particularly interesting, as it echoes the opening sequence by involving statues taking life too, in a kind of *mise en abyme* of the film.

In chapter 52 of book 1, Don Quixote sees a procession walking by, and, mistaking the statues for real life people, he decides to assault the marchers in order to set the oppressed "statues" free. Similarly, in the film, Don Quixote attacks a procession in today's Spain. Welles's use of this specific episode is utterly important on several grounds. Indeed, the procession establishes time continuity between Quixote's days and Welles's: time has gone by, but some things have not changed. The reference, however, is not just supposed to mean that Quixote should be considered as our contemporary, that one should look for the character today. The procession is still there but at least two elements have changed. First, while the procession misinterpreted by Quixote necessarily remained fictional in the book, despite Cervantes's efforts to make his characters more real, the procession shown in the film is far less fictional and therefore much closer to reality. Indeed, the sequence apparently uses documentary shots of real processions along with the fictional shots of Don Quixote. The character has not altered, but the reality around him has: the film of *Don Quixote*, unlike the book, deals with the relationship of fiction and reality without having to resort to fiction and only fiction. Second, because it echoes the end of the opening sequence, the procession creates a parallelism between Don Quixote and Orson Welles, who both give life to statues, although in different ways. Of course, as noted earlier quoting Michel Foucault, Don Quixote consults the books he has read to determine what he should say or do, and this is just what a film director adapting a book does. But, while the transformation operated by Quixote lacks verisimilitude, so that his psychological problem is constantly exposed by Cervantes, Welles manages to give life to statues in a much more credible and efficient way. The statue he brings to life is not the one Quixote sees, but the one Quixote is. Our days have fulfilled some of the conditions for Quixote's dream of literally adapting his favorite romances to come true.

The opening sequence, then, conveys that the relationship of fiction and reality has changed with the birth of the moving image and its increased illusionary powers. Consequently, Cervantes's reflection, based on the possibilities of the epic and the novel, cannot be valid anymore, unless it takes into account the new conditions created by moving pictures, i.e., unless it is applied to cinema. This is what Welles seems to be trying to do in his film.

The starting point of the novel, Quixote's desire to make books come true, is preserved, though Welles is now the most quixotic character in his movie. And whereas the book reflects on literary genres, Welles's film reflects on cinema. Indeed, for Cervantes, the role of the novel is to free literature from its *imitative* imperative. While the epic used to rest on the possibility for art to express life, the novel rests on the possibility for literature to *create* life. Welles's film, juxtaposing as it does real life sequences and adaptive sequences in the traditional meaning of the word, i.e., sequences which *imitate* what is in the novel, seems to deal with the same problem in the context not of literary genres, but of film genres. And of course, this new reflection, inspired by the book but translated into cinematic language, leads the director to new conclusions.

In the book, the reflection reaches conclusions mostly in book 2. Similarly, the film becomes more reflexive when it deals with the second part of the book. Indeed, in the second half of the movie, a film of *Don Quixote* is mentioned in the film, as a direct reference to the various mentions of books — one of which is a fake — also bearing the title *Don Quixote* in part 2. *The film within the film* intervenes several times and under various aspects. Unfortunately, a sequence in which Don Quixote assaulted a cinema screen on which his picture was projected, the equivalent of the episode of the puppet show in book 2, seems to have been lost. But a few other sequences give a good idea of how Welles wished to deal with the specular dimension of the book.

To take but one example, the film includes a sequence in which Sancho, now traveling alone to look for Dulcinea, "makes a couple of bucks by acting as an extra in a film," as the voice-over narrator puts it. The film, of course, is none other than Orson Welles's *Don Quixote*. The sequence provides a good translation of the book's central point.

In part 1 of *Don Quixote*, a character sees the outside world as the imaginary world described in the books he has read. In a few words, he reads the books into the world around. In part 2, we hear that Don Quixote and Sancho have become the main characters in a novel entitled *Don Quixote*, which is therefore a *book within the book*. As Lucien Dällenbach shows, in part 2, the characters of book 1 come across fictional doubles, and the immediate effect is that they appear to be more real for being less fictional than their literary counterparts, and perhaps not fictional at all.[21] Consequently, Cervantes bears a resemblance to Don Quixote, in that they both give life to fictional creatures. The important difference, of course, is that, thanks to the novel, Cervantes is able to do so with a lot more distance than his character does, because he is aware of his power to design lifelike creatures and uses the book to reflect on this illusionary power. In other words, the reflexive quality of the novel allows Cervantes to separate the confusion of subjectivity and objectivity (Don Quixote's ailment) on the one hand, and the creation of objectivity through subjectivity (the author's privilege) on the other hand. The consequence in terms of literary genres is that the one favored by Don Quixote, the epic, has become outdated, and should be replaced by the one used by Cervantes, the novel.

In the film, particularly in the shooting sequence, Welles also tackles the relationship between subjectivity and objectivity, although he has cinema, rather than literature, in mind as a topic for reflection. Indeed, just like in the novel, subjectivity intervenes in objective sequences in various degrees.

The first shot in the sequence is documentary-like, since it shows children in contemporary clothes playing, while the voice-over narrator asks for silence. The next shot is also a documentary shot, though the documentary, in this case, is not about Spain today, but about the shooting of a movie. In a long shot, we find on the left Sancho on a donkey walking away into the background, a camera center-screen recording the action, under the attentive gaze of the director, Orson Welles, standing right of screen. The shot might appear to be totally objective if the camera did not pan slightly as Sancho's donkey staggers under the weight of the rider, as if to underline some degree of directorial intervention even in the most "objective" shot. Then, after a medium close-up shot of Orson Welles wiping the sweat off his brow, the next shot is definitely subjective, since it shows, in a medium shot, Sancho riding away, as the camera in the previous shot, and the director, saw him. But the voice over is still there, shouting advice at Sancho, to remind us that this is not totally a shot from *Don Quixote* adapted, that it is still part of a documentary about shooting a film. The end of the sequence alternates shots of Sancho and shots of Orson Welles, until the latter goes away from the screen as if to put an end to the sequence.

The interest of the passage lies in the fact that, as subjectivity intervenes in the objective sequence, Sancho, presented as a real, contemporary character throughout the film, becomes more fictional, in a kind of inversion of the device used by Cervantes in book 2. In the book, Cervantes reflected on fictional heroes becoming more real. In the film, Sancho is real, and Welles has the power to make him become fictional: his characters, who have already become real in the book, are being turned into fiction again. The documentary-like sequence encompasses shots from a traditional adaptation, and therefore reflects on them in the same way as the novel produced a reflection on the epic. Welles's conclusion, regarding cinema, is similar to that drawn by Cervantes: it is useless to adapt *Don Quixote* by illustrating what is in the book, first because it would amount to doing just what Quixote himself does, and which is exposed by Cervantes, second because there is no need to demonstrate that the characters are real: you just shoot them documentary-style in a contemporary context, and they are. The power of the author used to lie in his ability to create truth out of fiction. The power of the film director lies in another kind of confusion between fiction and reality: the possibility to turn *real life* into fiction, and to create even greater confusion, which is the topic of Welles's *Don Quixote*.

Consequently, the film, even if it is not a traditional adaptation, should still be considered as a relevant adaptation of *Don Quixote*. Indeed, the use of what Welles calls the 'essay film' allows him to demonstrate that a traditional, literal adaptation of *Don Quixote* is impossible because it would necessarily fail to express the book's reflection on subjectivity and objectivity, for one simple reason: the advent of moving images has made fake objectivity much more easily attainable, thus changing all the data of the problem. A film merely talking about a character reading the outside world as one of his favorite books would totally miss the point. By using a documentary form including fictional sequences, Welles manages to keep the reflexive dimension of the book and *adapts it* to the context of our times and to cinema. His *Don Quixote* uses the re-adaptation process present in the book, and turns this literary device into film re-adaptation. Whereas Cervantes drew conclusions from this reflexive aspect in the field of literature, replacing the epic by the novel, Welles draws conclusions about cinema and, just like Cervantes, applies his conclusions to his own work: since, as the film shows, a traditional adaptation of *Don Quixote* is impossible today, a film of *Don Quixote* should adapt its own form to express the contemporary meaning of the book, which it does. Welles's conclusion in the film he could never finish is totally in keeping with the trend of his whole career, from fictional movies to 'essay films' such as *F for Fake*, and from direct adaptations of Shakespeare' plays to documentaries about adapting and about film-making, such as *Filming Othello*. The re-adaptation found in the book is then made to work again in order to produce meaning today. Cervantes found the greatest point of confusion between fiction and reality to lie in novels, not in epics. Readapting Cervantes, but differently, so as to keep the essence of the book, Welles finds the best powers of illusion not in fictional films or traditional adaptations, but in documentary movies which make it even easier to lie like truth.

NOTES

1. See Timothy Richard Wutrich, *Prometheus and Faust. The Promethean Revolt in Drama from Classical Antiquity to Goethe*, Westport, CT: Greenwood, 1995.

2. "C'est un livre impossible, sans cesse à faire et sans cesse à recommencer." Marthe Robert, *L'Ancien et le nouveau, De Don Quichotte à Franz Kafka*, Paris: Grasset, 1963, 13.

3. "Le *Don Quichotte* pourrait être lu dans n'importe quel ordre (Cervantès le suggère du reste), car il ne se développe pas à travers des situations découlant les unes des autres et, de ce fait, de plus en plus compliquées, mais se compose par l'accumulation de "sketches" analogues, mis bout à bout sans aucun lien de causalité." *Ibid.,* 125. ("*Don Quixote* could be read in any order (Cervantes suggests as much), because it doesn't progress through situations that are caused one by the other, and therefore are increasingly complicated, but rather is composed of an accumulation of similar "bits" placed end to end without cause or effect.") See also Juan José Saer, *Lignes du Quichotte*, Paris: Éditions Verdier, 2003, 10: "Quels que soient les avatars, les circonstances, les caractéristiques des aventures que connaît Don Quichotte, le modèle, le sens de chacune est toujours le même: la confrontation de son idéal avec une réalité qui est en conflit avec cet idéal. Et à chaque épisode, autant dans la première partie du livre que dans la seconde, la même situation se répète indéfiniment." ("Whatever the form, the circumstances, the characteristics of Don Quixote's adventures, the model and the meaning of each is always the same: the confrontation of his ideal with a conflicting reality; and in each episode, both in the first and in the second book, the same situation repeats itself indefinitely.") All translations are the editor's.

4. In chapter 72, Don Quixote and Sancho meet one of the characters in the fake sequel, who claims he knows the real Don Quixote and Sancho, then finally admits to lying and declares those in front of him to be the real ones.

5. "Il est le héros du Même." Michel Foucault, *Les Mots et les choses*, Paris: Gallimard, 1966, 60.

6. "Le livre est moins son existence que son devoir. Sans cesse il doit le consulter afin de savoir que faire et que dire, et quels signes donner à lui-même et aux autres pour montrer qu'il est bien de même nature que le texte dont il est issu." *Ibid.,* 60. ("The book is not so much his existence as his duty. Constantly he must consult it to know what to do and say, and which signs to give to himself and others to show that he is indeed cut from the same cloth as the text from whence he comes.")

7. "A lui de refaire l'épopée, mais en sens inverse: celle-ci racontait (prétendait raconter) des exploits réels, promis à la mémoire; Don Quichotte, lui, doit combler de réalité les signes sans contenu du récit. Son aventure sera un déchiffrement du monde: un parcours minutieux pour relever sur toute la surface de la terre les figures qui montrent que les livres disent vrai. L'exploit doit être preuve." *Ibid.,* 61. ("It is his responsibility to remake the epic, but backwards: the epic told (or pretended to tell) of real exploits, certain to be memorable; Don Quixote must fill the signs without content of the narrative with reality. His adventure will be to decode the world: a painstaking path to collect the world over the figures that show that the books are true. His challenge must be proof.")

8. "Le langage pourtant n'est pas devenu tout à fait impuissant. Il détient désormais de nouveaux pouvoirs, et qui lui sont propres. Dans la seconde partie du roman, Don Quichotte rencontre des personnages qui ont lu la première partie du texte et qui le reconnais-

sent, lui, homme réel, pour le héros du livre. Le texte de Cervantès se replie sur lui-même, s'enfonce dans sa propre épaisseur, et devient pour soi objet de son propre récit. La première partie des aventures joue dans la seconde le rôle qu'assumaient au début les romans de chevalerie. Don Quichotte doit être fidèle à ce livre qu'il est réellement devenu; il a à le protéger des erreurs, des contrefaçons, des suites apocryphes; il doit ajouter les détails omis; il doit maintenir sa vérité." *Ibid.*, 62. ("Language has not become completely powerless. It now has new powers, powers that belong only to it. In the second part of the novel, Don Quixote meets characters that have read the first part of the text and who recognize him, the real man, as the protagonist of the book. Cervantes's text folds in on itself, plunging into its own depths, and becomes for itself the object of its own narrative. The first part of the adventures plays the role for the second was taken on by tales of chivalry. Don Quixote must be faithful to the book that he has become; he must protect it from errors, from counterfeits, from apocryphal sequels; he must add omitted details; he must maintain his truth.")

9. "Don Quichotte a pris sa réalité. Réalité qu'il ne doit qu'au langage, et qui reste entièrement intérieure aux mots. La vérité de Don Quichotte, elle n'est pas dans le rapport des mots au monde, mais dans cette mince et constante relation que les marques verbales tissent d'elles-mêmes à elles-mêmes." *Ibid.*, 62. ("Don Quixote has taken his reality, a reality he owes only to language, and which remains within the words. Don Quixote's truth is not in the relationship between words and the world, but in the fragile and constant relationship that verbal markers weave amongst themselves.")

10. "Fascinante pour qui l'écrit, magique pour qui la lit, la littérature n'est pas mensongère parce qu'elle accrédite des fictions, mais à cause de cette complicité soigneusement tenue secrète grâce à quoi le fictif et le réel se soutiennent mutuellement au détriment de leurs vérités respectives." Robert, *L'Ancien et le nouveau*, 170. ("Fascinating for those who write, magical for those who read, literature is not false because it gives credence to fictions, but because of its carefully guarded secret complicity which allows the fictional and the real to support one another to the detriment of their respective truths.")

11. "Ce n'est pas un hasard historique si *Don Quichotte* fut conçu comme parodie des romans de chevalerie, et la relation qui l'unit à eux dépasse le plan de l'accident. Le roman de chevalerie avait succombé au sort qui attend toute épopée dès lors qu'à partir d'éléments qui ne sont que formels, elle prétend soutenir et prolonger la vie d'une forme au-delà du moment où la dialectique historico-philosophique en a déjà condamné les conditions transcendantales d'existence." György Lukacs, *La Théorie du roman*, Paris: Gonthier, 1963, 96. ("It is no historical coincidence that *Don Quixote* was conceived as a parody of romances, and the relationship that links it to them is no accident. The romance had succumbed to the fate that awaits all epics when, using only formal elements, it intends to support and extend the life of a form beyond the moment where the historic-philosophic dialectic has already condemned the transcendental conditions of existence.")

12. "L'homme qui a su trouver le secret d'une invraisemblable perfection n'est point le naïf écrivain Cervantès, mais bien plutôt le visionnaire intuitif d'un instant historico-philosophique unique et qui ne reviendra jamais. Sa vision a surgi au point même où se séparent deux époques." *Ibid.*, 130. ("The man who knew how to find the secret of an unreal perfection is not the naïve writer Cervantes, but rather the visionary who intuited a unique historical-philosophical instant which will never return. His vision appeared at the very point where two periods separated.")

13. "Le roman est l'épopée d'un temps où la totalité extensive de la vie n'est plus donnée de manière immédiate, d'un temps pour lequel l'immanence du sens à la vie est devenue problème mais qui, néanmoins, n'a pas cessé de viser à la totalité." *Ibid.*, 49. ("The novel is the epic of a time where the exhaustive totality of life is no longer given instantaneously, a time for which the immanence of the meaning of life has become problematic, but which nonetheless has not stopped aiming for that totality.")

14. "*Don Quichotte* est le commencement de cette séparation entre subjectivité et objectivité, idéal et réalité, fait et sens, intérieur et extérieur, fiction et vérité, dont, chez Welles même, *Citizen Kane, The Lady from Shanghai,* ou Mr. Clay voulant réaliser 'une histoire immortelle' seront les avatars." Youssef Ishaghpour, *Orson Welles cinéaste: Une caméra visible,* vol. 3, Paris: La Différence, 2001, 830. ("*Don Quixote* is the beginning of this separation between subjectivity and objectivity, ideal and reality, fact and meaning, internal and external, fiction and truth of which Welles's *Citizen Kane, The Lady from Shanghai,* or Mr. Clay wanting to make 'an immortal story' are the avatars.")

15. "Il ne s'agissait donc pas d'une réalisation directe, d'une "adaptation" cinématographique, à la manière du *Procès* ou des films shakespeariens, mais d'une référence obligée au livre, qui est — le premier grand roman de la littérature occidentale — lui-même autoréférentiel, un effet de référence à d'autres livres : imitation, redoublement et réflexion." *Ibid.,* 826. ("Therefore it was not a direct realization of a film adaptation, like *The Trial* or the Shakespearean films, but an obligatory reference to the book, which is — the first great novel in Western literature — autoreferential, an impression of reference to other books: imitation, doubling, mirroring.")

16. "La 'fidélité' au texte de l'auteur est-elle pensable comme telle, sans renversement de sens ? Pareille attitude de metteur en scène ne s'apparenterait-elle pas au projet aberrant de l'adaptateur bien intentionné décrit par Borgès, dans sa nouvelle *Pierre Ménard, auteur du Quichotte* ? Ménard imagine de réécrire 'mot à mot et ligne à ligne' le roman de Cervantès. [...] *In fine,* le *Quichotte* de Ménard se révélera plus riche et plus complexe que celui de Cervantès, composé 'un peu à la diable, entraîné par la force d'inertie du langage et de l'invention." André Helbo, *L'Adaptation du théâtre au cinéma,* Paris: Armand Colin, 1997, 17–18. ("Is the 'faithfulness' of the text to the 'author' imaginable as such, without changing its meaning? Would not such an attitude in a director suggest the well-intended director's aberrant project described by Borgès in his short story *Pierre Ménard, the author of Don Quixote*? Ménard imagines rewriting word by word and line by line Cervantes's novel. In the end, Ménard's *Quixote* will end up being a richer and more complex work than Cervantes's, 'a bit devilish, dragged along by the strength of language's inertia and inventivity.")

17. "La présence de ce théâtre dans le roman est justement ce qui devrait interdire l'adaptation, le spectacle donquichottesque n'étant en aucun cas une fin en soi – ce qu'il devient dès qu'on le porte à la scène–, mais un moyen dont la puissance est mise entièrement au service de la démonstration romanesque. [...] Un Don Quichotte *joué* est inévitablement pris à la lettre, il coïncide si parfaitement avec son personnage qu'il paraît *naturel,* alors qu'il joue et souligne ostensiblement la distance qu'il convient de maintenir entre lui-même et sa comédie." Robert, *L'Ancien et le nouveau,* 30. ("The presence of this theater in the novel is what should make its adaptation forbidden, as the Don Quixotean spectacle is in no case an end in itself— which it what it becomes once it's put on stage — but a tool whose power is entirely in the service of the novelistic demonstration. A Don Quixote *acted out* is necessarily taken literally; he coincides so perfectly with his character that he appears natural, whereas he is acting an ostensibly highlighting the necessary distance between himself and his comedy.")

18. Ishaghpour, *Orson Welles cinéaste,* 823.

19. Robert, *L'Ancien et le nouveau,* 13.

20. "The main thing is that our narrative should not depart an inch from the truth."

21. "[Dans *Don Quichotte,*] la fictivité affirmée dès l'abord transforme en scandale narratif le fait que les protagonistes, comme échappés du premier livre, prétendent dans une seconde partie — tributaire de la même source !— se faire juges de la première; moyen privilégié de jouer avec l'illusion, cette intrusion de lecteurs fictifs dans la sphère où seule leur fiction peut être lue permet précisément à ces derniers de tenter une sortie hors de leur monde." Lucien Dällenbach, *Le récit spéculaire. Essai sur la mise en abyme,* Paris: Éditions du Seuil,

1977, 118. ("In *Don Quixote*, the fictionality affirmed from the outset transforms the fact that the protagonists, as if refugees from the first book, become judges of the first, into a narrative scandal; it's an excellent means of playing with illusion — this intrusion of fictional readers in a world where only their fiction can be read allows the characters to attempt to exit their world.")

BIBLIOGRAPHY

Dällenbach, Lucien. *Le récit spéculaire. Essai sur la mise en abyme*. Paris: Éditions du Seuil, 1977.

Foucault, Michel. *Les Mots et les choses*. Paris: Gallimard, 1966.

Helbo, André. *L'Adaptation du théâtre au cinéma*. Paris: Armand Colin, 1997.

Ishaghpour, Youssef. *Orson Welles cinéaste: Une caméra visible*, vol. 3. Paris: La Différence, 2001.

Lukacs, György. *La Théorie du roman*. Paris: Gonthier, 1963.

Robert, Marthe. *L'Ancien et le nouveau, De Don Quichotte à Franz Kafka*. Paris: Grasset, 1963.

Saer, Juan José. *Lignes du Quichotte*. Paris: Éditions Verdier, 2003.

Wutrich, Timothy Richard. *Prometheus and Faust. The Promethean Revolt in Drama from Classical Antiquity to Goethe*. Westport, CT: Greenwood, 1995.

Bad Shakespeare:
Adapting a Tradition

Charles Holdefer

"Bad Shakespeare" can mean many things: a poorly executed play, a "corrupt" quarto, or a work like *Titus Andronicus*. (For the last, it often comes with special pleading, as in "No, really, it's not as bad as it seems...") But a more generic meaning is possible, too. I would like to use the term to refer to a self-conscious literary tradition which goes back for centuries, and which has continued into the film era.

Because of Shakespeare's privileged status in the canon, parodies and pastiche of his work have thrived, along with descriptions of imagined disastrous performances. Most of these are ephemera, intended as a bit of fun, soon forgotten, only to be replaced by more of the same. On occasion, they have known great success as popular entertainments, for instance John Poole's *Hamlet Travestie* (1811). They have also shown a chameleon-like ability to adapt to their local political environment, for example in America with minstrel show burlesques of *Othello*.[1] Sometimes these works are later judged of sufficient interest to be preserved: witness the recent republication of three volumes of imitations, parodies and forgeries composed between 1710 and 1820.[2]

More rarely, bad Shakespeare appears in works which have become, in their own right, canonical. One thinks of Mr. Wopsle's lugubrious Hamlet in *Great Expectations,* or of the King and the Duke's theatrical forays in *The Adventures of Huckleberry Finn*. In addition to providing comic relief, such depictions also contribute to their works in terms of tone and structure. They are an essential part of the tissue.

I would like to consider how this literary tradition has been adapted to film. Although an exhaustive description exceeds the bounds of this article,

I would like to compare representative examples and modes of allusion, rang-
ing from direct affiliation to selective quotation to performance as camp.
Adapting the bard involves high stakes, both aesthetically and politically.
What is gained by making him look bad?

A Dialogue with Tradition

Parody, more than other forms of allusion, accentuates an author's intentions. Speculation about intentionality is always risky, but parody advertises
its referent and its purpose. Ambiguities persist — such is the nature of language — but the dialogue between new text and source text is brought to the
foreground.[3] Because of Shakespeare's perceived position in the cultural hierarchy, responses to him often originate from the low burlesque. Conversations
are conducted while looking up.[4]

For this reason, bad Shakespeare is invested in the idea of good Shakespeare. "The act of transgression paradoxically depends upon preserving — at
least initially — some conception of an authentic, original, or proper Shakespeare so that it can then be symbolically defaced."[5] Good and bad need each
other.

Of course, there is no universal consensus about the future of this positive
template. Richard Burt, describing the American context, foresees a "post-
hermeneutic" situation, characterized by "unspeakable" products geared for
an infantile, dumbed-down culture, in which the perception of badness is
not a functioning acknowledgement of positive standards but an act of trans-
valuation toward a kind of dead-end "cool" which celebrates being a loser.[6]
Changing politics, patterns of education and new forms of commodification
are responsible for this brave new world. It is interesting to note that a mere
fifteen years before Burt's description, Terry Eagleton probably thought he
was being provocative when he speculated that "given a deep enough transformation of our history, we may in the future produce a society which is
unable to get anything at all out of Shakespeare."[7] Burt seems to suggest that
we are almost there.[8]

I do not believe we have yet reached such a watershed. The appropriations
of Shakespeare that Burt cites (many of them from television, many of them
self-consciously bad, or at least unambitious, which is not necessarily the same
thing) might not really be so new, aside from the manner of their dissemination. Unless one fully embraces the idea that the medium is the message, it
is possible to argue that these popular appropriations have precedents. For
instance, they might be roughly analogous to 17th century "drolls" or other

amusements. Although technological developments are far-reaching and potent, they do not necessarily invent unprecedented uses of Shakespeare. A dialogue with tradition — however it is valued, displaced, debased, palpably erased or celebrated — persists, at least in the examples of film adaptation studied here.

Direct Affiliation

One of the earliest film adaptations of intentionally bad Shakespeare appears in Richard Thorpe's version of *The Adventures of Huckleberry Finn* (1939). Thorpe had just been fired from directing *The Wizard of Oz*, which was struggling in production at MGM. Thorpe's *Finn*, like *Oz*, strives for more than formula: it is a self-conscious engagement with a much beloved work, a prestige product. Mickey Rooney was cast in the lead role.[9] Hugo Butler's screenplay attempts to be faithful to Twain's vision and though not a literal transposition, its relationship to its source might be described as a direct affiliation.

In Twain's account, the King and the Duke's bad Shakespeare is an eclectic affair, a sequence of calculated crowd-pleasers. It includes the balcony scene from *Romeo and Juliet* and the sword fight from *Richard III*, with a soliloquy from *Hamlet* as an encore. A version of this soliloquy is recorded in its entirety by Huck, and it turns out to be a disordered and nonsensical pastiche of famous lines from Shakespeare. Later, when the show flops in front of a backwoods audience, the Duke concludes that "Arkansaw lunkheads couldn't come up to Shakespeare."[10] This sets the stage for the King's painted nude cavortings in "The Royal Nonesuch."

In the film, as is usually the case in adaptations, the text has been compressed and the soliloquy pastiche is cut — an obvious choice, given the switch to a visual medium — and for the rest of the show, the only performance depicted is the balcony scene from *Romeo and Juliet*. In the novel, the King plays the heroine; in the film, Huck appears in drag. Mickey Rooney as Juliet is busty, lipsticked, and has a flower on each shoulder. When he misses a cue, he belches. The performance ends in a riot when a yokel in the audience suddenly realizes that Huck is not a girl, and cries out, "Sold."

In addition to matters of taste — what might seem absurd but inspired in the novel appears, in this film, somewhat puerile — there is the vital question of Thorpe's editorial choices. In the novel, the rehearsals of Shakespeare are described at some length, the soliloquy and theater posters are reproduced verbatim, and the unsuccessful performance is summarized: it is all part of

Twain's set-up of the Royal Nonesuch, the scam by which an entire village is "sold." In the film, the Royal Nonesuch is completely elided, and the balcony scene stands in isolation. Granted, in the era of the Hays Code, depicting the King's nude dance was not an option; but there is an even greater problem in the director's depiction of the villagers' outrage: the scene ends abruptly and bewilderingly and seems arbitrary even by the picaresque conventions of the story. As purposefully bad Shakespeare, it fits the description; but as an adaptation capturing the richness of the situation, the code-bending and cunning of these con men, it falls short. A later attempt such as Disney's 1993 version directed by Stephen Sommers shies away from the problem and eliminates Shakespeare and the Royal Nonesuch altogether. This is arguably a question of pacing but it comes at a price in terms of adaptation and perhaps attests, moreover, to the challenge of this kind of representation. My point here is not to disparage a weak film or to tut at a timid one, but to underline their aesthetic situation. A scene might be a travesty, but art still imposes its rigors. Tradition offers successful precedents, in light of which later efforts are judged. Or, to put it another way: it is not easy to be bad.

Selective Quotation

While Thorpe approaches Shakespeare via Mark Twain, and offers an adaptation of an adaptation, other directors go straight to the source, and conjure up their vision of badness to suit their own story. Ernst Lubitsch's *To Be or Not to Be* (1942), set in wartime Warsaw, uses Hamlet's famous speech for ends that go far beyond parody. "To be or not to be" is surely the most frequently cited line in Shakespeare, if not in all of English literature, and pops up in more winking examples than I can begin to enumerate.[11] One can nevertheless distinguish between a passing allusion or pastiche — for instance, when Woody Allen as a court jester in *Everything You Wanted to Know About Sex, But Were Afraid to Ask*, recites "TB or not TB" — and a sustained allusion such as in Lubitsch's work, which compresses the original text (one hears only the beginning of the soliloquy) but returns to it repeatedly. It is a running gag, but also much more, both integral to the plot (a wife's ploy in infidelity) and central to the character of Joseph Tura, a vain yet insecure actor as played by Jack Benny.

Lubitsch's film explores the idea of the ham, whose distinctive badness is achieved when the actor's efforts become so obvious to the viewer's attention that they compete with the role itself. Shakespeare, because of his lofty reputation, is irresistibly attractive to this most eager of theatrical animals; he also proves a veritable killing floor. Lubitsch delineates several types of hams: there is the expansive, overbearing variety, like the character Rawitch. Each time he is given a cue to speak, no space seems big enough. ("What you are," moans his Jewish colleague Greenburg, "I wouldn't eat.") And there is the quieter, more preening and self-regarding type of ham, such as Joseph Tura, whose performances convey an all-too-apparent neediness, which swells — and is punctured — each time he seeks his big moment with the "To be or not to be" soliloquy. In either case, the actor over-reaches, believing that Shakespeare's perceived greatness will somehow accrue to him personally.[12]

Such theatrical excess is refashioned by cinematic technique. For instance, Lubitsch's adroit shifts in camera perspective allow Tura's plight as a ham to be amusing and even endearing. The first time he enters as Hamlet and begins his speech — it takes only a few seconds — the perspective moves swiftly from the confined view of the audience (which is how one usually observes hams, and which is why they can induce an aesthetic claustrophobia) to a view *behind* the actor, which evokes the parallel world backstage, with all its problems and intrigues; and finally, to the actor's own view of the audience, and of a prompter improbably nudging him to say the famous lines. It is an invitation for sympathy for the *performer*, not for the character that the performer is playing. (The second time the scene is staged, it actually begins with a backstage perspective, further reinforcing this sentiment.) It contrasts, for instance, with another hammy Hamlet as described in Dickens' *Great Expectations*, where the reader has only Pip's account of the pitiable Mr. Wopsle. Everything is filtered through the audience's perspective. For instance, "On the question whether 'twas nobler in the mind to suffer, some roared yes, and some no, and some inclining to both opinions said "toss up for it.""[13] One can laugh at Wopsle, but there is no invitation, at the same time, to identify with him.

Lubitsch's adaptation of this soliloquy more vigorously asserts its independence from the original. It is less about Shakespeare than about itself, a springboard toward a contemporary story. Comparisons with Dickens' approach in *Great Expectations* offer a telling contrast: Chapter 31 of the novel begins with, "On our arrival in Denmark," whereupon Pip proceeds with an arch account of a sorry piece of theater that *stays* in the theater. For Lubitsch, however, the rottenness in Denmark recedes into the background, and is replaced by the invasion and occupation of Poland. Dobosh, the director of the theatrical company, frets, "I hate to leave the fate of my country in the hands of a ham." Made in 1942, the film artfully refracts Hamlet's existential question through a political prism. Will Poland survive, and somehow continue "to be"? Elsewhere in the film, an additional issue is raised when Greenburg performs Shylock's famous "Hath not a Jew eyes?" soliloquy from Act III of *The Merchant of Venice*. This is presented without irony, as an earnest adaptation in the spirit of "good Shakespeare." It is a selective quotation, too, but for decidedly different ends. Yet the "good" does not upstage the "bad," or vice-versa. Rather, the two modes complement each other.

Camp

Ever since Susan Sontag's 1964 essay "Notes on Camp," mainstream critical circles have been increasingly aware of camp sensibility and of its cultivation of semiotic excess. Bad Shakespeare lends itself readily to camp because, as Sontag observes, camp is "the sensibility of failed seriousness, of the theatricalization of experience."[14] Camp is a vast subject but it includes — for the purposes of this discussion — the idea of aesthetically studied badness. It is a slippery set of discursive processes which are readily queered and which enact, in Fabio Cleto's formulation, "a 'sham,' provisional, performative existence [...] translating its definitional 'fakeness' onto constructions which cannot but be based on categories provisional and partial — from a position, on behalf of a position."[15] Or, to put it another way: performing in tights might look silly, but what if you *like* it? (As performer, or observer, or more precisely, as *performing observer*.) What if this liking proves to be more than whimsical because its experience enrichens our perceptions of the conditions that created it? The chief difference between camp and the parodies described earlier is that the perspective moves even further away from its original source, in order to emphasize its performance of itself. "Both camp object and subject are made into a *situation*."[16]

Camp is already hinted at in the final scene of *To Be or Not to Be,* when Joseph Tura gets the honor of performing *Hamlet* in England, and enters in a dazzling new costume and foppish hairstyle. The character has never been more serious, but before he can utter a syllable, it is harder than ever to take him seriously. This is only a glimpse, involving a traditional camp persona,[17] but it is taken much further and applied more broadly in later adaptations of Shakespeare. For the sake of illustration, I shall concentrate on two examples: Douglas Hickox's *Theatre of Blood* (1973) and Baz Luhrmann's *William Shakespeare's Romeo + Juliet* (1996).

In *Theatre of Blood*, Vincent Price plays Edward Lionheart, a Shakespearean actor who is not only a ham but also a murderer, preying on critics who have panned him throughout his career. The film is packed with allusions to Shakespeare's plays, which provide Edward with the inspiration for the methods of his murders. Not only is Edward bad — as the film shows with snippets of his over-the-top acting — he is *bad*. He drowns a critic in a barrel of wine or chops off a head or removes a pound of flesh, among other exploits. This is intertextuality with a vengeance. *Theatre of Blood* employs a familiar story-line about a killer on the loose but it also breaks with convention by inviting the viewer to sympathize with Richard, to root against the cops and critics, and to marvel at the scenes he devises. Although poorly received at the time of its release, there is no doubting *Theatre of Blood*'s graphic originality. As Deborah Cartmell has observed,

> *Theatre of Blood* calls attention to an aspect of Shakespeare which is often forgotten, perhaps because to think of Shakespeare as "bloody" sullies our pure, high culture conception of Shakespeare as something that is good for you and should not require a Parental Guidance certificate. *Theatre of Blood* daringly implies that Shakespeare is bad for you.[18]

This film aggressively questions "bardolatry" and politically correct humanisms. To Cartmell's appreciation of substance I would like to add a remark about style: Hickox's *Theatre of Blood* can be viewed as participating in film traditions of both conscious and naive camp. Although Sontag's distinction between these two modes is problematic, because of the difficulties in decoding authorial intention,[19] it still offers a way to address the complexity of reception. For conscious camp (think of Jayne Mansfield in *The Girl Can't Help It*), we have not only Price playing the diva and Robert Morley as an effete critic with poodles, but Diana Dors, too, conspicuously herself. For naive camp (earlier examples cited by Sontag include the musical numbers by Busby Berkeley), we have the exquisitely awful seventies decor and fashions, which figure so largely in recent appreciations of Elvis and Abba. In *Theatre of Blood*, it is if the ham quality of the actors has been embraced by the film's director — or even, unthinkingly, by its *era* — and adapted to the entire film.

This is a risky business, for a 100-minute movie. A common trait of the bad Shakespeare examples mentioned earlier was their status as parts within a whole. They were set pieces or citations, characterized by brevity — perhaps because even successful badness can become cloying like candy and, in quantity, too much of a good bad thing. The conscious camp of Vincent Price as a murderous, prancing gay hairdresser in an Afro wig, reproducing the execution of Joan of Arc as depicted in *Henry VI* but doing it, in this adaptation, with an electric hair-dryer, or the naive camp implicit the film's period detail, for instance, its prodigious sideburns — to mention but a few examples — give *Theatre of Blood* a semiotic excess of vast interpretative possibilities, if one can sort them all out. It is a maximalist piece of work.

In contrast, Baz Luhrmann's *William Shakespeare's Romeo + Juliet* (1996) is informed by camp sensibility but embraces it with ambivalence. It is at turns more sophisticated and less coherent. Its movement toward a post-verbal Shakespeare is nothing new (the first film adaptations, after all, were silent, not to mention adaptations in other sound genres by composers like Prokofiev); but it is true that some of this film's most successful moments come from visual puns, rooted in a camp sensibility. For instance, the opening credits introducing the cast of characters in Verona City (a taste of cheesy television) or quick sight gags like a "L'amour" advertising billboard fashioned like the logo for Coca-Cola, offer the studied frivolity of camp. The speed with which these images sail by would be impossible to reproduce in theater: they are a forceful expression of cinema.

But as the film progresses, camp style makes room for other styles, and the screen becomes rather crowded. For instance, the choreographed violence is aestheticized in an earnest and banal manner, and is often indistinguishable in presentation from the kinds of shows that earlier were being "sent up." The explosions and fireballs are quite sincere. Even Mercutio as a drag queen — a camp archetype if there ever was one — is sullied by seriousness when, after a costume change, the adapted script cuts some of the joking ironies at his death scene, in favor of playing it straight with a swelling soundtrack which tries to milk the emotion. This pattern is repeated elsewhere and as a result, much of the film, while flirting with camp, settles for kitsch,[20] or even descends into schlock.[21] As Richard Burt has remarked, "the film is less an account of the play than it is of Romeo and Juliet's mediatization, their legacy as star lovers of Western culture."[22]

For Luhrmann and his co-writer Craig Pearce, this eclecticism is not a problem; interviews suggest that many of these modes are conscious choices and may even arise out of a desire to be faithful, in their estimation, to the profusion of influences and styles in the original.[23] Shakespeare, it is well known, was not averse to a turn of bad Petrarch. But one can also argue that *William Shakespeare's Romeo + Juliet* drifts into an aesthetic jumble, and instead of getting more, the viewer experiences a dilution. After camp's initial frisson of style, the film loses its ability to surprise. It seems intent on hedging its bets.

In conclusion, bad Shakespeare shifts the focus from the original source and its ostensible purpose, and puts it on the very idea of representation, and on the potential appeal of interesting failure. In one of the first full-length critical studies of adapting Shakespeare, Jack J. Jorgens remarked, "Many have written of the *problems* of rendering Shakespeare on film, but few of the *possibilities*."[24] The film adaptations cited above reveal that there are also possibilities in the problems.

What is gained by making Shakespeare look bad? As the character Green-burg remarks in *To Be or Not to Be,* when another cultural icon is ridiculed (this time, Hitler), "a laugh is nothing to be sneezed at." And, in addition to laughs (which, indeed, should not be underestimated), bad Shakespeare brings with it a salutary critical distance. It is part of an ongoing conversation with the most potent sign in English-language literature.

Film can continue the literary traditions of parody and pastiche while at the same time exploring the techniques particular to the medium, to construct a tradition of its own. This tradition is a flexible network of direct affiliation, selective quotation or camp — categories that are neither exhaustive nor mutu-ally exclusive. In being bad, and in trying to be good at being bad, critical values are brought to the fore, made explicit and sometimes re-examined. Bad Shakespeare is a performance of a performance that shakes up our habits of seeing, and has the potential to make the work new again.

NOTES

1. Douglas Lanier, *Shakespeare and Modern Popular Culture,* Oxford: Oxford University Press, 2002, 38.
2. Jeffrey Kahan, ed., *Shakespeare Imitations, Parodies and Forgeries,* 3 vols., Oxford: Routledge, 2004.
3. Robert Alter, *The Pleasures of Reading in an Ideological Age,* New York: W.W. Norton, 1996, 132–33.
4. One could imagine a mock-heroic treatment of bawdy bits of Shakespeare, but fashion and ideology have tended otherwise.
5. Lanier, *Shakespeare and Modern Popular Culture,* 19.
6. Richard Burt, *Unspeakable ShaXXXspeares: Queer Theory & American Kiddie Culture,* New York: St. Martin's, 1998, 213.
7. Terry Eagleton, *Literary Theory: An Introduction,* Minneapolis: Minnesota University Press, 1983, 11.
8. At least in regard to Burt's stated priority of using Shakespeare for progressive polit-ical discourse, 244.
9. Rooney earlier played Puck in Max Reinhardt and William Dieterle's *A Midsummer Night's Dream* (1935), but the directors' intentions were not "bad."
10. Mark Twain, *The Adventures of Huckleberry Finn* (1884), London: J.M. Dent, 1997, 144.
11. A July 2006 Google search for this phrase claimed approximately 2,660,000 hits.
12. In Alan Johnson's 1983 remake of *To Be or Not to Be,* Mel Brooks plays the same role as ham *and* hoofer, performing Broadway-style song and dance, along with various turns of slapstick. The antic behavior, however, tends to drown out hammy neediness.
13. Charles Dickens, *Great Expectations* (1861), New York: W.W. Norton, 1999, 193.
14. Susan Sontag, "Notes on Camp" (1964), in Fabio Cleto, ed., *Camp: Queer Aesthetics and the Performing Subject: A Reader,* Edinburgh: Edinburgh University Press, 1999, 62.
15. Fabio Cleto, "Introduction: Queering the Camp," in *Camp,* in Fabio Cleto, ed., 36.
16. *Ibid.,* 25.
17. Related representations occur in later films like Herbert Ross's *The Goodbye Girl* (1977) and Bob Clark's *Porky's 2* (1986), but they are characterized fear and self-loathing,

not hammy enjoyment. See Burt, *Unspeakable ShaXXXspeares*, 44–51. In John McTiernan's *The Last Action Hero* (1993) and Robert Burnett's *Free Enterprise* (1999), Arnold Schwarzenegger and William Shatner respectively have fun with Shakespearean trappings but these moments are mainly a pretext for them to camp with received public images of *themselves*.

18. Deborah Cartmell, *Interpreting Shakespeare on Screen,* Basingstoke: Macmillan, 2000, 10.

19. Sontag, "Notes on Camp," 58.

20. Cartmell, *Interpreting Shakespeare,* 46–47.

21. "While schlock is truly unpretentious [...] and is designed primarily to fill a space in people's lives and environments, kitsch has serious pretensions to artistic taste [...] The producer or consumer of kitsch is unaware of the extent to which his pretensions are alienated in the kitsch text, or else is made to feel painfully aware of this alienation in some way. Camp, on the other hand, involves a celebration, on the part of the cognoscenti, of the alienation " Ross, "Uses of Camp," in Fabio Cleto, ed., *Camp,* 316.

22. Burt, *Unspeakeable ShaXXXspeares,* 160.

23. See the interviews with Luhrmann and Pearce on the 2000 DVD release of the film.

24. Jack J. Jorgens, *Shakespeare on Film,* Bloomington: Indiana University Press, 1977, ix.

Bibliography

The Adventures of Huck Finn. Stephen Sommers, dir., scr. Buena Vista, 1993.

The Adventures of Huckleberry Finn. Richard Thorpe, dir., Hugo Butler, scr. Metro Gold-wyn-Mayer, 1939.

Alter, Robert. *The Pleasures of Reading in an Ideological Age.* New York: W.W. Norton, 1996.

Burt, Richard. *Unspeakable ShaXXXspeares: Queer Theory & American Kiddie Culture.* New York: St. Martin's, 1998.

Cartmell, Deborah. *Interpreting Shakespeare on Screen.* Basingstoke: Macmillan, 2000.

Cleto, Fabio, ed. *Camp: Queer Aesthetics and the Performing Subject: A Reader.* Edinburgh: Edinburgh University Press, 1999.

Dickens, Charles. *Great Expectations* (1861). New York: W.W. Norton, 1999.

Eagleton, Terry. *Literary Theory: An Introduction.* Minneapolis: Minnesota University Press, 1983.

Jorgens, Jack J. *Shakespeare on Film.* Bloomington: Indiana University Press, 1977.

Kahan, Jeffrey, ed. *Shakespeare Imitations, Parodies and Forgeries,* 3 vols. Oxford: Routledge, 2004.

Lanier, Douglas. *Shakespeare and Modern Popular Culture.* Oxford: Oxford University Press, 2002.

Theatre of Blood. Douglas Hickox, dir., Anthony Greville Bell, scr. Metro Goldwyn-Mayer, 1973.

To Be or Not to Be. Ernst Lubitsch, dir., Edwin Justus Mayer, scr. Romaine Film Corporation, 1942.

Twain, Mark. *The Adventures of Huckleberry Finn* (1884). London: J.M. Dent, 1997.

William Shakespeare's Romeo + Juliet. Baz Luhrmann, dir., Craig Pierce, Baz Luhrmann, scrs. 20th Century–Fox, 1996.

Readapting "the Horror":
Versions of Conrad's
Heart of Darkness

Gene M. Moore

The word "horror" occurs in one form or another (horrid, horrifying) some fifteen times in the course of Joseph Conrad's *Heart of Darkness*. The "aunt" who helps Marlow to find employment in Africa speaks of "weaning those ignorant millions from their horrid ways,"[1] and at the first Company station, the "grove of death" where Africans are left to die leaves Marlow "horror-struck."[2] These references culminate of course in Kurtz's famous last words — "The horror! The horror!" — which are repeated three times in the text, as if horror were the essence of savagery. But Marlow takes special pains throughout the story to remind us that the horror is not confined to the dark places; his very first words are an assertion that "this, also [meaning England] has been one of the dark places of the earth,"[3] and Marlow brings Kurtz's "horror" back with him into his encounter with Kurtz's Intended in the sepulchral city of Brussels, when he tells her that Kurtz's last words were her name.

Adaptations of the story can be understood in terms of where "the horror" is located and how it is defined: whether its meaning in a given adaptation is more specific and narrow than in Conrad's story — horror applied to a particular form of savagery, or to a specific "dark place" — or whether man's capacity for horror is seen in more general terms. Is the horror always to be found "there" but never "here," or is there darkness in everyone's heart? Like Marlow's aunt, some adaptations take the horror as a symbol of ignorance and savagery which attaches to "those ignorant millions" but not to us. In terms of horror, the opposition between "us" and "them" is difficult to overcome, and even those adaptations that seek to do full justice to Marlow's realization that all places have been dark tend, paradoxically, to colonize this realization and define the horror as specially or exclusively *ours* in a manner that excludes *them* from consideration altogether.

The notion of "horror" in Conrad's story is itself not very clear. The narrator tells us that the meaning of Marlow's tale "was not inside like a kernel but outside, enveloping the tale which brought it out only as a glow brings out a haze, in the likeness of one of these misty haloes that sometimes are made visible by the spectral illumination of moonshine."[4] In other words, the meaning of the story becomes visible without becoming clear; it can be perceived only as a haze lit by moonlight. There is a lot of haze in *Heart of Darkness*, a story which has been hailed as "one of the most scathing indictments of imperialism in all literature"[5] and also condemned as an "offensive and totally deplorable book."[6] Marlow's journey upriver is both the story of a Faustian overreacher and a descent into Hades in the classical footsteps of Hercules and Aeneas, not to mention Don Quixote. Perhaps most relevant for modern audiences is its pursuit of an "idea" to justify the horrors of world conquest, an "idea" embodied in a remarkable man named Kurtz. It is a liminal story, a voyage to the edge of experience, to what Marlow calls "the farthest point of navigation and the culminating point of my experience"; it was "not very clear [...] yet it seemed to throw a kind of light."[7]

What kind of light do the film adaptations and re-adaptations of *Heart of Darkness* seem to throw? Efforts to tell the story come oddly in pairs, beginning with the two matching notebooks that Konrad Korzeniowski kept on his voyage up the Congo river in 1890: one notebook was organized in terms of space, observing landmarks and making notes on navigation; the other was a diary organized in terms of time, noting the various "horrors" he encountered on his journey upriver: a "horrid" albino woman, a skeleton tied to a post, a 13-year-old boy with a gunshot wound to the head.[8] Six years later, just married and starting a new career as an English novelist under the name of Joseph Conrad, he wrote two stories based on his African adventure. "An Outpost of Progress," his own favorite among his short stories, describes the effects of isolation on two ordinary Belgians sent into the jungle to trade for ivory. It was followed two years later by *Heart of Darkness*, which reworked the same idea, but this time with a more elaborate narrative frame and with a "remarkable man" as the protagonist. In this sense, *Heart of Darkness* is itself already a re-adaptation of Conrad's personal experience. Although Conrad's subsequent works involve racism, colonialism, and exploitation in places like South America and the Malay Archipelago, he never returned to Africa in his fictions. Nor did he seem to look back upon *Heart of Darkness* or make claims on its behalf: when it was published in book form in 1902, the volume in which it appeared was entitled *Youth: A Narrative, and Two Other Stories*, and *Heart of Darkness* was simply one of the "two other stories." Although his literary friends expressed great admiration for its power and its technique, it was not recognized as a classic text in Conrad's lifetime, and the first translations did not appear until 1924, the year of his death.

Since then, it has been adapted more than half a dozen times for film or television.[9] The two most serious attempts to bring the story to the silver screen are again characterized by a tendency towards re-adaptation or reduxification. Orson Welles adapted the story twice for radio: once for his Mercury Theatre on the Air in 1938, and again to launch a short-lived series of radio dramas called *This Is My Best* in the spring of 1945. In between, Welles tried to bring Conrad's novella to the silver screen as his first Hollywood film, to make visible what he could only suggest audibly in the earlier radio version. The film was scrapped in pre-production, but we know that Welles wanted to use a so-called "subjective camera," so that the viewer would see everything from Marlow's first-person viewpoint (an experiment that would not be realized until seven years later, in Robert Montgomery's *Lady in the Lake* and in the first part of the Bogart film *Dark Passage*). In Welles's film, as the riverboat journeys upstream and into the past, the jungle would become increasingly sparse and dead, ending in a stagnant cypress swamp that owes more to the world of Faulkner than Conrad. In the midst of the lake there would be a "temple" festooned with skulls in which Kurtz is himself sits enthroned as an idol who has achieved absolute power and confronted the absolute corruption of Lord Acton's dictum.

In Conrad's story we learn that "all Europe contributed to the making of Kurtz," and that England played a substantial role in his formation: "His mother was half–English, his father was half–French" and he "had been educated partly in England."[10] Welles's film was being made in the fateful autumn of 1939, however, and Welles demonized Kurtz by making him explicitly and exclusively German — Eric Kurtz — and by silently transplanting the heart of Kurtz's darkness from King Leopold's Congo to an unspecified German colony. The Thames estuary of Marlow's frame tale is replaced with New York harbor — which for 400 years has been one of the dark places — and Marlow becomes an American, while the nameless company officials in Conrad's story are all given Prussian-sounding names like Stitzer or De Tirpitz. The racism that worried Chinua Achebe is here the racial ideology of the Third Reich, and Welles's dying Kurtz leaves no doubt about the analogy with the Führer when he remarks that "there is a man now, in Europe, trying to do what I have done in the jungle." After the film project was scrapped, Welles re-used much of the structure and dialogue in his second radio adaptation broadcast on 13

March 1945. In effect, his three adaptations for radio and film came increasingly to adapt Conrad's tale as a timely vehicle for anti–German propaganda, locating the heart of darkness in the Third Reich or its former colonies. This narrow interpretation was tied to a specific time and place, and once the war had ended, there was no further need to invoke Conrad's tale as a contribution to the fight against fascism.

The first visual adaptations of *Heart of Darkness* to be completed were both made for CBS television in the 1950s, the days of live television drama: a 60-minute version for "Camera Three" in 1955 in the static style of a live radio broadcast, with speakers reading their parts before a curtain, was followed three years later by a 90-minute "Playhouse 90" performance starring Roddy McDowell as Marlow, singer Eartha Kitt as an African Queen, and Hollywood's famous Frankenstein monster, Boris Karloff, as Kurtz ("The horror! The horror!"). Although recorded for television, both of these productions were essentially adaptations for the theater, and neither used the visual potential of television or film to bring out the meaning of Marlow's tale.

By far the most famous adaptation of *Heart of Darkness* is *Apocalypse Now*, which was already a re-adaptation even before it was reduxified. John Milius read Conrad as a 17-year-old and wrote a script in film school about the Vietnam War that was "inspired by" Conrad's tale. As Coppola explains in the commentary now available on the DVDs of *Apocalypse Now: The Complete Dossier*, he directed the film with Milius's script in one hand and Conrad's text in the other, trying to re-adapt Milius's war movie to bring it back more closely to Conrad's original. The militarization of Conrad's tale was a brilliant stroke, and one that lays bare the aggression at the heart of colonial exploitation; but rewriting Conrad's tale as a war film also invoked all the stereotypical expectations associated with war films. Milius' script was to end in a blaze of gunfire and glory, with a great apocalyptic battle and the obliteration of Kurtz's compound by an air strike.

The militarization of Conrad's tale had other consequences as well. In Conrad's story Marlow goes upriver not to "terminate" Kurtz, but to rescue him. This is a major difference — the difference between life and death — and Marlow's efforts, however futile, are presented as an example of relatively civilized behavior. Captain Willard's situation is far more dubious. In the context of an increasingly senseless journey descending into what Coppola calls "surrealistic weirdness," Willard clings stubbornly to his "mission" to assassinate a Green Beret officer who has in effect become an independent contractor on the margins of the war. Why does the CIA want Kurtz to die? The details that we and Willard learn from his dossier suggest only that he has become an embarrassment to the CIA because of his remarkable efficiency in rooting out communist agents. The fact that he is seen as a god and has chopped off many heads may well be a sign of unsound method or lack of restraint, but it in no way limits his effectiveness in the war effort, and he is certainly not being assassinated in the name of human rights or the rights of his subjects.

Among other things, *Heart of Darkness* is a study in moral atavism. For both Conrad and Coppola the journey upriver is a journey back in time, reversing the proud chronology of Western progress and civilization. In *Apocalypse Now*, the technology becomes increasingly primitive as the journey advances: helicopters and napalm give way to spears and arrows, and automatic rifles are replaced with ceremonial swords. Colonel Kilgore's Air Cavalry helicopters could easily have dropped Willard directly and promptly into Kurtz's compound; the entire long journey of the riverboat or PBR (Patrol Boat River) is necessary for the narrative but not for Captain Willard's "mission," and is itself a sign of technological anachronism and inefficiency.

One of the key phrases of the upriver journey is "Don't ever get out of the boat," because the world outside the boat is a jungle filled with the horror of tigers, savage and deadly. Contact between the boat and the shore was necessarily closer in Conrad's story: Marlow has an African helmsman, and his crew consists of cannibals brought in from elsewhere. They are obliged to moor daily and go onshore to chop wood for the boilers. The white "pilgrims" riding as passengers respond to attacks by shooting blindly into the bush, but Marlow is troubled by a sense of kinship with the wild men on shore: "They howled and leaped, and spun, and made horrid faces; but what thrilled you was just the thought of their humanity — like yours — the thought of your remote kinship with this wild and passionate uproar."[11] This sense of kinship is utterly absent from *Apocalypse Now*. The Vietnamese, dehumanized into "dinks" and "slopes," remain as invisible in the film as they often were to American soldiers in reality, their presence revealed only by the wreckage they have caused: crashed helicopters, or the tail of a downed B-52. The "plantation" sequence restored to the *Redux* version of the film was meant to recreate the world of French colonists that ended with defeat at Dien Bien Phu in 1954, but it also illustrates the barriers that separate a vanished world of Proustian dining tables from the gross cultural illiteracy of the American soldiers, including Willard, who are unable to think outside the ahistorical and monolinguistic box (or boat) defined by their "mission."

This within-the-boat mentality is also evident in the distinctions drawn between the black and white soldiers on the PBR. When (in the *Redux* version) Willard trades fuel for sex with stranded Playboy bunnies, all of whom are white, only the white crewmembers are included in the deal. In Conrad's story, the death of the African helmsman is one of a good many occasions for an affirmation of human if unequal contact: "I had to look after him, I worried about his deficiencies, and thus a subtle bond had been created, of which I only became aware when it was suddenly broken. And the intimate profundity of that look he gave me when he received his hurt remains to this day in my memory — like a claim of distant kinship affirmed in a supreme moment."[12] When the helmsman's counterpart, the Chief, is killed by a spear in Coppola's film, his look is murderous as well as profound, and his last gesture is both a desperate hug and an attempt to impale Willard on the point of the same spear that has just pierced his own breast.

Apocalypse Now is a spectacular film in many respects, and Coppola and his wife have constructed a personal myth in which he appears as a Kurtzian film director struggling to find an ending for the film without going insane. This ending was ultimately found by stepping outside the frame of the war into a realm of primal ritual that seems to confirm Conrad's point about kinship by drawing all humankind into a common history of sacrificial bloodshed and "horror." Kurtz's *montagnard* people are played in the film by the Ifugao, the *montagnards* of the northern Philippines, whose contract included provisions for a regular supply of chickens, pigs, and buffalo to be used for both food and ceremony. Coppola realized that the sacrifice of an animal could be rendered cinematically equivalent to the termination of Kurtz and the accomplishment of Willard's mission. Montage is Coppola's signature: the *Godfather* films culminate in a montage that equates murder — the settling of Mafia scores — with rituals like the baptism of a baby or Italian opera, covering gunshots with glorious music as if to remind us that individuals may die but the music of life goes on. In *Apocalypse Now* the montage suggests that the king or god must die to make way for a new ruler, according to rituals understood as universal, as "ours" because they date back to the beginning of human culture. Coppola appropriates the Ifugao ceremony visually but replaces its music with the ending of "The End," the song by The Doors that opened the film.

This sequence is cinematically dazzling, and seems to bear out the universalist implications of Conrad's tale, although Willard becomes not a successor god but a *deus absconditus* who abandons his people once his mission is accomplished. His face may blend with a stone idol, but in effect he has never gotten out of the boat of his Western concerns. I cannot find a single instance in the three hours of the *Redux* version where actual contact or conversation occurs between any of the Americans and the indigenous Vietnamese or *montagnards*. The most extended encounter between the soldiers and the Vietnamese is a gruesomely gratuitous scene based on the My Lai massacre, where the barriers of language and culture have deadly consequences. The motives of Willard's role in this ritual sacrifice of Kurtz have nothing to do with the needs or desires of Kurtz's native subjects.

And what about "the horror"? In one of the most curious passages in the novella, Conrad's Marlow insists that Kurtz's last outcry had a positive and redeeming value: "It was an affirmation, a moral victory, paid for by innumerable defeats, by abominable terrors, by abominable satisfactions. But it was a victory!"[13] It is hard to understand how the death of Colonel Kurtz can be seen as a "moral victory" for anyone. Given Kurtz's moral isolation and the armed bubbles from within which Americans tend to view the rest of the world without ever getting off the boat (or the high-tech body armor they wear when they do go on land), the moral of Coppola's film suggests that the earth's dark places are darkened only by our own unwillingness to recognize any kinship with those outside the boat. In this sense, Coppola's film has nothing to do with Vietnam and everything to do with the "horror" of American vanity and hubris, splendid isolation and rugged individualism. At the level of ageless ritual we can recognize that Kurtz's "horror" is Willard's and our own, but the montage serves only to accentuate the difference between the "ignorant millions" and ourselves, between a godlike Willard and 500 submissive tribesmen for whom one white god is apparently as good as another. We may recognize Kurtz's "horror" as our own, yet the universality of ritual slaughter implies no recognition of human kinship except on terms that remain exclusively "ours." In Coppola's film, the recognition that "we" are also capable of horror implies no common bond of humanity.

The "horror" at the heart of Conrad's tale has offered film directors a malleable device for portraying the atavistic or evil forces that threaten mankind. The challenge for filmmakers is to evoke a sense of horror that is fully and globally "ours," one that does not ultimately fall victim to the melodramatic conventions of propaganda or horror films.

Heart of Darkness *Adaptations:*
A Chronological List

1938   6 November: first radio adaptation by Orson Welles for Mercury Theatre on the Air

[**1939   *Heart of Darkness*.** RKO Pictures. Dir. Orson Welles. Ran over budget and was never filmed. Scripts and related materials are held in the Orson Welles Collection, Lilly Library, University of Indiana, Bloomington, Indiana, and in the UCLA Arts–Special Collections Library.]

1945   13 March: Second CBS radio adaptation by Orson Welles for *This Is My Best.*

1955   *Heart of Darkness.* 60 mins. Dramatized for "Camera Three" by WCBS-TV in co-operation with the New York State Education Department. Dir. Francis Moriarty. Broadcast 15 Oct 1955. Viewing copy available at the Museum of Television and Radio, New York.

1958   *Heart of Darkness.* 90 mins. CBS-TV "Playhouse 90" live drama from Television City, Hollywood. Dir. Ronald Winston. With Roddy McDowell (Charles Marlow), Eartha Kitt (The Queen), Oscar Homolka (The Doctor), and Boris Karloff (Kurtz). Introduced by Sterling Hayden. Broadcast 6 Nov 1958, 9:30–11 P.M. EST. Sponsored by the American Gas Assn. Viewing copy available at the Museum of Television and Radio, New York.

1968   *Riusciranno i nostri eroi a ritrovare l'amico misteriosamente scomparso in Africa?* Documento Film, 124 mins. Dir. Ettore Scola. With Alberto Sordi (Fausto Di Salvio), Bernard Blier (ragionere Ubaldo Palmarini), Nino Manfredi (Oreste Sabatini). Filmed partly on location in Angola.

1977   *Le Crabe-Tambour* (based on Pierre Schoendoerffer's novel inspired by *Heart of Darkness* and other works of Conrad). BELA Production — A.M.L.F. — LIRA — TF1, 119 mins. Dir. Pierre Schoendoerffer. With Jean Rochefort (Le Commandant), Claude Rich (Le Médecin), Jacques Perrin (Willsdorff, Le Crabe-Tambour).

1978   *El corazón del bosque* (inspired by *Heart of Darkness*). Arándano Films, 105 mins. Dir. Manuel Gutiérrez Aragón. With Norman Briski (Juan), Angela Molina (Amparo), Luis Politti ("El Andarín").

1979   *Apocalypse Now* ("structured on" *Heart of Darkness*). Omni Zoetrope, 147 mins. Prod. and Dir. Francis Ford Coppola. With Marlon Brando (Col. Walter E. Kurtz), Robert Duvall (Lt. Col. Kilgore), Martin Sheen (Capt. Willard). Filmed in the Philippines. Redux version released 2001.

1988   *Cannibal Women in the Avocado Jungle of Death* (*Heart of Darkness*). Guacamole Films, 89 mins. Dir. and screenplay, J. D. Athens (pseud. of Jonathan Lawton). With Shannon Tweed (Dr. Margo Hunt), Adrienne Barbeau (Dr. Kurtz), Bill Maher (Jim). A "comedy reverse-gender version of *Heart of Darkness*" shot in eleven days on a budget of $100,000.

1994   *Heart of Darkness.* TNT (Turner Network Television), 101 mins. Dir. Nicholas Roeg. With John Malkovich (Harry Kurtz), Tim Roth (Marlow). Filmed in Belize and London.

NOTES

1. Joseph Conrad, *Heart of Darkness,* in *Youth / Heart of Darkness / The End of the Tether,* London: J. M. Dent and Sons, 1946, 59.
2. *Ibid.,* 67.
3. *Ibid.,* 48.
4. *Ibid.*
5. Adam Hochschild, *King Leopold's Ghost: A Story of Greed, Terror, and Heroism in Colonial Africa,* New York: Houghton Mifflin, 1998, 146.
6. Chinua Achebe, "An Image of Africa," in Robert D. Hamner, ed., *Joseph Conrad: Third World Perspectives,* Washington, D.C.: Three Continents, 1990, 126.
7. Conrad, *Heart of Darkness,* 51.
8. Zdzislaw Najder, "To the End of the Night," in Gene M. Moore, ed., *Joseph Conrad's Heart of Darkness: A Casebook,* New York: Oxford University Press, 2004, 125–134, 137.
9. A brief list of these adaptations is provided at the end of this essay. Further details on these and other films are available in "A Joseph Conrad Filmography" in Moore, ed., *Conrad on Film,* pp. 224–249.
10. Conrad, *Heart of Darkness,* 117.
11. *Ibid.,* 96.
12. *Ibid.,* 119.
13. *Ibid.,* 151.

BIBLIOGRAPHY

Achebe, Chinua. "An Image of Africa." Robert D. Hamner, ed., *Joseph Conrad: Third World Perspectives.* Washington, D.C.: Three Continents, 1990.
Bachmann, Holger. "Hollow Men in Vietnam: A Reading of the Concluding Sequence of *Apocalypse Now.*" *Forum for Modern Language Studies,* vol. 34, n° 4, 1998, 314–334.
Chatman, Seymour. "2½ Versions of *Heart of Darkness.*" Gene M. Moore, ed., *The Cambridge Companion to Conrad on film.* Cambridge: Cambridge University Press, 1997, 207–223.
Conrad, Joseph. *Heart of Darkness. Youth / Heart of Darkness / The End of the Tether.* London: J. M. Dent and Sons, 1946.
Elsaesser, Thomas, and Michael Wedel. "The Hollow Heart of Hollywood: *Apocalypse Now* and the New Sound Space." Gene M. Moore, ed., *The Cambridge Companion to Conrad on film.* Cambridge: Cambridge University Press, 1997, 151–175.
Hochschild, Adam. *King Leopold's Ghost: A Story of Greed, Terror, and Heroism in Colonial Africa.* New York: Houghton Mifflin, 1998.
Lothe, Jacob. "The Problem of Narrative Beginnings: Joseph Conrad's *Heart of Darkness* and Francis Ford Coppola's *Apocalypse Now.*" *Revue des Lettres Modernes: Histoire des Idées et des Littératures,* 2002, 35–58.
Miller, John Hillis. "The Interpretation of *Lord Jim.*" *Harvard English Studies,* vol. 1, 1970, 211–228.
Moore, Gene M., ed. *Conrad on Film.* Cambridge, Cambridge University Press, 1997.
Najder, Zdzislaw. "To the End of the Night." Gene M. Moore, ed., *Joseph Conrad's Heart of Darkness: A Casebook.* New York: Oxford University Press, 2004, 125–152.
Norris, Margot. "Modernism and Vietnam: Francis Ford Coppola's *Apocalypse Now.*" *Modern Fiction Studies,* vol. 44, n° 3, 1998, 730–766.
Watt, Ian. *Conrad in the Nineteenth Century.* London: Chatto & Windus, 1980.
Welles, Orson. *Heart of Darkness,* "This Is My Best." CBS Radio, 13 March 1945, online at http://www.radiocrazy.com/shows2/T/ThisIsMyBest/HeartOfDarkness.mp3, 14 June 2007.

Three *Scarfaces*: Documents, Messages and Works of Art

Dominique Sipière

His name is always Tony and the three versions of *Scarface* repeat the rise and fall of a gangster inspired by Al Capone, with the distant memory of Macbeth as a prototype. In the end, Tony Guarino (in the novel), Tony Camonte (Hawks) or Tony Montana (De Palma) die in front of an operatic display of automatics and machine guns, but everybody knows that their model, Capone, actually died in his cell.

While adaptations concern only two texts (a book and a film), re-adaptations suppose a longer period and at least a threefold comparison between a novel and two films, the second film often belonging to a very different period, country or frame of mind. For example, De Palma's *Scarface* (1983) comes more than fifty years after Hawks's reading of Armitage Trail's book (1931). Our questions and our tools will be a little different then from the ones suggested for a mere two-term adaptation. Instead of a descriptive study of the way the diegesis is adapted (time, space, characters, narration and motifs) and of the different steps of a film production (script, location and casting, scenography, filming, editing...) this study will concentrate on the possible *uses* of narratives. A novel or a film will then be considered according to its different levels of existence for the different people who study it. *Scarface*, for example, suggests three steps: a) it can be studied as a historical *document* belonging to the period it was made; b) it delivers a multi-layered (and contradictory) *message*; c) and it can be considered as a *work of art* whose ambition is to escape its own time(s) although it promotes a specific style belonging to a specific period. These are the three levels we are now going to describe with *Scarface* in mind.

It is obvious here that the relationship between the two films and their respective sources is of a very different nature: even though the first film took great liberties with the story in 1932, Howard Hawks explicitly adapted Armitage Trail's novel and mentioned it in the credits. On the contrary, Oliver Stone and Brian De Palma simply seemed to ignore the novel. What we have then is a very loose *adaptation* in 1932 and a provocative *remake* in 1983 instead of a case of readaptation, and the novel is only a virtual hypotext in the 1983 version. De Palma, however, insists that he "thought it was very important that (they) dedicated the movie to Howard Hawks and Ben Hecht because that was always the inspiration of it" (DVD bonus).

Scarface *as a Document*

Scarface provides a significant example of the way events, characters and settings borrowed from real facts can be reorganized and warped by very strong preexisting *narrative segments*. The afore-mentioned case of the narrative pattern of *rise and fall* inherited from Elizabethan tragedy, for example, proves stronger than the known fact that many gangsters — and Capone in particular — died very undramatic deaths. This makes the attention given by the novelist and the filmmakers to realistic details and the would-be 'authenticity' of the three versions of the same story paradoxical. Armitage Trail (whose real name was Maurice Coons) described an environment he knew quite well: "Maurice Coons gathered the elements for *Scarface* when living in Chicago, where he became acquainted with many Sicilian gangs. For a couple of years, Coons spent most of his nights prowling Chicago's gangland with his friend, a lawyer..."[1] Ben Hecht too had lived in Chicago, and Howard Hawk's personal enquiries when he prepared his film are well-documented.[2] Oliver Stone (who wrote the 1983 script) also insists on his careful research in Cuba, Miami and Columbia.

This may serve as a first step in the game of difference versus equivalence in the three versions of *Scarface*. The tale — born in Chicago — was reinterpreted by Hawks, who added his own narrative segments (the Borgia tradition, etc.); then it was significantly delocalized to Miami in a modernized environment for De Palma's rendition. What was already felt to be exotic in 1932 traveled from the United States to Cuba and South America.

Chicago by night filmed in black and white is replaced by what seems to be its opposite: Miami in the sun and its flowered shirts, in a counterpoint to the black striped suits (with an occasional white suit) at night in the Babylon restaurant, because the fictional gangster must be smartly dressed and showing off his wealth. Stone and De Palma not only replace Sicily with Cuba, they very soon give up alcohol for cocaine, a much more deadly motif affording a new system of colors: while Coppola put red blood at the heart of some of his films (*The Godfather* and *Dracula*), De Palma plays a threefold game of black, red and *white*. Immigrants have changed too: they are no longer the hopeful Irishmen or Italians using and abusing their freedom in a "land of opportunities," but merely the consequences of a dirty trick played by Fidel Castro on the United States as he drained his jails of hundreds of killers and madmen and sent them north.

As a consequence, the gangster's *ethnicity* is transformed: while it gave Trail's book an atmosphere, it achieved a new pinnacle in Hawk's *talking movie* along with the sound of bullets and the screeching tires of automobiles, but it becomes a more ambiguous sign of Tony's difference in 1983. De Palma's Montana not only carries a gun, he also belongs to a tradition of psychopaths; he is a metaphor embodying contagion, a mirror held up to contemporary American society.

But, again, the story also presents a telling picture of the actual criminal organizations. The three versions insist on Scarface's rise from several generations of gangsters and a *hierarchy* suggesting a kind of typology of the powers of crime. Tony always begins by eliminating an old time gangster — James Colosimo in Al Capone's Chicago, Al Spingola in the novel, Big Louie in Hawks — or a mere wild beast from another world in 1983 ("Chainsaw" Hector, who calls to mind the dinosaurs King Kong kills in his own jungle as a hint of the sort of world he comes from). Tony is then appointed as a confidence man by a new boss who exemplifies the present situation (John Torrio in the historical America of the 1920s, then Johnny Lovo, both in the novel and in Hawks, and Frank Lopez in De Palma). Indeed, in John Torrio, Johnny Lovo's real-life counterpart and Colosimo's antipodal successor, the public received a respectful lesson in the capabilities of the efficient up-to-date businessman. Torrio embodied the relentless drive that Colosimo fatally lacked, and the story of his gang celebrated the replacement of small, local enterprises by diversified, far-ranging, and highly organized corporations in the larger economy.[3]

Likewise, Tony always courts his boss's wife (Poppy or Elvira) as a token and a sign of his new power. Then he kills his rival who tried to get rid of him. The three versions add a powerful external rival (Irish Gaffney and Bolivian Sosa) but the two films differ here: Hawk's Tony Camonte graphically eliminates Gaffney (played by Boris Karloff) in a bowling alley and is then killed by the police, whereas Tony Montana kills Mel Bernstein, the corrupted cop, and gets killed by a group of killers sent by Sosa. We will see how narrative laws supersede the picture of the real criminal environment in our last part.

Message

Some tales openly deliver a "message," others simply imply it, but most messages are ambiguous and they require a multi-layered reading that takes into account the contradictions of their own times and the uses they afforded in later periods. The gangster saga of the thirties is a typical example of such contradictions between an official message and several contradictory implications the contemporary audiences understood perfectly. De Palma's film belongs to another period and it does not claim to deliver any "immediate" message — other than a hymn to graphic violence.

"Colorful": both the 1932 and 1983 films use the same word but with very different meanings. When De Palma says (in the DVD bonus) that "they may be killers, but they're kind of *colorful*" he obviously thinks of their narrative and aesthetic potential, their "picturesque" force. This is exactly what the police officer (a character imposed by censors) refused in the thirties:

> Colorful? What color is crawling louse? Say listen, that's the attitude of too many morons in this country. [...] Colorful? Did you read what happened the other day? A car full of them chasing another down the street in broad daylight. Three kiddies playing hopscotch on the sidewalk get lead poured in their little bellies. When I think what goes on in the minds of these lice, I want to vomit [*Scarface* 1932].

Of course, this attack on the naïve admirers of crime was not written by Hawks, but the film (like its contemporary Warner counterparts) is sincerely shocking in its portrayal of the death of children, of the ridiculous upstarts and of the "lessons" given by arrogant fools (the two Tony characters *and* their model Capone). However, the gangster saga repeatedly delivers a *contradictory message* of repression versus admiration. Most films of the thirties owe a great deal to their ambivalent fascination for violence and their obvious exhilarating display of machine guns. It is probably because they are *simultaneously* appalled and delighted that these films still hold up so well today.

Beyond the well-known struggle with the censors, two reactions of the contemporary press confirm this ambiguity. First *Harrison's Report*— aimed at provincial distributors who did not want embarrassing protests from local censors — gave them fair warning:

> This is the most vicious and demoralizing gangster picture produced. There is no doubt that it will be resented by civic, educational and religious organizations; and rightly so, for both in action and in talk it is brutal and obscene. If ever an argument was needed by reform bodies in favor of censorship, this picture will furnish it. Even though the hero is killed in the end, there is no moral in the story. [...] There is not one character in the picture that arouses sympathy [April 23, 1932].

Variety was wiser and more prophetic:

> Presumably the last of the gangster films, on a promise, it is going to make us sorry that there won't be anymore. [...] It isn't for children. And it's pretty strong even for adults. But to keep people away from the theatre where it plays will be about the same as keeping 'em out of speakeasies [...] the punch is on the violence, the killings, the motives and the success of the cast in giving the director what he wants [May 24, 1932].

Of course they already knew that *Scarface* is much more attracted by violence than its Warner counterparts, particularly if one compares it with the rather muddled ethics of some Cagney stories (such as *Angels with Dirty Faces*, for example). Two examples of *messages* about the way violence is made more palatable for the audiences may help here: the origins of evil in the three *Scarfaces* and the way the gangster finds excuses for his acts.

The Origins of Evil

In the novel, Tony's brother is a policeman. The narrator comments on the "blue uniformed legs" above young Tony[4]:

> To Tony, the only difference between a policeman and a gangster was a badge. They both came from the same sort of neighborhoods, had about the same education and ideas, usually knew each other before and after their paths diverged, and always got along well together if the gangster had enough money.[5]

Armitage Trail's description of the Guarino family deliberately opposes two reactions to the same social environment. Tony has hated the police since he was a kid:

> There were other factors, of course, that contributed strongly in making Tony a gangster. His attitude toward the law, for instance. His first contact with it had come at the age of six when, hungry, he had snatched a pear off a push-cart and a policeman had chased him. Thus, from the first, he had known the law as an enemy instead of a protection, as something which stood between him and the fruition of his desires.[6]

The novel shares an even more important event in Tony Guarino's 'formation' with later Warner films (*The Roaring Twenties*): he is one of the many soldiers who came back from World War I with a broken face and a deranged mind. But (with an ambiguity similar to that of will Montana's Cuba in 1983) the war came as an epiphany for this particular soldier and he actually loved it!

> Tony Guarino made a good soldier. They put him in a machine gun company and he loved it.
> They gave Tony the D.S.C. and the Croix de Guerre for that night's work...[7]

The war, then, does not explain everything and the narrator insists that Tony was "a born gangster."[8] Tony is a madman, but a thoroughly *professional* one, the sort of man Howard Hawks admired. But Hawks was not interested in causes and it might explain why his film begins *in media res*, without any explanation for Tony's behavior (contrary to *The Public Enemy,* but not unlike *Little Caesar,* its two contemporary rivals).

De Palma's Tony is also introduced as a wild beast from an alien world which is both very near Florida and dangerously exotic: Fidel Castro's Cuba in the eighties. Tony's mother bitterly reminds him he already was 'a bum' there and that communist jails are only an alibi for his violence.

And a Few Justifications of Evil

Hawks's film probably invented the exhilarating projection of the spectator through the screen by putting huge 'spitting' machine guns in Tony's hands. This was only the beginning of a kind of inflation if one considers current video games encouraging the player to insult and to shoot his enemies in a strong identification with Scarface (in the game, the player *is* Scarface himself). But De Palma's spectator has also narrative reasons to "understand" and indeed, almost shares Tony's violence: first because it is urged by revenge — or is it retribution? — and then because it only threatens despicable, dangerous or unreal opponents. This was already suggested in the two first versions of the story, but it became systematic in 1983. A list of Tony's targets is quite revealing:

1. He executes Rebenga "because" he was a traitor and Castro's executioner.

2. He slaughters a group of Columbians who dismembered Angel, his young aide.

3. He witnesses Omar's dramatic hanging from a helicopter after his (alleged) betrayal.

4. He scornfully orders Frank Lopez's execution by Manny when he realizes his former boss planned his own death.

5. He coldly shoots corrupt cop Mel Bernstein who actually deserves no respect (and could be an embarrassing witness).

6. He unexpectedly shoots contract killer Alberto as he was about to blow a car up, because there also were two children in it.

Tony is a killer with a soft heart. In each case Tony may feel justified although his own interests seem to coincide with his "mission." Towards the end of the film, the deaths belong to a different phase as he is on his inevitable decline (as Elvira says, "We're not winners... We're losers!"). These killings are *blunders* caused by passion (he kills his best friend Manny) and cocaine. The film progressively becomes a slow dark operatic tragedy which eventually reaches a nadir if one remembers the novel's sympathy for the young couple made by Tony and his girl friend (Jane Conley, the Irish Gun girl), according to a typical pre–Bonnie and Clyde pattern: "They rose and moved out on the small crowded floor, quite the handsomest couple in the place [...] And yet they were not murderers, except legally. In their own minds, they felt completely justified for everything they had done."[9] Even when he died, this Tony took things with style and lightness: "Tony saw the revolver flash, then his head snapped back from the impact of the bullet. Anyway, he had always faced it."[10] Or, as Jane puts it: "Well, what the hell. A girl only lived once and she might as well get all the kick she could out of life."[11]

This is why the novel gives the lightest and happiest image of the gangster, albeit in a totally corrupted world he seems to transcend. De Palma's message also includes a rejection of a society that produces crime, but his vision is much darker: "the movie was supposed to be shocking... It's a shocking world" (Bonus). In such a world "Montana is a virulent disease, fatal to all who contract it,"[12] including spectators. This catching disease has to do with the systematic exhibition of violence: "I wanted to establish a level of violence that nobody had ever seen before" (Bonus).

Of course, when they deal with violence, the three versions of *Scarface* do not share the same approach: Trail unfolds an urban picture that owes much to nineteenth-century tales of big cities and a taste for underground mysteries (Sherlock Holmes is not very far away); Hawks, with producer Howard Hughes, invents a dynamic style mixing documentary, message and an aesthetic project (as we see in the formalist use of crosses signifying death); De Palma seems to start with form itself and use narration as a mere pretext.

Narration and Art

Both the *documentary* approach and *message analysis* are concerned with *Scarface* as a dated object providing information about specific periods. The third level of analysis addresses a more timeless and universal approach connected to the idea of "classicism" in literature and art: the ambition to be read, seen and "used" by audiences belonging to much later periods. This is where we go back to pre-existing *narrative segments* (or stereotypes) and *aesthetics*.

As was already the case in popular tales of the nineteenth century, descriptions of a real world are organized and influenced by famous narratives that seem to invest all versions of *Scarface*. We have already mentioned *Macbeth* and his story as a brilliant professional blinded by his ambition, involving his best friend (Banquo, Guino, Manny...) and his wife (Lady Macbeth, Poppy, Elvira ... though each of these are quite different). *Scarface* is thus invested by several different narrative segments that could be entitled "*Two Brothers*," "*Bonnie and Clyde*," "*Borgia and His Lucretia*," "*A Revenger's Tragedy*," etc.

The novel, for example, collects real-life details, but organizes them into a typical pulp fiction narrative. Of course, it seems to come after our knowledge of the story as it was told in Hawks's film and the two first sentences already indicate massive differences when compared with the films: different characters, Tony's formation as a killer, the narrator's status, or an interaction between fictitious and real gangsters... "Tony Guarino, destined to be the greatest of all America's notorious gang leaders was eighteen when he committed his first serious crime. And the cause, as is often the case, was a woman [Vyvyan Lovejoy]."[13]

The original Tony shares his name with Ben Guarino — the very policeman who is to kill him at the end of the story. In Armitage Trail's novel, "Scarface" Tony is the policeman's brother and the reader is to imagine that the scar prevents the police, his family, his *moll* and his friends — even his mother — from recognizing him! Of course, they seem to hesitate for a few seconds and Tony *Camonte* (an assumed name) fears they will associate the infamous killer with their previous friend, brother or son. Tony comments, "Jeez! What a fine family mess I got into."[14] This is nineteenth-century melodrama with a hint of self-conscious comedy.

Hecht and Hawks also tell a family story, but they interweave two love stories or, to be accurate, two love triangles that Stone and De Palma will preserve in 1983: the narrative logic of the novel borrowed games of mistaken identities from melodrama, whereas both films use the incestuous Borgia plot between Tony and his sister Cesca; Hawks was probably thinking of Donizetti's opera which was very popular in the late twenties. This means that the old logic of masks ("What a blessing it was that most people actually knew so little")[15] was replaced by a more structured logic of symmetrical triangles: on a conscious level, Tony is Lovo's rival and he kills him to get Poppy as a token of success (triangle of ambition); on a less conscious level Tony kills his best friend (Guino) because he cannot accept the love affair with his sister Cesca (triangle of unconscious desire). The love triangles make the film gangster much more complex and interesting.

De Palma keeps the same structure and only changes names: Lovo becomes Frank Lopez and Guino is Manny. Tony Montana's fall is again triggered by the death of his friend Manny and by Gina's reaction, but the 1983 version adds a slow subplot reminiscent of *The Public Enemy* with the police only in the background and the sort of paranoid obsession of revenge that brought Tom Powers (James Cagney) to his end. Hawk's Tony was killed by the police (Guarino) whereas De Palma's Scarface never seems to be actually threatened by the law but by other gangsters (Sosa's killers) who come to "punish" him as a traitor (he failed to kill a dangerous witness) in a new twist of the revenge subplot.

The end of the novel was totally different: the Guarino brothers — gangster and policeman — were shown in a final duel and Scarface fell under his brother's bullets. Guarino expressed his surprise: "'But God! Wasn't it lucky his gun jammed? He was a dead shot, that guy; for a minute I thought sure I was goin' to wake up with a wreath on my chest. But you never can tell about an automatic.'" And the narrator concluded: "But even an automatic can't jam when the trigger hasn't been pulled."[16]

All these changes of places, dates, contexts or narrative devices make some borrowed passages very different. For example Tony's job as a "salesman" (he collects money for his boss) is described in both films. Hawks shows him in a sequence of very short visits to Chicago bars by night in order to make sure they sell his beer. He uses verbal, then physical violence, before he bombs a reluctant pub or more radically shoots everybody in the *Shamrock*. In 1983, these four short scenes are replaced by a ten-minute set piece of bravura opposing a quiet sunny avenue in Miami to the claustrophobic bathroom scene, with its extreme violence of a chainsaw "negociation" with Hector, the Bolivian dealer. This is not only meant as a time adjustment (violence and cocaine) but as an almost autonomous set piece. The narrative material becomes less interesting than the telling itself.

Art. The three versions of *Scarface* share the same artificial atmosphere mingling luxury and violence. But both films introduce an innovating aesthetic conception in their time. Some visual metaphors travel from one film to the other, like the paranoid urge for protection against an enemy who is bound to transgress all barriers: Macbeth does not believe the witches when they predict Dunsinane forest will walk; in the novel, Tony reinforces his lorries; in the first film the police bullets ricochet on Tony's lead window blinds; and Al Pacino lives among a sophisticated TV system but fails to see a group of killers invading the house because of his sister. Guino's (George Raft) spun coin disappears in De Palma, but Hawks's "The World Is Yours" sign is back, first on a *Goodyear* airship, then above his rather pathetic pool where he floats dead. But these short-lived echoes enhance deeper differences between the films.

Hawks's *Scarface* should be compared to the somewhat ill-famed aesthetic Italian Futurist movement (rather than its British equivalent *Vorticism*, which proved far more verbal and sophisticated). Howard Hawks and his "mouthpiece" Tony — inspired by reverberated images of Chicago gangsters — write their stories with *objects*, machine guns for example, the so-called "Chicago Typewriters."[17] Tony is so fond of them that he shouts "I'm gonna write my name all over this town with it in big letters."[18] *Scarface* is a dynamic homage to metal and fire and it embodies an aesthetic of machines, speed, town noises and triumphant steel. In Europe, Marinetti's leanings of Futurism towards Fascism totally disqualified the strong and ambiguous gaze which Hawks himself would probably have discarded. But Marinetti's *Futurist Manifesto* merits reading and affords a few interesting meeting points with the gangster movies of the early thirties:

1. We want to sing the love of danger, the habit of energy and rashness.

2. The essential elements of our poetry will be courage, audacity and revolt.

3. Literature has up to now magnified pensive immobility, ecstasy and slumber. We want to exalt movements of aggression, feverish sleeplessness, the double march, the perilous leap, the slap and the blow with the fist.

4. We declare that the splendor of the world has been enriched by a new beauty: the beauty of speed. A racing automobile with its bonnet adorned with great tubes like serpents with explosive breath [...] a roaring motor car which seems to run on machine-gun fire, is more beautiful than the Victory of Samothrace.

5. We want to sing the man at the wheel, the ideal axis of which crosses the earth, itself hurled along its orbit.

6. The poet must spend himself with warmth, glamour and prodigality to increase the enthusiastic fervor of the primordial elements.

7. Beauty exists only in struggle. There is no masterpiece that has not an aggressive character. Poetry must be a violent assault on the forces of the unknown, to force them to bow before man.

8. We are on the extreme promontory of the centuries! What is the use of looking behind at the moment when we must open the mysterious shutters of the impossible? Time and Space died yesterday. We are already living in the absolute, since we have already created eternal, omnipresent speed.

9. We want to glorify war — the only cure for the world — militarism, patriotism, the destructive gesture of the anarchists, the beautiful ideas which kill, and contempt for woman.

10. We want to demolish museums and libraries, fight morality, feminism and all opportunist and utilitarian cowardice.

11. We will sing of the great crowds agitated by work, pleasure and revolt; the multi-colored and polyphonic surf of revolutions in modern capitals: the nocturnal vibration of the arsenals and the workshops beneath their violent electric moons: the gluttonous railway stations devouring smoking serpents; factories suspended from the clouds by the thread of their smoke; bridges with the leap of

gymnasts flung across the diabolic cutlery of sunny rivers: adventurous steamers sniffing the horizon; great-breasted locomotives, puffing on the rails like enormous steel horses with long tubes for bridle, and the gliding flight of aeroplanes whose propeller sounds like the flapping of a flag and the applause of enthusiastic crowds.[19]

De Palma's *Scarface* was badly received at first and only reached cult status later. The director comes from a totally different background from Hawks, and his interests lie elsewhere, not in the reverence for modernity in the 1932 film. His general conception of filmmaking is concentrated on a Hitchcock-like manipulation of audiences. In his short but stimulating book, John Ashbrook distinguishes between early Hitchcock-inspired films and the later works that he finds more mainstream and commercial; he claims the demarcation line coincides with *Scarface*. This means that De Palma's *set pieces*—"separate high gloss pearls strung together by thin threads of plot"— use narrative patterns as a pretext and that his *Scarface* is not really a *remake*. But Ashbrook concludes: "then things changed with *Scarface*. This was very much a film about people with frailties, and it led to a different kind of drama. Human drama."[20] As a consequence, De Palma's film is simultaneously an exercise in audience direction (in the Hitchcock tradition), an homage to Hawks's style, and an aesthetic manifesto in itself.

Oliver Stone, like Hecht 50 years before, claims his script does not owe much to other people: "I didn't want to do a remake." The film was to be directed by Sidney Lumet and in that case would probably have been more politically oriented. But De Palma was better known at the time than Stone himself and he got the job: "I liked the material specifically because to me, it was sort of like a modern metaphor for *The Treasure of the Sierra Madre* where cocaine becomes gold." Oliver Stone's shift from alcohol prohibition to cocaine implied a radical change of atmosphere: "It is like the capitalist dream gone bizarre and berserk and as crazy as it can get, and completely self-destructive" (De Palma, Bonus). The operatic excess already sketched in 1932 goes much further than the Tony character when he advises Guino to "think big." Its "epic expansion" (Jean Loup Bourget, 78) extends to the whole film. Bordwell adds: "after Richard Corleone's slide into melancholic corruption a gangster would have to be more flamboyantly aggressive"[21]; Bregman, who produced the film, calls it an "operatic, theatrical film" and Al Pacino says he's delighted to act in "a larger than life approach" (Bonus).

This leads to a paradox: in De Palma's *Scarface* the characters keep asserting their *authenticity* while they are living in an incredibly artificial world, both by day (Florida) and by night (luxury). Hence the improbable image of the Tiger[22]—epitomizing immediate presence and Truth—in Tony's garden when he gets married. Scarface sees himself as a tiger and he wants Elvira because "she's a tiger, she'll belong to me" [65]. Tony's values are thus authenticity, individual courage, and honor, in the form of his word and his loyalty to his friends. The film ruthlessly shows how he will eventually betray all these values (except, possibly, his "courage"—but then again this could be because the man is constantly high...) He could at least preserve the illusion of his supreme value: "fun." But his face expresses the exact opposite and the long coda suggests a melancholy and disastrous opera.

Now, De Palma's tools in order to express this tension between a craving for authenticity and the obvious artificiality of Tony's life suggest three different levels of analysis: a study of language, the typically visceral relationship of the audience with the film and the use of colors. We'll conclude with a short allusion to language and colors.

Language, in the 1983 *Scarface*, is so rude that it becomes almost epic, far beyond the usual four letter words in such films:

> COPS: Castro is [...] shitting all over us.
> FRANK LOPEZ, ABOUT SOSA: Let me tell you something about that greaseball cocksucker [...]
> TONY: This town is like a great big pussy just waiting to get fucked [...]

I'd like to suggest that when they reach such a degree of aggression, words seem to escape from reality and they become as *artificial* as the lyrics of an opera. Likewise, the artificial disconnection of words (which pull the film downwards towards the more lowbrow) is paradoxically echoed by the extreme sophistication of De Palma's *filming* (digitized split screen, etc ... with the help of John A. Alonzo), which pulls upwards towards "arthouse cinema," leading us perhaps to a final reflection on the highly symbolic nature of De Palma's colors. Cuba's real life is painted pale green, cream, and pastel with flowered shirts, and Miami by night is orange (real or photographed sunsets) and black. However, Tony's world is white, black and red. White is evil (because of the ever present cocaine), black is linked with luxury and red is originally a sign of change, a sign of movement, expressed by shed blood. That ubiquitous blood, incidentally, is the same red as the velvet curtains of the theater.

NOTES

1. Armitage Trail, *Scarface* (1930), London: Bloomsbury Film Classics, 1997, 1.
2. Joseph McBride, *Hawks on Hawks*, Berkeley: University of California Press, 1982, 46. "McBride: 'What kind of research did you do?' Hawks: I made a contact with one of

the best newspapermen in Chicago so that we could use the newspaper wire. I could ask him about people and things. If a man came into my office and said, "My name is James White, I was connected to the gang in Chicago. I wonder if I could talk to you," I'd say, "I'm sorry, Mr. White, I'm so busy. Will you come tomorrow?" And by that time I would have gotten in touch with Chicago and said, "Who the hell is James White?" So when he came in I'd say, "I know all about you." He'd say, "How do you know?" And I'd say, "oh... I know. I know that you started as a bouncer and became a pimp, you ran a saloon, you carried a gun for so-and-so, did such-and-such a murder." I'd get through and he'd say, "I wasn't no pimp." And I'd say OK... [...] "How did you do such-and-such a thing?" And he told me quite a lot. Five or six of them came around and told me their stories. Of course, we took liberties; we did what we wanted to do.'"

3. David Ruth, *Inventing the Public Enemy*, Chicago: University of Chicago Press, 1996, 125.

4. Trail, *Scarface*, 7.

5. *Ibid.*, 8.

6. *Ibid.*, 15.

7. *Ibid.*, 42, 44.

8. *Ibid.*, 17.

9. *Ibid.*, 108.

10. *Ibid.*, 185.

11. *Ibid.*, 182.

12. *Ibid.*, 13.

13. *Ibid.*, 1.

14. *Ibid.*, 146.

15. *Ibid.*, 155.

16. *Ibid.*, 186.

17. Ruth, *Inventing the Public Enemy*, 132.

18. The sexual connotation is never entirely absent: "Get out of my way," he warns Lovo, "I'm gonna spit."

19. F. T. Marinetti, in *Le Figaro*, Feb. 20, 1909.

20. John Ashbrook, *Brian De Palma*, Harpenden: Pocket Essential, 2000, 9.

21. David Bordwell, *The Way Hollywood Tells It*, Berkeley: University of California Press, 2006, 25.

22. An allusion to John Garfield in *Body and Soul*?

BIBLIOGRAPHY

Ashbrook, John. *Brian De Palma*. Harpenden: Pocket Essential, 2000.
Bordwell, David. *The Way Hollywood Tells It*. Berkeley: University of California Press, 2006.
Bourget, Jean Loup. *La Norme et la marge*. Paris: Colin, 2005.
Mast, Gerald. *Howard Hawks, Storyteller*. New York: Oxford University Press, 1982.
Munby, Jonathan. *The Public Enemies, Public Heroes: Screening the Gangster from Little Caesar to Touch of Evil*. Chicago: University of Chicago Press, 1999.
The Public Enemy. William A. Wellman, dir., Kubec Glasmon, John Bright, scrs. Warner Bros., 1931.
Ruth, David. *Inventing the Public Enemy: The Gangster in American Culture, 1918–1934*. Chicago: University of Chicago Press, 1996.
Scarface. Brian De Palma, dir., Oliver Stone, scr. Universal Pictures, 1983.
Scarface. Howard Hawks, dir., Ben Hecht, scr. The Caddo Company, 1932.
"Scarface." *Harrison's Report*. April 23, 1932.
"Scarface." *Variety*, May 24, 1932.

Sipiere, Dominique. *Quatre films exemplaires*: Scarface, Angels with Dirty Faces, Force of Evil, The Asphalt Jungle. Nantes: Le Temps, 2002.

Trail, Armitage. *Scarface* (1930). London: Bloomsbury Film Classics, 1997.

Warshow, Robert. "The Gangster as Tragic Hero." *The Immediate Experience: Movies, Comics, Theatre, and Other Aspects of Popular Culture* (1962). New York: Atheneum, 1977, 97–104.

Lost in Adaptation —
A Producer's View[1]
Roger Shannon

I'm extremely delighted to have been invited to attend this very interesting international conference. Literature and film have always been abiding and enduring passions in my life (well, there is a third and fourth and that's football and The Beatles, both relating to my home city of Liverpool, and completely inappropriate in this context, though I think they do have connections to the other two —film and literature —which may become apparent).

Literature is the subject that got me out of a possibly uninspiring and stultifying future on a council estate in Liverpool, and was also the subject that I took my first degree in. The work of Raymond Williams, that exemplary Welsh cultural theorist, led me to an expansive understanding of culture beyond literature, and onto a Masters Degree at the Centre for Contemporary Cultural Studies at the University of Birmingham, after which film production, film policy and film study became my profession and career. Like many folk of my generation in Britain, we came to the film and television industries via the unlocking of the social and intellectual imagination that literature provided. So, to talk at a conference where film and literature are combined — it's like a double whammy for me, a win-win scenario. Thank you.

I'm going to talk about some of the issues that arise for a producer when faced with adaptations. The title of the talk is taken from a mini Festival I set up and ran in Birmingham in 2005 —*Lost in Adaptation*, the exchange between literature and film/books and movies, when the following writers, directors and producers discussed their work:

- Gurinder Chadha, who had just directed her Bollywood version, which was titled *Bride and Prejudice*, of Jane Austen's *Pride and Prejudice*;

231

- Helen Cross, whose debut novel *My Summer of Love* had been adapted into an award winning movie by Pawel Pawlikowski;
- Frank Cottrell Boyce, a screenwriter turned novelist who had just adapted his original screenplay for the film *Millions* directed by Danny Boyle into an award-winning novel;
- Jonathan Coe, who firstly discussed candidly his difficult experience of adapting his own work *The Dwarves of Death*, and who secondly commented on the adaptation of his novel, *The Rotters Club* for BBC television.

Gurinder Chadha was our opening speaker, and as closing speaker we were graced with a fascinating interview with novelist, screenwriter, and Birmingham resident, David Lodge, who took us through an overview of his relationship between his novels and his screen adaptations of them, most notably *Nice Work*.

This mini Festival was an insight into the way that the originating writer — the novelist — viewed the exchange that went on to transform their novel into a film.

The session that encapsulated this exchange in a 360 degree way was the one where Helen Cross — the novelist of *My Summer of Love*— discussed the film of her book with the Executive Producer of the film, Emma Hayter. The process of creative origination in a bed sit followed by publishing success, the take up and optioning by the film industry and eventual filming by director Pawel Pawlikowski is mapped in the round in this discussion. Helen Cross is clear about the process and her relationship to it: "I'd seen Pawel's first film, *The Last Resort*, and thought it fantastic, poetic, brave and unusual. Even so, the idea of any film was alarming, rather like sending your baby away for plastic surgery."

In other sessions, the writers' take on this relationship is very different with a number of commentaries indicating closeness or detachment to the creative borrowing. Mil Millington and Mike Gayle are two novelists whose work has been optioned by American producers but so far not produced. Mil Millington says, "My advice is Let. Go. Even though I'm writing the screenplay of my own novel *Things My Girlfriend and I Have Argued About* the film isn't really 'mine.' It's the studio's. As a writer all you have the power to do is plead. Let. Go." Mike Gayle is more relaxed: "I'm not worried about creative control because I'm well aware that whatever they need to butcher in the book, they will do so without a second thought."

Another view is offered by David Lodge who has written a feature film script of his novel *Therapy* and adapted his own *Nice Work* and *The Writing*

Game for British television: "The downside is that you don't have total control over the final product as you do over a novel. The upside is that performance, visual imagery, and music can enhance and transform your story in ways that words alone can't achieve."

Helen Cross's comment about "sending your baby away" always make me think of "adoption" instead of adaptation. Perhaps there's a kernel of truth in that metaphorical elision into ideas of fostering, alternative parenting, and bringing up baby differently.

In an interesting step after the *Lost in Adaptation* event film maker Gurinder Chadha went from Austen (the author not the American city) to Texas to make *Dallas* (the American city and the soap), which will be an adaptation onto the movie screen of the legendary TV show.[2]

But what of producers?

For most producers, adapting a novel far outweighs beginning with a brand new idea. A buzz already gilds the novel; there's "brand" recognition; an already existing fan club; a never ending list of references on Google. You meet a financier, commissioning executive, film fund head and they all love to hold in their hands the book, the novel, the memoir. You can get into production that much quicker and the budgets are generally higher than for risky, untried, less trodden ideas. With a well-trodden path already marked out (plot, structure, characters), things are clearer.

Well not always. Many screenwriters assuming that it's an easy run approach a screen adaptation by leaving the source material dead on the page. By that I mean that screenwriters often forget the important rule that telling a story in prose fiction and telling a story for the screen are two completely different crafts, with different audiences and vastly different expectations.

In a nutshell, the personal transaction enjoyed by a reader who can skip passages of description, vault back and forth to renew a nuance, cheat a look at the end etc., is not available for the screen audience who aspire to be embraced by the story and the characters until the very end. Adaptations that are simply translating the original source do not as a rule work for the screen because the writer is uncertain about what to exploit visually and what to leave out. Sometimes this is excused as remaining loyal to the original, a sort of faithful monogamy. However, what a producer is looking for in an adaptation is a script that fillets the novel, keeping an accurate shape of the story, an accurate recollection of the spirit of the novel, and a truthful complimentarity in screen to the author's literary intentions.

So, how does a producer arrive at an adaptation that eschews a simple and direct translation of the original material? What assessments are made to determine the necessary elements to exploit and explore? He or she, aided by their screenwriter, need to know the material inside out; they need to compile a list of signature elements that comprise the novel: a synopsis; a brief summary of its hook, its appeal; a deconstruction of the book into structure, characterization, themes, visual style, audience appeal etc. Understanding how it works as a book, and why it is effective in this format, is part of the process of understanding how an adaptation might work and how it might be renewed for the screen.

The process of encapsulating the plot in a two to three page synopsis sounds tortuous, but this is an exercise in boiling down the plot to its essentials, to the active ingredients that make up the story — the turning points, the reversals, the climaxes etc. What this exercise can reveal is the thinness of a plot — the meagerness of a story line without incident and character development to carry a 100 min film — or alternatively, and more interestingly, it may be the tipping point toward an adaptation, as the synopsis can also reveal complexity, vibrancy, character development and incidents a plenty. Such a synopsis can also highlight — especially in a period piece — the relevant themes that might appeal to a contemporary audience. When Andrew Davies adapted for the BBC *The Way We Live Now*, much was written about how the climate then mirrored the extremes of financial speculation of the contemporary "dot com" bubble.

Subsequent stages pay attention to the structure of the novel and whether that will be the same in the screenplay. Will it follow the linearity of the source, or aim for something more complex — flashbacks, taking the viewpoint of the story from another character, vaulting between time zones, chaptering the screenplay to highlight characters...? Films like David Hare/Stephen Daldry's *The Hours* and Anthony Minghella's *The English Patient* respond to these challenges in interesting ways.

The next focus for the producer is to get the characterization right. Are the characters clearly defined? Are they engaging for an audience? Are there too many characters? Can their functions be merged into one? (This is the road that the producer took on the film *My Summer of Love*.) Regarding your main character, the producer will wish to have identified their "outward want," something which will be explicit from the start of the piece, and their needs, something which though not clear at the beginning unfolds as the narrative does. A way to express this need visually will be considered to help transport characters off the page and onto the screen.

Of course, an important consideration for a producer to take stock of is whether the source material feels cinematic or televisual. Will it appeal to a director, or is it too cerebral, depending on a character's thoughts too much?

A final piece of analysis a producer will want to undertake is to identify the pitch and the appeal of the source material. Who might be attracted to commission a screenplay? Is it a classic series beloved by the BBC for its main channel, or a more cutting edge and contemporary tale mores in line with the zeitgeist ambitions of a Channel 4 production? The producer needs to know what type of work fits where.

There is a myth that adapting a novel is an easy option for a screenwriter and producer. However, when you consider the pressures of audience expectation, what needs to be added or taken out, the demands of the film/TV market, there is perhaps an unavoidable truth that good adaptations are just as difficult to write as original screenplays.

As a producer I'm frequently looking for new film projects to develop. Most of the films that I have been associated with as a script developer, financier or executive producer have been original screen plays —films that have been based on an idea emerging directly from a director or screenwriter's imagination —films like *Lawless Heart*, written and directed by Neil Hunter and Tom Hunsinger and produced in 2001. However, in fact even this film does not escape completely from considerations of adaptation or even re-adaptation, as it is in many ways a re-working of the French director Eric Rohmer's *Rendez-vous à Paris*.

I have begun to add to my slate of projects in development a group of scripts emerging from contemporary British fiction and all of which are in various forms of adaptation. These include novels by the following writers — Jim Crace, Helen Cross and Niall Griffiths.

Jim Crace is a leading British novelist, an award winner for such novels as *Continent* and *Quarantine*. So far none of his novels have been adapted for the screen, though Stanley Kubrick did option *Quarantine*. Atom Egoyan, the Canadian director, had his eye on *Being Dead* and Harvey Weinstein of Miramax fame is currently pursuing Crace's latest novel, *The Pesthouse*. The novel I have had adapted is *Signals of Distress*, an early 19th century story set in Cornwall, Great Britain. It has been adapted for me by Laurence Coriat, the French screenwriter based in Britain who wrote *Wonderland* for the British director Michael Winterbottom.

The other two novelists represent a younger generation than Jim Crace and tackle modern themes in a more direct way than Jim Crace's well-regarded British version of "magical realism." Niall Griffiths has been described as a "Welsh Irvine Walsh" and in a sense this is a valid comparison as Griffiths's style is reminiscent of *Trainspotting* in its focus on a Welsh criminalized and drug-taking (and enjoying) *demi-monde*. Griffiths writes frequently about life in North Wales, the part of that country close to the city of Liverpool. His novel *Stump* is a story on the road from Liverpool to Aberystwyth, following two young criminals in their pursuit of a one-armed man who has lost his other arm to heroin, and who owes them money. I have asked Niall Griffiths to write the screenplay of his own novel and that is what he is doing, though it's frequently cautioned against having a novelist adapt their own work due to their obvious proximity to the material, and a possible unwillingness to fillet the book in the way that adaptations require.

The third adaptation is a new novel by Helen Cross whose debut novel *My Summer of Love* was an award-winning adaptation. Her third novel *Shopping and Sex* is to be published later this year and having seen a manuscript from her agent I'm very keen on pursuing this for the screen with Helen Cross adapting.[3]

It is clear in Britain and internationally, that there is an increasing demand for good adaptations. In both the publishing and film industries and also in academic environments, there is greater interest being expressed toward screen writing and adaptations. Much more attention than I think was evident in previous years it seems to me. This conference in Lorient is an example of that awakening of interest, as is the setting up of the Association of Literature on Screen Studies which had an inaugural event last year 2006 in Britain at the DeMontfort University in Leicester. My own mini Festival, *Lost In Adaptation*, was responding to this interest, as also are the newly launched annual Screenwriting Festival in Cheltenham and the fact that the prestigious Edinburgh Film Festival has announced that this year in August 2007 their theme will be Screenwriting, within which focus will fall on Adaptations. A further index of this increasing attention is the film industry's immediate buzz, as indicated in the film trade paper *Screen International*, whenever a short list for a literary prize is announced. The lists for the Mann Booker Prize, the Orange Prize, the Whitbread Prize are all immediately publicized and discoursed about in the trade papers to determine which of the novels are considered "oven-ready" for adaptation. This attention to adaptation is evident also in the newly arranged forum that takes place at the annual and prominent Frankfurt Book Fair, where the Berlin Film Festival now collaborates on the showcasing of a new movie, based on an adaptation, at the Book Fair, and uses the event to generate increased "heat" about the relationship between literature and film. In fact as I prepared to visit Lorient all the press emerging from the largest literary festival in Britain, at Hay-on-Wye, is all about film adaptations, especially the news that Andrew Davies, Britain's uber adaptor, intends to sex up Jane Austen's *Sense and Sensibility* by in his words "butching up" the male leads. Davies wants to encourage viewers to forget Ang Lee's version of the same novel.

The international box office in recent years has seen an increase in the reliance of the film industry on the known formulae that adaptations represent. Maybe this is an acknowledgement of retrenchment in the face of competing attractors from other media platforms, and the fact that the emerging generation is, in the vernacular, "platform agnostic" and do not look upon the cinema as the premier screen of choice. Maybe it's a sign of conservative times and the reduction of risk and innovation.

The international box office reveals a parade of adaptations from a plethora of sources, be they fiction, graphic novels, stageplay, musical, personal/familial memoirs, personal/public memoirs etc. Films such as *Dreamgirls, Spiderman, Fracture, Bridget Jones, Harry Potter, Lord of The Rings, Narnia, The Devil Wears Prada, Casino Royale* etc., all exemplify this scenario. There does seem to be an increasing number of movies in international distribution reliant on existing literary sources. Perhaps more than ever before I wonder. Or maybe it's always been so high. In Britain in recent years we have seen the screens dominated by adaptations, either by new versions of the classics, that each unfolding generation seems to want to put their specific fingerprints on (such as Dickens, Shakespeare, Jane Austen etc.) or by fast turnaround of recent literary successes (such as *My Summer of Love, Notes on a Scandal, The Last King of Scotland*, etc.).

There is also an emerging trend, no doubt partly influenced by the rise of the celebrity culture, of adaptations of personal stories, memoirs and biographies, especially where there is an insight into world events (e.g., Michael Winterbottom's film *A Mighty Heart* which premiered in Cannes with Angelina Jolie playing Mariane Pearl, based on Pearl's memoir of her husband's capture, captivity and subsequent death in Pakistan) or where one person's small drama resonates into a universal echo (e.g., Blake Morrisson's memoir *And When Did You Last See Your Father?*, now made into a film of the same name by director Anand Tucker). No doubt soon we'll have adaptations of blogs, when the blogosphere will become a valid source of original material for film makers. Maybe it's already been done? The personalization of culture as evident in My Space, You Tube and Second Life will soon be appearing in the development trays of film executives as they respond to the existing recognition factor in the millions of such virtual and visible transactions. In fact, it's possibly almost there, in the sense that the blog of the London call girl, the happy hooker, known as Belle de Jour became a book, and film rights are now being competed for. Perhaps at this moment in the development of the on line world, the transformation into filmable form had to take a literary pit stop first in order to gather a certain cultural cachet. In future, no doubt the book will be short-circuited and the adaptation will be direct from blog to film; from personal life to public dissemination.

Likewise, how will the new business model for the cultural industries as sketched out in the book *The Long Tail* by Chris Anderson have an effect on the availability of source material ready for adaptation, when the era of the niches rather than the blockbuster takes a grip? The boon for a producer with an existing source is the fact that it has a large-scale recognition factor built in (a sort of creative DNA that has already survived one process of evolution), but what happens when the digital revolution finally settles down and "endless choice creates unlimited demand"? The proliferation of the niches, as outlined by Chris Anderson, proposes an ecology of a greater number of available cultural products rather than the dynasty of a relatively small number of blockbusters. Maybe what's happening is that the traditional film industry is responding to these emerging changes by clinging to proven successful formulae such as adaptations, and reducing the financial risk in a threatening environment, while the lower budget area of film making which has embraced the digital world responds to the changing times by emphasizing original screenplays that have no prior creative reference points, and are independent therefore in terms of film making vision. I'm thinking here of the Dogma momentum of filmmaking advocated by the Danish director, Lars von Trier.

However, in an age of speeded up cultural exchanges between books, film, television, music, games, the web etc., and in a world where intertextuality is prevalent, a cross between and within cultural forms and an ever increasing proximity of sampled creativity, it perhaps becomes an increasingly difficult endeavor to ascertain where and when originality and adaptation begins and ends. Perhaps the "blending" that happens is leading to the need for a new metaphor to be invented. Adaptation proposes an evolutionary process, whereas contemporary interlocking of cultural forms suggests a metaphor resonating with robustness, vibrancy, rupturing, ripping and tearing.

NOTES

1. The following is a transcription of the talk given by Roger Shannon during the conference on adaptation organized in May 2007 in Lorient, France.

2. Editor's note: This film was replaced by a reboot of the television series in June 2012.

3. Editor's note: Helen Cross's third novel, entitled *Spilt Milk, Black Coffee,* was published by Bloomsbury Publishing in 2009.

Bibliography

This bibliography is of course far from exhaustive; it seeks rather to credit a certain number of texts that have either directly or indirectly influenced the preceding essays.

General Film Theory

Andrew, Dudley. *Concepts in Film Theory*. Oxford: Oxford University Press, 1984.

Balázs, Béla. *Theory of the Film: Character and Growth of a New Art* (trans. from the Hungarian by Edith Bone). New York: Dover, 1970.

Bazin, André. *Qu'est-ce que le cinéma?* (1975). Paris: Éditions du Cerf, 2002.

Deleuze, Gilles. *Cinéma 2: L'image-temps*. Paris: Éditions de Minuit, 1985.

Francaviglia, Richard, and Jerry Rodnitzky, eds. *Lights, Camera, History: Portraying the Past in Film*. Arlington: Texas A&M Press, 2007.

Higson, Andrew. *English Heritage, English Cinema: Costume Drama Since 1980*. Oxford: Oxford University Press, 2003.

Metz, Christian. *Essais sur la signification du cinéma*. Paris: Klincksieck, 2003.

Monk, Claire, and Amy Sargeant. *British Historical Cinema*. London: Routledge, 2001.

Stam, Robert. *Film Theory: An Introduction*. Malden, MA: Blackwell, 2000.

Stokes, Melvyn, and Richard Maltby, eds. *Hollywood Spectatorship: Changing Perceptions of Cinema Audiences*. London: British Film Institute, 2001.

Trotter, David. *Cinema and Modernism*. Malden, MA: Blackwell, 2007.

Adaptation Criticism

Boozer, Jack, ed. *Authorship in Film Adaptation*. Austin: University of Texas Press, 2008.

Boyum, Joy Gould. *Double Exposure: Fiction into Film*. New York: Universe Books, 1985.

Cardwell, Sarah. *Adaptation Revisited*. Manchester: Manchester University Press, 2002.

Cartmell, Deborah, and Imelda Whelehan, eds. *Adaptations: From Text to Screen, Screen to Text*. London: Routledge, 1999.

_____, and _____. *The Cambridge Companion to Literature on Screen*. Cambridge: Cambridge University Press, 2007.

Corrigan, Timothy. *Film and Literature: An Introduction and Reader*. Upper Saddle River, NJ: Prentice Hall, 1999.

Costanzo Cahir, Linda. *Literature into Film: Theory and Practical Approaches*. Jefferson, NC: McFarland, 2006.

Desmond, John M., and Peter Hawkes. *Adaptation: Studying Film and Literature.* Boston: McGraw-Hill, 2006.

Elliott, Kamilla. *Rethinking the Novel/Film Debate.* Cambridge: Cambridge University Press, 2003.

Forrest, Jennifer, and Leonard Koos, eds. *Dead Ringers: The Remake in Theory and Practice.* New York: SUNY Press, 2001.

Giddings, Robert, Keith Selby, and Chris Wensley, eds. *Screening the Novel: The Theory and Practice of Literary Dramatization.* Basingstoke: Macmillan, 1990.

Harrison, Stephanie, ed. *Adaptations: From Short Story to Big Screen, 35 Great Stories That Have Inspired Great Films.* New York: Three Rivers Press, 2005.

Horton, Andrew, and Stuart McDougal, eds. *Play It Again, Sam: Retakes on Remakes.* Berkeley: University of California Press, 1998.

Hutcheon, Linda. *A Theory of Adaptation.* New York: Routledge, 2006.

Jeffers, Jennifer M. *Britain Colonized: Hollywood's Appropriation of British Literature.* New York: Palgrave Macmillan, 2006.

Leitch, Thomas. *Film Adaptation and Its Discontents: From* Gone with the Wind *to* The Passion of the Christ. Baltimore: Johns Hopkins University Press, 2007.

McFarlane, Brian. *Novel to Film: An Introduction to the Theory of Adaptation.* Oxford: Oxford University Press, 1996.

Naremore, James. *Film Adaptation.* New Brunswick, NJ: Rutgers University Press, 2000.

Sanders, Julie. *Adaptation and Appropriation.* London: Routledge, 2006.

Seger, Linda. *The Art of Adaptation: Turning Fact and Fiction into Film.* New York: Henry Holt, 1992.

Stam, Robert. *Literature Through Film: Realism, Magic, and the Art of Adaptation.* Oxford: Blackwell, 2005.

_____, ed. *Literature and Film: A Guide to the Theory and Practice of Film Adaptation.* Malden, MA: Blackwell, 2005.

Stam, Robert, and Allesandra Raengo, eds. *A Companion to Literature on Screen.* Malden, MA: Blackwell, 2004.

Tibbetts, John C., and James M. Welsh, eds. *Novels into Film,* 2d ed. (1998). New York: Facts on File, 2005.

Verevis, Constantine. *Film Remakes.* New York: Palgrave Macmillan, 2006.

Vincendeau, Ginette, ed. *Film/Literature/Heritage: A* Sight and Sound *Reader.* London: British Film Institute, 2001.

Zanger, Anat. *Film Remakes as Ritual and Disguise: From* Carmen *to* Ripley. Amsterdam: Amsterdam University Press, 2007.

About the Contributors

Florence **Cabaret** is an associate professor with ERIAC at the University of Rouen. Her research focuses on English-language Indian novels, as well as Indian film adaptation of classic Anglophone literature. Her recent work includes "Representations of Power Shifts Between Great Britain and the Raj in *The Jewel in the Crown*" in the online journal *TVSeries* and "Variations on Diasporic Viewpoints in *The Namesake* by Jhumpa Lahiri" and Mira Nair's Filmic Adaptation of the Novel" in *India and the Diasporic Imagination* (2011).

Deborah **Cartmell** is a professor of English at De Montfort University and founder and co-editor of the journals *Shakespeare* (Routledge) and *Adaptation* (Oxford University Press). Recent publications are *Screen Adaptation: Impure Cinema* (with Imelda Whelehan, Palgrave, 2010), *Screen Adaptations: Jane Austen's* Pride and Prejudice (Methuen, 2010), and an edited volume, *The Companion to Literature, Film and Adaptation* (Blackwell, 2012).

Karim **Chabani** teaches literature and translation at the Maison de l'Éducation de la Légion d'Honneur at Saint-Denis, where he prepares advanced students for elite French universities (*Classes Préparatoires Grandes Écoles*). His research interests include the interaction between text and image (film, graphic novels, painting).

Hélène **Charlery** is an associate professor in business, film and American studies at the Université de Toulouse 2 — Le Mirail. She is the author of several articles on the representations of race and gender identities in contemporary mainstream films. Research interests include re/deconstructions of racial, sexual and beauty standards in visual media.

Nicole **Cloarec** is a lecturer in English at the University of Rennes 1. She is the author of a doctoral thesis on Peter Greenaway's films and a number of articles on British and American cinema. Her latest research work focuses on the cinema of Stephen and Timothy Quay, Guy Maddin, Derek Jarman and British women filmmakers.

Kevin **Dwyer** is a lecturer in American studies at the University of Artois. He wrote his Ph.D. dissertation in film studies on representations of food in film and is researching the aesthetic and narrative uses of food and eating in the arts. Recent publications include an analysis of cannibalism in Italian cinema.

Kamilla **Elliott** is a senior lecturer at Lancaster University. She is author of *Rethinking the Novel/Film Debate* (Cambridge University Press, 2003), *Portraiture and British Gothic Fiction: The Rise of Picture Identification, 1764–1835* (Johns Hopkins University Press, 2012), as well as other essays and chapters on literature and film.

Joyce **Goggin** is an associate professor of literature at the University of Amsterdam where she also teaches film and new media, and an emeritus member of Amsterdam University College where she served as head of studies for the humanities from 2008 to 2010. Her research focuses on literature, film, painting and new media, and she has published articles on gambling, addiction, and finance in various cultural media.

Sarah **Hatchuel** is a professor of early modern literature and English-speaking cinema at the University of Le Havre. She is the author of *Shakespeare and the Cleopatra/Caesar Intertext: Sequel, Conflation, Remake* (Fairleigh Dickinson University Press, 2011), *Shakespeare: From Stage to Screen* (Cambridge University Press, 2004) and *A Companion to the Shakespearean Films of Kenneth Branagh* (Blizzard Publishing, 2000), and the coeditor of several other works on Shakespeare.

Charles **Holdefer** is an American writer based in Brussels. His latest novel is *Back in the Game*. His short fiction, essays and reviews have appeared in the *New England Review, Los Angeles Review, North American Review, New York Journal of Books* and other publications.

Ariane **Hudelet** is an associate professor in the English Department of the Université Paris–Diderot (LARCA research unit). She specializes in film adaptation and contemporary TV series. Beside several articles on film adaptations, she wrote *Pride and Prejudice: Jane Austen et Joe Wright* (Armand Colin, 2006) and *The Cinematic Jane Austen* (with David Monaghan and John Wiltshire, McFarland, 2009). With Shannon Wells-Lassagne, she edited *De la page blanche aux salles obscures* (PUR, 2011).

Sébastien **Lefait** is a lecturer in English at the University of Corsica. He completed a Ph.D. on Shakespeare and Orson Welles, in which he treated Welles's works as adaptations *of* and *to* Shakespeare's thought. He has published articles about the new forms of film adaptation and is researching the use of surveillance in films, in which he sees a socio-analytical instrument and an aesthetic tool.

Delphine **Letort** teaches American civilization and film studies at the University of Le Mans. She published *Du film noir au néo-noir: mythes et stéréotypes de l'Amérique 1941–2008* (L'Harmattan, 2010). Her research focuses on issues of representation in American films, including gender, race and ideology.

Laurent **Mellet** is a senior lecturer in 20th and 21st century British literature and cinema at the University of Burgundy in Dijon. He is the co-author with Shannon Wells-Lassagne of *Étudier l'adaptation filmique: Cinéma anglais, cinéma américain* (PUR, 2010), and the author of *L'Œil et la voix dans les romans de E. M. Forster et leur adaptation cinématographique* (PULM, 2012).

Gilles **Menegaldo** is a professor of American literature and film at the University of Poitiers. He is the co-author of *Dracula, la noirceur et la grâce* (Atlande, 2006), and editor or co-editor of 27 volumes of collected articles. Recent publications include *Les Nouvelles Formes de science-fiction* (2006), *Les Imaginaires de la ville entre littérature* *et arts* (Presses Universitaires de Rennes, 2007), *Cinéma et histoire* (Michel Houdiard, 2008), and *Manières de noir* (Presses Universitaires de Rennes, 2010).

Gene M. **Moore** teaches English and American literature at the Universitty of Amsterdam. His publications include *Conrad on Film* (Cambridge University Press, 1997), *Conrad's Cities* (Rodopi, 1992), a casebook on *Heart of Darkness* (Oxford University Press, 2004) and the *Oxford Reader's Companion to Conrad* (Oxford University Press, 2000). He helped to edit Conrad's letters for Cambridge University Press.

Roger **Shannon** is a producer of films with his Birmingham-based company Swish Films, and a professor of film and television at Edge Hill University. He has served as head of production at the British Film Institute, the UK Film Council and Scottish Screen.

Dominique **Sipière** is an emeritus professor at the Université de Paris Ouest Nanterre la Défense. He wrote several books dealing with film adaptation, and co-edited studies about *A Streetcar Named Desire* (Temps, 2003), *Dracula* (Ellipses & Armand Colin, 1995), and *Jane Eyre* (PUF, 2008). He is a former president of SERCIA and the current president of the jury for the Prix de la Recherche (SAES and AFEA).

Donald **Ulin** is an associate professor and director of English at the University of Pittsburgh's Bradford campus, where he teaches British and Irish literature, film and environmental studies. He has published mainly on travel and tourism in the 19th century and is currently editing a collection of immigrant correspondence.

Shannon **Wells-Lassagne** is an associate professor in British literature and film adaptation at the University of South Britanny. She has published articles on Elizabeth Bowen, Graham Greene, and Ford Madox Ford as well as on classic and heritage film adaptations and television series. She is co-author of *Étudier l'adaptation filmique* and co-editor of *De la page blanche aux salles obscures*, both published by Presses Universitaires de Rennes, in 2010 and 2011, respectively.

Index